THE FAMILY
IN THE
MODERN AGE

THE FAMILY
IN THE
MODERN AGE

More than a Lifestyle Choice

Brigitte Berger

Transaction Publishers
New Brunswick (U.S.A.) and London (U.K.)

Library of Congress Catalog Number: 2001052508
ISBN: 0-7658-0121-3
Printed in Canada

Library of Congress Cataloging-in-Publication Data

Berger, Brigitte.
The family in the modern age : more than a lifestyle choice / Brigitte Berger.
p. cm.
Includes bibliographical references and index.
ISBN 0-7658-0121-3 (cloth : alk. paper)
1. Family. 2. Postmodernism—Social aspects. I. Title.

HQ518 .B45 2002
306.85—dc21   2001052508

Acknowledgements

This book came out of a project of the Institute for the Study of Economic Culture at Boston University supported by a grant from the Lynne and Harry Bradley Foundation. Early work on the project was also supported by the Randolph Foundation through the good offices of Heather MacDonald.

Contents

Preface   ix

Part 1 The Assault on the Family

1.   The Family: From Basic Institution to
        "Just Another Lifestyle" Choice   3

2.   Modernization and the Family: Theorists on
        the Road to Postmodernism   33

Part 2 The Modern Family: Its Nature and History

3.   The Family: The Primary Institution of
        Individual and Social Life   69

4.   The Conventional Nuclear Family and the
        Rise of the Modern World   99

Part 3 The Conventional Family Today and Its Future

5.   The Modern Family Today   139

6.   Critical Contemporary Issues   177

7.   The Family in the Postmodern Age   223

Subject Index   241

Author Index   243

Preface

This is a book about the modern family, its nature, its status, and its future. Its main purpose is to identify those structural and ideational factors that have made for its strength and dynamism in the past and to explore the modern family's viability in a world in transition. This endeavor takes the reader on a long journey that begins with a brief portrayal of those social shifts that have caused many to doubt the family's capacity to meet the needs and desires of modern men and women and it concludes with a renewed appreciation of its resilience and importance in the life of individuals and society alike. Fashionable assertions to the contrary, this volume sets out to document that the modern family has shown itself to be an extraordinarily adaptable and vital social institution despite the broad changes that have occurred in the ways we live, work, and conduct ourselves. Beyond that an attempt is made to shed light on the reasons why the vast majority of modern men and women continue to aspire to the ideals and the lifestyle that have distinguished the modern family from the beginning and, in looking to the future, a rationale is presented of why it is reasonable to expect that the family that stood at the cradle of the modern social order some three hundred years ago will continue to provide the basis for any society concerned with the happiness, liberty, equality, and prosperity of all its members. Rather than being condemned to the dust heap of history, as critics of all stripes have been inclined to assume, it is the book's sum argument that the modern family is more than a lifestyle choice.

What is at issue today is the viability and future of the conventional nuclear family of a father, a mother, and their children, who live together and who are tied to each other by mutual bonds of love and obligations. Distinctive in structure and ethos, this type of family has long served Western societies as the unifying principle for the organization of individual and social life. In the voluminous literature a number of labels can be found that describe its distinguishing features: social historians and demographers prefer the term "proto-industrial" to describe the structural features of the nuclear family in its preindustrial incarnation; in the nineteenth century, when it was thought useful to emphasize the importance of the lifestyle and the ethos of the nuclear family, the terms "domestic" and "conventional" family came into vogue; and in the twentieth century one encounters a tendency to combine features of structure, lifestyle, and ethos under the rubric of "the family of the middle classes." While conservatives tend to laud conventional family virtues, Marxists, who have a strong distaste for both its nuclear structure and its individualistic ethos, speak of the "bourgeois family" only to find their pejorative use of the term strongly contested by social historians like Simon Schama who argue that it is high time to liberate the bourgeois family from its negative Marxist connotations.[1] Yet regardless of the labels used, legions of analysts are in agreement today that unrelenting forces of change have weakened the family's nuclear structure as well as its broad moral claims. Some, like the theorists of postmodernism who deny the validity of all guiding principles that have long organized individual and social life are even prepared to celebrate and promote its decline and doom. Weakened and embattled, many argue that the modern family is an anachronistic institution whose demise is only a question of time.[2]

When one looks at the rise and future of the modern world through an analytical lens different from the one we are accustomed to it becomes readily apparent that many aspects of the conventional nuclear family and modern family life have been sorely miscast. One-dimensional and frequently flat, the currently prevalent analytical perspectives have given rise to a view that sees the modern family to be restrictive in form and poorly equipped to deal with the challenges of a postmodern world looming on the horizon. A wealth of new materials derived from disparate fields of inquiry and a reinterpretation of an avalanche of research data available today, however, suggest that this view is in urgent need of redress. In emphasizing the role of social institutions in individual and social life, this volume arrives at a very different assessment of the role of the modern family and its future. While it is taken for granted that political factors and the economy can and do influence the lives of people wherever they may live, the book sets out to demonstrate why the relationship between private life and the macro institutions of society is considerably more complex than it is commonly assumed. In paying careful attention to the distinguishing features of the modern family it is illustrated how its inner dynamics sways and inspires each generation anew regardless of external changes. As a consequence of this analytical endeavor, it is concluded that the modern family is an institution in its own right that follows its own dictates and unfolds its own culture-creating dynamics. Not only can an argument be made that the rationality of modern private life is qualitatively different from the rationality that governs the macro-institutions of modernity but it can also be demonstrated that the behavioral patterns and the distinctive ethos peculiar to the modern family have provided the modern world with its organizing principles and moral charter. Following the logic of these findings the book submits that it is important not to see the modern family as a helpless pawn of powerful forces flowing from the organization of technology, the economy, and the law, but to recognize that the dynamics of everyday family life tend to "colonize" the macro institutions of the modern world, rather than the other way around.[3] If these two propositions hold—as I think they do—it may not only be argued that the modern family is far less fragile than it has been commonly assumed, but that today, as in the past, public life lies at the mercy of private life.[4] Taken together, these propositions have important theoretical as well as practical implications.

In developing this argument, issue is taken with a plethora of recent studies that have led to claims that a bewildering variety of alternative lifestyles has crowded out the behavioral codes that have long governed the ways in which individuals organize their personal lives. Although masses of statistics undoubtedly indicate that sexuality is no longer normatively prescribed by rules of marriage, and individuals appear to be more inclined to tailor their domestic arrangements to personal needs and desires than in the past, the book attempts to show that these reported behavioral shifts undermine neither the continued viability nor the ideal of the family in its conventional nuclear form. By the same token, the book also reasons that it is safe to assume that exploding rates of cohabitation and divorce do not necessarily imply that marriage is on the way out or that the two-parent family has lost its attraction for the vast majority of ordinary people today. Neither does it give much credence to fashionable arguments that modern individuals are adrift in a whirlwind of change or that they have abandoned their moorings in the conventional family and its equally conventional morality. While it agrees with findings that reflect that individuals in many ways have come to rely to a greater extent on the state and outside professionals, it strongly disagrees with trendy arguments that families today are inclined to relinquish their nurturing and pedagogical mission. If anything, a reinterpretation of the available empirical data indicates that more than at any other period in history families today are to a much greater degree and for a much longer period of time involved with their children and concerned with securing those conditions which they hope will promote their well-being and progress.

Specific public policy proposals advocated by the three political camps dominating the debates in the public arena today—the liberal, the conservative, and the postmodernist—are also challenged. From the perspective developed in the book, all three leave a lot to be desired: the liberal faith in the salutary effect of governmental intervention has a distinctly hollow ring in the face of a record of measured failure; yearnings for the restoration of the traditional family have predisposed conservatives to mythologize the family to a degree that its political agenda frequently bears little relationship to the exigencies of the present; and the entire postmodernist interpretational scheme is based on such flawed assumptions that it is intellectually impossible to take its claims seriously. In a review of major current policy issues, an attempt is made to present a position that is informed by an understanding of contemporary social life in which the family is neither glorified nor castigated, nor condemned to the dust heap of history. In contrast to current practices, the perspective developed in this book permits a sorting out of specific policy recommendations in terms of their potential to undermine the continued viability of the modern family, rather than endorsing the agenda of either political–cultural camp.

The line of argumentation revolves around four major concerns: (1) to let the reader see how the short shrift given to the institutional dimension of the family has misconstrued the importance and the role of the family today; (2) to document the close cognitive fit between the core elements of the modern family and modern society and to signal that any society that forgets this connection does so at its own peril; (3) to inquire to what degree currently identified problems have the potential to endanger the modern family's vital individual and social functions; and (4) to explore what reasonable projections can be made about the future of the family that has been so instrumental in the creation of a politically democratic and economically prosperous world.

To this end the first two introductory chapters seek to provide a brief account of "the career" of the conventional family in the twentieth century. Chapter 1, "From Basic Institution to 'Just Another Lifestyle Choice'," looks at the ways whereby the conventional family came into disrepute in the course of a few fatal decades, while Chapter 2, "Modernization and the Family—Theorists on the Road to Postmodernism" looks at its correlative career among theoreticians.

Chapters 3 and 4 develop a view of the family that is distinctly different from the one found in the literature today. In Chapter 3, "The Family: The Primary Institution of Individual and Social Life," an analytical framework is presented that serves to guide the explorations of the subsequent chapters. While avoiding becoming ensnared in arguments from biology and "nature," the chapter illustrates the necessity for the institutionalization of basic human propensities through the agency of the family. While an element of control is peculiar to *all* institutions, the culture-creating and liberating dimension of particular institutional configurations receives special emphasis in this connection. Chapter 4, "The Conventional Nuclear Family and the Rise of the Modern World" sets out to redress the short shrift given to the singular role of the conventional nuclear family in the creation of liberal democracy and the market economy, and tries to show how the conventional family, with its emphasis on personal autonomy, responsibility, individual freedom along with nascent notions of justice and equality, inspired those grand social themes that have come to move the modern world.

In Chapter 5, "The Modern Family Today," the discussion turns to recent demographic shifts in behaviors relating to sexuality, marriage, family structure, family values, relationships, and family functions. The chapter examines the degree to which the turmoil of recent decades has destroyed the core elements of the modern family and illustrates that contemporary yearnings for personal freedom, independence, equality, and the achievement of one's own identity do not necessarily conflict with equally strong desires for a life revolving around love, marriage, and family.

Chapter 6, "Critical Contemporary Issues," looks at some of the hotly contested contemporary issues relating to the family—the definition of the family, the institution of marriage, cohabitation, gay marriage, divorce, abortion, women and work, childcare, and assorted issues of poverty, crime, and education—through the analytical prism advocated in this book. Here great care is taken not to fall prey to currently popular definitions and conceptualizations that define the conventional family out of existence, conventional marriage a thing of the past, and family relationships in terms of the exchange of goods and services. At the same time, equal care is also taken not to be guided by visions of a mythical past where things are held to have been of "the whole cloth" and therefore more natural and better.

And finally, in a brief concluding chapter, "The Family in the Postmodern Age," the argument is made that despite the industrial system's numerous permutations and the far-reaching social adjustments they exacted, the norms and the cognitive style peculiar to the modern family are likely to remain the core features of any dynamic democratic social order organized around the market. What is more, there are no credible reasons to expect that this is likely to change in the future. With all its tedium and problems, the modern family's unique capacity to reinvent itself with every new phase of the modern order, to provide individuals with a secure anchor in periods of turmoil and meet the ever-changing requirements of an increasingly complex world, gives reason to expect that this type of family will retain the loyalty of modern individuals whoever they are and wherever they may be.

A few comments on the use of the concept of "modernization" and the political agenda of this book are in order. Though it has become distinctly unfashionable in academic circles in recent decades to use the term modernization, I shall continue to make use of the concept nonetheless. It has to be emphasized, however, that the term modernization, or "being modern," as used in the present context, should not be understood as signaling the superiority of one form of existence over another, but rather as a mark, a point, on a rising and falling scale. We know only too well that the twentieth century has been full of stunning events—running the full spectrum from the great and wonderful to the horrible and unimaginable— that make it impossible to use the term "modern" as a sign of tribute or approbation. At the same time, "being modern" also conveys that the majority of people—and not only the elite—live longer, healthier, and enjoy a standard of living and a degree of freedom unimaginable to people of an earlier age. For the purposes of the book, "modern" simply implies that the majority of people work in industrial settings, use advanced technology as a tool, live in cities or suburbs, have a comparatively high standard of living, and participate in a form of government that in its democratic form is rather different from previous ones. By the same token it is of considerable importance to recognize that culture is not destiny. Civilizations resting on very different family cultures—as many in Africa, Asia, and Latin America do—and whose traditions appear to be resistant to modernization, have not only the capacity to change, but, in fact, do change. Yet for that change to occur and to succeed, it must be anchored in accompanying changes in the family.

If the book has a political agenda, then its overarching aim is to capture a middle ground in the currently polarized political climate. In being leery of both a liberal faith in the power of the state to solve all social and personal ills as well as conservative yearnings to return to pastoral beatitudes, it hopes to show that an intellectual and political middle-ground position is not only possible but also the only viable one morally and politically.

Notes

1.	Simon Schama, *The Embarrassment of Riches*, (New York, Alfred A. Knopf, 1987).

2.	The use of the term "conventional family" in contrast to other terms such as the "traditional," "Victorian," or "domestic" family is preferred in this book as it is able to combine its structural as well as its ideational features without confining it to a particular geographical location or historical period. When indicated, use is made of other labels such as the "proto-industrial," the "domestic," and the "middle-class" family as well, depending upon which of the particular dimensions of this type of family needs to be emphasized. As it will become apparent in subsequent chapters, what sets the conventional family apart from other family forms, including the "amoral familism" characteristic of traditional societies regardless of time and space, is precisely its novel combination of structural and ideational features that engendered new economically productive behavior patterns, a growing civic consciousness, and an intensified respect for individuals and their rights.

3.	If one cares to use Marxian terminology, it could be argued that the time has come to provide a "material" (i.e., family) base for Juergen Habermas's famous dictum of the "colonization of the private by the rationality of the public."

4.	This argument has been most forcefully made by Allan C. Carlson in *Family Questions: Reflections on the American Social Crisis*, (New Brunswick, N.J., Transaction Publishers, 1988).

Part 1

The Assault on the Family

1

The Family: From Basic Institution to "Just Another Lifestyle" Choice

Until a few decades ago most people almost intuitively knew what the term "the family" meant, a father and a mother and their children living together, tied to each other by mutual bonds of love and obligation. While there may have existed a tendency to look at "the family" through rose-tinted glasses and surround it with romanticized notions of marital bliss, no one doubted that this is what a family looks like and, what is more, *should* look like. If by force of circumstance individuals were compelled to live in different arrangements—as was the case with orphans and widows—they were to be pitied and deemed to be in need of help.

Social scientists, for their part, always recognized that reality frequently falls short of the ideal. Ethnographers, in particular, took great pleasure in impressing upon us that there exist a great variety of ways in which life is organized in cultures different from our own. Nonetheless, all agreed that today, as in the past, some social arrangement one may call a "family" could be recognized in all societies across the globe. Wherever they turned they discovered regularized patterns of conduct that were expressed in more or less enduring forms passed on from one generation to the next. Despite a multitude of intercultural variations, these forms, or structures in technical parlance, were found to be strangely similar. On the basis of a very large number of cases—more than two hundred at the time—ethnographers went on to identify six bedrock features characteristic of the family:[1]

1.   the organization of human sexuality by means of some form of marriage that serves to socially legitimize the sexual union, regardless whether manifested in the form of monogamy or polygamy and its subcategories;

2.   a taken-for-granted acceptance that the core function of this union revolves around the procreation and protection of children;

3.   an acknowledgment of the rights and duties between the spouses as well as those of the spouses to their children;

4.   some clearly-designated residential arrangement for husband, wife, and children commonly called a household;

5.   a set of more or less precisely established reciprocal economic obligations between husband and wife and of both to their children; and finally

6.   a socially-legitimated system of reckoning descent.

While in modern societies these bedrock features were found to be encoded in the law, in pre-modern societies seemingly immutable traditions served to secure the fundamental features constitutive of the family perhaps even more forcibly. In all instances these regularized patterns of human life were defined by more or less cogently expressed value systems that revolved around the family regardless of its particular structural manifestation. In every case, family values not only provided shape and meaning to individual behavior but they also equipped domestic behavior patterns with normative, and, at times, even coercive powers. Because in all societies ethnographers encountered it was taken for granted that individuals would organize their behavior along socially-sanctioned familistic lines, they concluded that the family is a massive social unit in which human nature and human needs are indelibly intertwined with the basic requirements of social life. In the shorthand fashion of academics, social scientists dubbed these enduring structures of conduct and their corresponding social expectations and symbolic meanings "the institution of the family."

To be sure, in their research in the far corners of the globe, ethnographers also came across some borderline cases that led them to question the universality of the institution of the family (the Nayars of the Malabar Coast of India are probably the most frequently cited example). Yet for a long time social analysts agreed that if the institution of the family is not universal, it is probably almost universal and the just-listed features are its recurrent constituent parts. It was full well recognized that human groups differ in many ways: in the forms of marriage and the ways mates are selected; in the types of restrictions imposed on sexuality (such as those governing premarital sex, adultery, incest, and homosexuality); in the social roles assigned to husbands and wives as well as the power and deference accorded to each; in the different structures of kinship and residence; as well as in the different ways children are reared. Yet considering the many ways in which human life differs in almost every other respect, scholars were amazed by the lack of variation in the fundamental characteristics defining the institution of the family. Everywhere, or almost everywhere, these firmly ensconced institutionalized patterns were found to run through human societies like a scarlet thread. Until very recently then, ethnographers celebrated "the family of man" and there existed little disagreement among them that this family-based thread served to tie human life together regardless of race, ethnicity, and differences in time and place.

The Western "Nuclear" Family under Pressure

The family patterns of Western societies, and in particular those of the societies of North-Western Europe and the United States, were found to differ from other family patterns in that the organization of individual and social life revolved around the family in its nuclear form. As pointed out earlier, the term "nuclear" family in the language of the social sciences refers to a family pattern that typically consists of a married couple—husband and wife—and their children, living together in a common or "conjugal" household, that is to say, separate from the wider kinship group. In this nuclear unit individuals are tied to each other by mutual bonds of affection and obligation, and they are dependent upon one other in many ways.

The origin of the conjugal nuclear family is shrouded in mystery. Historically we encounter some variant already in the Hebrew Bible and social historians are able to trace its "career" and permutations through the centuries down to our own time. As we shall see in a later chapter, the behavioral and normative requirements of the nuclear family became the conventional way for the organization of individual and social life in the course of a few centuries. At this point in our argument, however, it is important to appreciate that the nuclear family of Northwest European origin is of long historical standing and the record shows that it antedates the Industrial Revolution by centuries. Though the onset of industrialization in the societies of the West transformed the ways in which people live, work, and consume with cataclysmic speed, the most distinctive structural features of the conventional family long remained unchanged. Neither the progressively declining economic role of the household nor the "sentimental revolution" of the nineteenth century were able to challenge the esteem this type of family enjoyed; and inside and outside of the academy scholars were intrigued by its extraordinary staying power. By the late nineteenth century a sizable literature on the uniqueness of the nuclear family filled the libraries of Western countries. When one reads through this literature today, one is impressed by the degree to which academics, like the vast majority of the population, were convinced that this type of family was not only based on facts of nature but that it was also held to be superior to any other family form.[2] Long into the early decades of the twentieth century it was taken for granted in all societies of the West that the family in its conventional nuclear form was the central institution of modern life. Neither symptoms attesting to the existence of internal tensions nor the rising tide of all sorts of problematic behaviors in the society at large did much to undermine the persisting faith in its superiority. By and large such symptoms were held to be an inevitable, and perhaps temporary, consequence of the modernization process and, with the notable exceptions of conservatives and radical Marxists, they were expected to abate with the maturation of the industrial order.

As the twentieth century progressed, however, personal and social problems seemed to multiply rather than decrease. As a consequence, fears about the conventional family's capacity to handle its many functions began to mount. Nowhere were such fears more strongly expressed than in the United States. Here in "the first new nation," where the forces of industrialization, urbanization, and immigration—the "triple revolution" of modernity—intersected in visibly dramatic ways, the conventional family appeared to have lost its "functional utility" to a special degree. With masses of immigrants streaming into America's rapidly growing industrial urban centers, social observers feared that families bereft of the traditional support of kin and community were ill-equipped to adequately meet their central functions and it became customary to tacitly assume that the social isolation of migrants in the exploding cities was responsible for the soaring rates in crime, delinquency, alcoholism, drug addiction, and an increase in family breakup. The newly-established discipline of sociology, in particular, seemed to be able to document with a fair measure of certainty that the conventional family was ill-suited to absorb the fallout from the broad changes sweeping through the industrializing world. Confronted with such empirical data, progressive intellectuals began to argue ever more forcibly that it fell upon the modern state—both for moral as well as economic reasons—to design and provide public mechanisms to compensate for the conventional nuclear family's inferred shortcomings.[3] The Aid to Dependent Children and the Social Security legislation of the 1930s may be cited as the most outstanding public policy achievement motivated by this new understanding of the role of the state. Other public measures ranging from the establishment of child guidance clinics to an assortment of family support programs were enacted as well for the purpose of shoring up a family increasingly held to be in need of support. Proliferating numbers of trained experts who made the family their vocation and profession, the "friendly intruders" in the language of the time, set out to bring individual behavior held to be problematic under control by getting involved in the inner workings of the family.

It is of some importance to realize that the policy model developed during the first part of the twentieth century focused, in the main, on the behavior of the individual rather than on the family as a social unit. Though America's individualistically-based political philosophy undoubtedly promoted this particular mode of intervention, it also reflected the country's peculiar propensity for quasi-psychotherapeutic explanatory approaches. That is to say, all individual deviations from idealized behavioral norms tended to be reduced to psychological malfunctions that were held to have their origin in defective family interaction. In this manner untested and often competing psychologistic notions about the factors shaping individual behavior were introduced into the public discourse. Without fail this modus operandi made for a situation in which professionals increasingly came to understand their services as rescue missions designed to extricate individuals from destructive family relationships, however vaguely defined. In the relevant literature of the time one reads a lot about the problems caused by authoritarian fathers and overbearing mothers—or, in a competing reading, about the noncaring father and the overindulgent mother. Unintentionally, though perhaps inevitably, the doors were thereby opened to what the sociologist Philip Rieff has called the "triumph of the therapeutic." Increasingly individuals were no longer held to be responsible for their own behavior, they now were seen to be hapless victims of destructive family dynamics. In short order it became accepted practice to blame the family for all manifestations of individual behavior that gave cause for concern. The growing trend fueled not only a phenomenal rise in the prestige and discretionary power of the growing legions of family professionals; it also promoted the expansion of governmental authority to intervene in intimate matters of personal and familial life. This deep-seated predisposition for individual-centered psychologistic explanations contributed in no small measure to the way in which the conventional family came to be viewed in subsequent decades.

By the time the 1960s came around it had become increasingly evident to policymakers that many of the well-intentioned public measures designed to upgrade the functions of families held to be in distress remained elusive. Their failure manifested itself to a palpable degree in the attempt to integrate minority groupings into the economic and cultural mainstream of American society. With this recognition something akin to a "paradigm shift" a la Thomas Kuhn occurred in that the focus switched from the individual to factors of social life. Though the psychologistic mode of intervention was never fully abandoned, a trend established itself to attribute individual problematic behavior to the persistence of racial discrimination and the unequal distribution of political and economic power. Poverty and inequality, rather than faulty family interactions, were now identified as the "root cause" of all personal and social ills.

The "paradigm shift" progressed in distinctive stages, with one phase replacing the next in rapid succession. With the enactment of the Johnson administration's "Great Society" programs, the policy focus shifted from viewing problematic individual behavior as a consequence of family shortcomings to viewing it as a product of long-entrenched discriminatory practices racial minority groups had experienced in the past. As many politicians and policymakers became increasingly convinced that only greater governmental involvement could provide a solution to mounting problems, a rousing call for national action issued forth and a "war on poverty" was declared. All that was needed to make social dysfunctional behavior, racial discrimination, and persisting poverty a thing of the past was a combination of national will, money, and good old American know-how, meted out by credentialed experts. Was America not the richest and the most caring nation in the world, and the smartest one to boot? Or so the argument went. Far-reaching legislation was introduced to do away with the most egregious discriminatory practices that had plagued the American political system for all too long. Using the powers of the federal government, racial segregation—which subsequently was extended to include segregation by gender, age, and the sexual propensities of individuals—was outlawed and mechanisms were put into place that aimed to make up for the most damaging consequences of past discrimination. Soon a large network of programs began to span the country from coast to coast and the courts set out to hold individuals and organizations transgressing against the new laws legally responsible.

There can be little doubt that the civil rights legislations of 1964 targeting discrimination and the lack of access to opportunities and resources succeeded in many ways. A number of Great Society cornerstone programs—such as the enactment of Medicare and Medicaid—must even be seen as genuine and long overdue achievements. Yet in other important areas of social life the well-intentioned legislations failed to achieve its goals. So for instance, it did not take long for it to become evident that few of the antipoverty and antidiscrimination policies had the desired effect on the ways in which individuals conducted their personal lives. Poverty rates, despite minor fluctuations, persisted and the climbing rates of delinquency, crime, alcoholism, drug addiction, truancy, divorce, desertion, illegitimacy, and so forth, signaled to any one who had eyes to see that the link between poverty and destructive personal behavior was not as clearcut as had been assumed. Some prescient policymakers soon recognized that it was an altogether different thing to declare war on poverty through legislation that outlawed discriminatory practices in employment, politics, and housing, from bringing about actual and lasting changes in individual behavior. More importantly, however, few at the time were inclined to link the de facto growth of worrisome behavioral trends to the ambivalent role the new public policy had assigned to the conventional family. In fact, it was to take more than two decades, some major social upheavals, and two further phases in the paradigm shift, until it became admissible to give voice once more to the inherent linkage between the two.

While it was self-evident for most ordinary people that the family plays an indispensable role in the socialization of children and their preparation for a productive role in society, the creeping disillusionment with the effectiveness of Great Society programs motivated idealistic poverty warriors to look for remedies in an altogether different direction. By coincidence rather than design, a number of adversary cultural and political movements jumped onto the public stage precisely at the time when their ineffectiveness could no longer be denied. In a fateful confluence of countercultural sentiments and New-Left politics the public discourse was swiftly radicalized and in an amazingly brief span of time a point was reached in the late 1960s when an all-out war against the conventional family became the agenda of the day.

Under the influence of theoretical perspectives meted out in academic disputes it became customary in progressively-inclined elite circles to portray the old liberal domestic policy approach of the first part of the twentieth century as one dominated by a set of policies and mechanisms concocted by the ruling classes—the powerful and the rich—for the purpose of controlling the lower classes and those deviating from the cultural mainstream. With energy and resolve a slew of studies was conducted to uncover class-based social controls in education, social work, medicine, psychiatry, the criminal justice system, and the juvenile courts. So, for instance, it was argued that public welfare programs, far from being motivated by humanitarian impulses, were a manipulative device of the elite classes for the purpose of creating a pool of cheap wage labor and preventing revolutionary upsurges.[4] It was further claimed that the proliferation of jarring individual and social problems should not be understood as a failure of individuals to adapt to existing social norms and requirements, but rather that such problems and inabilities must be seen as symptoms of the failure of "the system." With increasing certitude the new scholarship averred that the widening array of worrisome behavior—delinquency, crime, alcoholism, drug addiction, truancy, divorce, desertion, illegitimacy, and so forth—must be understood as the inevitable consequence of the unequal distribution of income and power rampant in societies organized under the capitalist market economy. In other words, rather than "blaming the victim," it was the system that had to be blamed, for it was the system that had turned ill-fated individuals into victims.[5]

The multitude of state-organized, state-financed, and state-delivered social intervention programs that had come into existence in the wake of the Great Society campaign had already prepared the ground for the elevation of a vision of social life that in essence was hostile to the modern family in its conventional nuclear form. Though it would be a grave injustice to blame the assault on the family on Great Society policy efforts to fight poverty and discrimination, it can be shown that by divorcing issues of poverty and individual malfunctioning from the exigencies of the conventional family, a dynamic was set into motion that turned welfare into a support system individuals could count on regardless of the destructive consequences of their actual behavior. While a noticeable loosening in traditional norms had already occurred long before the sixties, countercultural exhortations to "do your own thing" and to "let it all hang out" greatly served to encourage behavior patterns that stood in direct opposition to the exacting norms that are part and parcel of the modern nuclear family. What is more, the counterculture's vision of a life free of boundaries and restrictions made it virtually inevitable that the lifestyle and values of this type of family came to be seen as the major obstacle standing in the way of its realization. In other words, what started with a redefinition of the causes of poverty and discrimination ended in short order with a rousing call to "turn the world upside down." Since many of these sentiments continue to linger in the public discourse to this day, a little more has to be said about how it happened that in the brief span of a few tumultuous years the unenviable status of being responsible for all the ills of the Western way of life came to be assigned to the nuclear family in its conventional form.

The Countercultural Revolution and the Rise of the Politics of the Family

To this day, the suddenness and vehemence with which the countercultural revolution of the 1960s came to dominate the public discourse continues to be a puzzle to scholars and ordinary people alike. In addition to the celebrated literary paragons of the countercultural movement, those setting the tone were the student revolutionaries in education and sociology, radical existential psychiatrists and psychologists, and the radical members of the clergy in the schools of theology and the churches. Their message of the dehumanizing function of social boundaries and traditions in time penetrated into the lower ranks of professionals and semi-professionals where suspicions about the inadequacy of the conventional family had been rife for some time. While it is impossible to trace the history of the countercultural movement here, it is of some importance for the arguments of this book to decipher the general process whereby a coalition of special interest groups came to declare war on the conventional family and nearly succeeded in driving it into the underground.

It is important to keep in mind that from the very beginning the countercultural movement was more than merely a movement determined to battle this or that particular manifestation of injustice and inequity. Amazingly candid in its revolutionary formulations, and without apology, it was a passionate crusade for the transformation of the full array of institutional arrangements distinctive of the Western way of life. In those unsettling days of the "new politics" of the 1960s and 1970s, its revolutionary fervor swept like a brushfire through all democratic industrial societies of the West and in crossing national borders it did not take long for a view to consolidate in opinion-setting elite circles that the nuclear family, conventional and incorrigibly bourgeois, presented the major obstacle to the emergence of a more just and more equitable society. Bourgeois capitalism, bourgeois democracy, and the bourgeois family, along with all the presuppositions upon which these institutionalized forms rest, simply had to go.

The strong liberationist sentiments floating about at the time served to unite an otherwise motley group of Left-wing political activists, rebellious students, feminists, gays, lesbians, and other refugees from mainstream society. Despite divergent, and often contradictory, understandings of the causes of oppression, they were tied together by a savage dislike of America's present, and, for that matter, its past as well. In their destructive rage and imbued by grievances too many to enumerate, they showed themselves willing to tear down all the obstacles they held to stand in the way of a better future. All the institutional cornerstones that for long had been the hallmark of Western societies had to be removed posthaste, none could be spared. Reminiscent of Edmund Burke's observation of several centuries ago that those who destroy everything are certain to remedy some grievances, the American political philosopher Benjamin Barber warned at the time with considerable prescience that "to redress by eradication is to eliminate the present and reject the past without creating a future."[6]

In the volatile climate of the sixties and seventies, with war raging in Vietnam, racial unrest threatening to tear American society apart, and the Cold War entering into a new phase, it became fashionable to blame the conventional nuclear family for virtually everything held to be wrong with the modern world and anti-system protests swept through all the industrialized democratic nations of the West. Nowhere, however, was the animus against the "system"— and the conventional family by extension—more virulently expressed than in the United States. Every aspect of modern American family life that used to be understood as an expression of human nature in a taken-for-granted manner—definitions of masculinity and femininity, the necessity of marriage, the wish of having children, the rights and obligations of children and parents to each other, and so forth—was now subjected to question and attack.[7] The attacks were so venomous at times, and for the most part so irrational, as to merit the description of a witch-hunt. Few popular songs expressed the cultural mood of the time better than Bob Dylan's famous "The Times They Are a-Changin'." To the alluring tunes of an electric guitar, mothers and fathers throughout the land were reprimanded not to criticize what they didn't understand. They were commanded to get out of the way as their behavior and morals were conjectured to be demonstrably obsolete and standing in the way for a more equitable, more just, and, above all, a more unencumbered life to emerge.[8]

In retrospect one can only marvel at the speed in which attitudes and behavior, that at first seemed to be outlandish if not repellent to mainstream America, came to be tolerated and finally accepted. Under the drumbeat of an adulatory media, it became the received wisdom of the day that to survive in an unjust and heartless world modern men and women were compelled to tailor their domestic arrangements to their personal needs and preferences. The once taken-for-granted conventional family with its stringent normative requirements was thus reduced to just one lifestyle choice among many, and a frequently reviled and anachronistic one at that.

As the countercultural revolution gained momentum, its claims and visions came to be ever more radicalized. With this radicalization the war against the family entered into a phase that went far beyond demands for the liberation from the restraints imposed by this type of family. An instructive case in point is the way in which radical feminists transformed a movement initially concerned with the revision of the position of women in modern society into an intemperate attack on virtually every aspect of conventional family life that ultimately culminated in a war against human nature itself.

From Women's Liberation to Liberation from Nature

A convenient event by which to date the inception of the new women's movement is 1963, when Betty Friedan's *The Feminine Mystique* was published.[9] This book was an indictment of the middle-class woman's "imprisonment" in the kind of domesticity Virginia Woolf once described as "the cottonwool quality of daily life." In Friedan's views the requirements of the conventional nuclear family that had been institutionalized in the course of centuries served to stifle a woman's capacity for personal growth and prevented her from conquering her rightful place in the economy and in politics. The public domain, she insisted, was controlled by males ruthlessly determined to keep women in their "proper place," that is to say in the home and primarily in charge of the care of children and the "finer things of life." With her observation that if asked the question, "Who am I?" a woman answers: "I am Johnny's mother and Bob's wife," a woman is in serious trouble.

The way in which Friedan formulated the contemporary Western woman's problems served to enthrone a politics of identity that pitted the interests of women against the interests of their families, that of their husbands and children alike. Friedan's solution to the modern woman's identity problem was unambiguous and infectious: women had to move out of the household into the world of work where their essential identity could be found. Freedom for women in Friedan's mind meant freedom from the family.

While Friedan was writing her book, however, women had already been entering the workforce in ever-larger numbers. While in the 1950s 20 percent of all married women worked outside of the home, by 1972 the figure had climbed to over 40 percent, with women with young children making up the bulk of the rise. (By the 1990s the percentage of married women in the labor market had climbed to over 50 percent, reaching the level of over 60 percent at the turn of the millenium.) What was new in this shift was the social location of the women moving into the labor market. While in earlier periods the paid female labor force consisted primarily of working-class women, it was the highly-educated women of the middle classes, who for more than a century had celebrated domesticity as the proud badge of their middle-class status, who were now determined to be liberated from the confines of family and home. In the gilded cages of America's suburbs, (the middle-class woman's "comfortable concentration camp," in Friedan's revealing phrase), a good number of the highly-educated and ambitious young women felt increasingly constrained by family obligations that prevented them from pursuing the careers they felt they were prepared for. No longer satisfied with the limiting world of children and home, they strained hard to find meaning and purpose (and income!) outside of the family. In retrospect it may seem more than a little ironic that middle-class women recklessly denounced the very lifestyle their working-class "sisters" had fervently wished to gain for so long.

Yet as ever more highly-educated women moved into the labor market, they encountered what some perceived to be massive discrimination. It was among this group that Friedan's battle cry to "turn the world upside down" found special resonance. Her message had both a political as well as a psychological impact. Politically, it set off a fierce struggle for equality in all spheres of life. Psychologically, it encouraged personal self-assertion and a quest for self-realization that opened the doors to a struggle between the genders. In the general climate of the period, both aspects became radicalized to a degree whereby what first appeared to be a reasonable, even legitimate cause, was rapidly turned into an agenda of an altogether different kind. By the mid-seventies a new feminist ideology had been firmly established that differed from the feminist ideology of the earlier period in many ways. Most importantly, however, it was now distinguished by pronounced antifamily prejudices.

In the research centers and think tanks set up at the time, academics set out to supply the appropriate ammunition for the demolition of long-established, commonsensical views of the family and human nature. In focusing the laser beam of their attention on those aspects of modern family life that could help to legitimate countercultural claims, they set out to deconstruct what in essence is difficult, if not impossible, to deconstruct. A good number pursued this agenda with gusto and, at times, even with considerable ingenuity. A case in point is the work of Mary Jane Sherfey, a New York psychiatrist, who, in combining new findings in biology with new data on sexual responsiveness, popularized the notion that insofar as embryonic development was concerned males develop from females and not the other way around.[10] While these and other new findings of modern science are perhaps able to expose the biblical story of creation as mythical, it is difficult to see how they can be used to buttress feminist arguments in general. To conclude, as Sherfey does, that for reasons of anatomy there exists an inherent conflict of interests marking all relationships between women and men surely defies logic.[11]

Yet questions of the logic of the argument hardly entered into the feminist equation. Without providing further qualifications it soon became fashionable to argue that human nature no longer implies destiny, that a person's gender is a matter of individual choice which can be changed at the edge of a surgeon's knife, and that any cultural taming of human sexuality is an authoritarian, and hence objectionable, enterprise. Empirical observations on the nature of early infantile behavior and parental response, for instance, which permit both to be considered within the framework of mutually interactive signaling systems peculiar to humans, were declared to be ideologically tainted. The existence of a maternal instinct upon which the care of infants depends was found to be a myth, and the notion of motherhood itself was argued to be a legend conveniently constructed for the purpose of keeping women in bondage. In a widely-read and influential book by Elizabeth Badinter, for instance, it was averted that women had for long been miscast as vessels of maternal instinct. Providing example after example of feminine ambivalence and indifference, if not hostility, toward children and the young, Badinter sought to demonstrate that the maternal instinct is neither natural nor universal but learned and historical, subject to manipulation. And as to be expected, the claim of its existence was argued to be a prime tool in the subjugation of women.[12] In the same vein other feminist writers claimed that the significance of mother-child bonding rests on shoddy research and that the value of human bonding is a perilous mystification.

In a crescendo of voices the family itself soon came to be declared to be a pathogenic agent. Perhaps nowhere were these sentiments more clearly reflected than in the writings of the radical psychologists R. D. Laing and David Cooper, whose pronouncements had ramifications far beyond the limited professional circles of clinical psychologists and their half-baked followers.[13] In their various publications the two writers depicted the family not only as an institution in which humans find themselves entrapped through the accident of birth, the powerlessness of childhood, and the false beliefs inculcated by their dependency, but they also declared the conventional nuclear family as the prime agent of every conceivable pathology. What is more, Laing and Cooper spearheaded a view of social life in which each member of any group, but that of the family group in particular, is a tyrant vis-à-vis every other member. With self-discovery and self-fulfillment pronounced to be the ultimate purpose of human life, a notion of human nature came to be propagated in which the existence of its most noble potentials were belittled, if not denied. David Cooper, for instance, presented a particularly sharp case against human potentials for self-sacrifice, altruism, and nurture when retelling—approvingly—the Japanese tale of the monk Basho who, upon finding an abandoned child on the river bank, performs the true act of self-fulfillment by leaving the child to die on the river bank and continuing on his journey.[14]

When one looks back at the events of these crucial decades it is not difficult to empathize with the civil rights' agenda of the women's movement in its early phase. A woefully long record attested to the ways in which women had been disadvantaged in terms of education, employment, social status, and legal and political rights through the ages and across cultures. Although a fair number of the movement's attempts to rectify the historical record leave much to be desired, the fact remains that modern women had good cause to demand broader societal commitments and to redress their many grievances. When under the doctrine of equal rights a surprisingly small group of feminists set out to fight for the equal treatment of women in the workplace, in politics, and in the culture as a whole, many Americans—perhaps even the majority of people in the societies of the West—felt the women's agenda to be fair and perhaps also necessary. On the psychological level as well, a large number of men and women thought it was high time to combat traditionalist and Freudian tendencies (epitomized by Helene Deutsch's notion of the existence of a distinctive feminine passivity rooted in biology) to use the female anatomy and psyche to legitimate social practices that relegate women to a life spent in the nurture of children, the care of the household, and to apply themselves to charity, the arts, and a select variety of traditional women's causes. In sum, women had many and real grievances.

Yet emboldened by the initial successes of their requests during the heady days of liberation, the assertions and demands began to accelerate. Prominent activists began to outdo each other with claims that women are by nature the "most oppressed of all people." In finely-wrought tracts feminists writers used their considerable talents to conjure up a vision of social life in which women were enslaved into a permanent state of servitude by hateful men and in making use of dubious materials when it suited them, but with no real effort to search for the truth itself, quite a few set out to ensconce their message in the public mind. So for instance, Juliet Mitchell's message that women are "the most oppressed of all people," soon escalated into Kate Millet's claim that "sexist oppression is more endemic to our society than racism," only to be topped by Shulamite Firestone pronouncement that "sexism represents the oldest, most rigid class-caste system in existence." And finally, it fell to Yoko Ono to declare that "woman is the nigger of the world." Book titles such as *Is Marriage Necessary?*, *The Marriage Trap*, *The Female Eunuch*, and *The Death of the Family* soon began to crowd the shelves of every corner drug store. Garish headlines such as "Is This the Last Marrying Generation?," "Women United Against Marriage," and "Breaking Free by Breaking Out" were flaunted from every newsstand. This new trend was surely quite an escalation of Friedan's original critique! No longer did it suffice to protest against this or that aspect of discrimination, now a *reinterpretation* of history and of the human condition itself was demanded as an indispensable prerequisite if human felicity was to be gained. And as the rhetoric escalated, the conventional family and everything connected with it came to be the prime target of the feminist wrath. With pronouncements such as "heterosexuality is rape," "motherhood slavery," and "all relations between the sexes are a struggle for power," arguments were carried to a point that ultimately culminated in one huge outcry against being female. The family—and the conventional nuclear family in particular—was declared to be Western society's paramount instrument for holding women in a state of base subjugation.

This outcry reached its peak in the early 1970s when the radical feminist perspective on family life merged with other countercultural visions floating about at the time. The ensuing massive onslaught solidified an existing propensity among the cultural elite that the time had come to abandon not only the conventional family as a cultural ideal, but as a model for social policy as well. With the 1979 White House Conference on the Family, the loudly touted "Year of the Family," much publicized countercultural dispositions became part of the mainstream public discourse. However, unexpected and unpredicted, the fateful meetings of this conference served not only to provide the status of legitimacy to the countercultural agenda, it also served to galvanize the rise of a conservative pro-family movement which in time was to gain momentum and support from unexpected quarters. Yet the fierce opposition of culturally more conservative delegates not withstanding (a courageous group simply walked out), the major achievement of the White House Conference on the Family of 1979 amounted to nothing less than an officially sanctioned redefinition of the family. To accommodate a wide variety of domestic arrangements— ranging from single-parent households, blended families, same-sex families, cohabiting couples to more exotic makeshift groupings—that had made their entrance during the preceding decade, the term "family" was replaced by the term "families" without further ado. All domestic arrangements, and were they yet the most fleeting and far-fetched, were now held to be equally acceptable and, of course, deserving of public recognition and support.

It may be useful at this point in our brief account of the successful degradation of the conventional family to reflect for a few moments on what the coalition between an out-of bounds Left-wing liberalism and radical feminism has wrought, though some proponents, I am sure, are still reluctant to face up to the all too real personal and social consequences of their rhetoric and demands.

What the Radical Counterculture Has Wrought

As we have seen, the countercultural "liberationists" took themselves and their agenda very seriously. Inflamed claims to start out with quickly escalated into a rhetoric that left neither room for distinction nor for the recognition of the many and real changes that had occurred in the life of Western women during the past centuries. Leaving questions of historical accuracy aside, to deny the fact that the women of the highly-industrialized, democratic societies of the West are today by all measures better off than their counterparts in traditional China or those living in the strife-ridden societies of contemporary central Africa, is as misguided as it is pernicious. Western women have enjoyed a much higher degree of respect and freedom in the past than many feminists are willing to admit. One only has to read a few pages of Emmanuel Le Roy Ladurie's much noted book *Montaillou*, a carefully documented account of late-fourteenth-century life in the south of France, or Steven Ozment's *The Buergermeister's Daughter*, an equally fascinating description of the life of a very contrarian fifteenth-century German woman (not to mention the rich documentation of English, Dutch, and German family life in early modern times), and a very different picture of women's lives in the Western past emerges.[15] Yet perhaps even more importantly, the persistent inability of radical feminists to differentiate between the "plight" of highly-educated women living in the comfort of American suburbia and the plight of the prisoners of the Warsaw Ghetto or Stalin's Gulags reveals an astounding ignorance of history and is morally reprehensible. Claiming that sexism represents the oldest, most rigid, and vilest form of oppression and to use the language of oppression as carelessly and indiscriminately as feminists have done, has led to a situation in which the legitimate grievances of women have begun to fall on deaf ears. With their contempt for marriage and the family and their inability to distinguish between what are the problems of life and what are the problems of women radical feminists have done modern women a great disservice.

The process whereby the feminist tendency to reduce the many obstacles women encounter in social life to an all-pervasive sexism manifests itself most revealingly in the denial of the existence of biological differences between the genders. To bolster their legitimate arguments on behalf of women, radical feminists found it necessary, in short order, to aver that there do not exist any biological differences between men and women at all. They vociferously argued that both genders have the same capacities, the same impulses, the same propensities, and the same aspirations. One may well squabble with some of the specifics of a naturalist definition of the genders that holds that men and women are equally endowed in energy, impulses, sexual appetites, and cognition, as more biologistically-inclined critics have done. Yet the tendency to reduce women—and men, for that matter—to generic categories that allow no accounting for the extraordinary diversity in the manifestation of human behavior reveals the near willful ignorance of the fanatical ideologue. It is one thing to reject traditional ideas about the nature of women and men, such as women being by nature passive and men aggressive, yet it is an altogether different thing to make generalizations that bear no relationship to objective reality. When claims are made that a woman can only achieve equality if she denies her female nature—and then only in isolation from men and children—social life becomes an impossibility. Sisterhood may be powerful, yet when a vision triumphs that denies the possibility of the existence of those characteristics of human nature that in their complimentariness provide the "glue" without which social life is impossible, something unreal and infinitely disturbing enters into the equation of human existence.

When one plods through the immense volume of publications of the time, it does not take long to realize that during the peak days of the countercultural movement quite a few liberationists seriously believed that enduring human felicity could be gained if social life would be remade to the measure of their own imagination. Celebrating life outside of established boundaries and structures, all social forms, roles, expectations, continuities, and certainties, almost by definition, came under suspicion. The systematic demolition of existing boundaries was argued to be a necessary preamble for the creation of an ideal society, a society in which individuals are allowed to discover their "basic humanity," whatever that may mean. While in retrospect it may sound merely quaint that large numbers of young enthusiasts agitating for a juster, more equitable, more brotherly society in which wicked things like war, racism, exploitation, and all forms of human suffering can be eliminated by taking to the streets, protesting, holding sit-ins and teach-ins, it strikes the present-day reader as positively bizarre that such intoxicating ambitions presupposed a prior liberation from family and human nature.

There is no space here to discuss in any detail the many twists and nuances of the arguments that carried the day in quick succession. What matters is to understand that a consistent attempt was made to present a powerful case against the necessity of the family and, by extension, against the limitations imposed by human nature. Perhaps the most disturbing aspect of the flood of publications was the persistent tendency to reframe every inquiry to fit the agenda of the politics of gender. Many of the publications that saw the light of day during this turbulent period had less to do with an honest effort to gain a better understanding of human nature than with the unmasking of the "lies" generations of middle-class white males of European origin were alleged to have foisted on unsuspecting and long-suffering women. There can be no doubt that it is the incontestable task of every scholar to examine the truthfulness of existing bodies of knowledge through the lens of newly-collected and secured information and, when indicated, to modify, expand, or even discard that part of our stock of knowledge that can be demonstrated to be wrong. Yet very little is gained when the new "truths" are even more unsecured and more sweepingly framed than was the old stock of knowledge. To be sure, some new interpretations were able to draw renewed attention to the importance of culture in the shaping of human behavior. Yet others have made better and more convincing arguments along these lines long before and after. Rather than proving the significance of cultural factors, the ideology-driven countercultural research agenda produced the opposite effect. And this is a great pity, for the recognition of the impact of cultural and social factors on the lives of individuals and social groupings remains an unfinished intellectual task. Whatever the merits of some counterculturally-inspired studies may be, the fact remains that a type of scholarship was enthroned that will prevent for some time to come the coalescence of diverse strands of knowledge into a workable and balanced research paradigm for the study of human nature.

In today's more sober climate much of the hype of the countercultural movement may strike many as exaggerated, if not outlandish. Yet its linguistic excesses provided second-wave feminism with its biting edge and drew widespread public attention to its message. Under the drumbeat of an ever-willing media, radical feminists succeeded to block out more reasoned voice—at least for a while. In hindsight one is left with a new appreciation of the power of language. That is to say, language may not only reflect social reality; language also shapes social reality to a considerable degree. Definitions, philosophers tell us, have real consequences. This observation holds *a fortiori* for the family.

Reality on the Rebound: The Family in the 1980s and 1990s

It is of some importance to appreciate that the vast majority of ordinary men and women—in all walks of life and from the most varied ethnic backgrounds imaginable—continued to stay loyal to a vision of life defined by the criteria of the conventional family. Though confused and troubled by the turmoil set into motion by the countercultural Left, most refused to embrace the more extreme positions flaunted by the intellectual firebrands who had been turned into cultural icons by an adulatory media. Yet during those tumultuous years it had become increasingly difficult for many to close their eyes and ears to countercultural claims, particularly when these claims were officially sanctioned and accompanied by prospects of unimagined personal freedom. By the middle of the 1970s the stage had thus been set for the paradoxical situation in which the cultural elite was eager to deinstitutionalize the family in its conventional form and celebrate the rich variety of lifestyle options available, while ordinary people remained to be guided by more conventional ideals. The data clearly bore this out: most people continued to fall in love, marry, have children, and to aspire to a family life that strikingly resembled the ideals of an earlier generation. Few expressed these existing cultural cleavages better than Shulamite Firestone, who in her call for a radical feminist revolution bewailed the confounding reality that "just as God has been pronounced dead quite often, but has this sneaky way of resurrecting himself, so everyone debunks marriage and the family, yet ends up married."[16]

At the same time, the unrelenting attacks on the legitimacy of the conventional family and its demanding ethos left their mark on many ordinary people. While large segments of middle America felt at times to be in danger of being condemned to live a life in the cultural underground, the officially sanctioned anticonventional family view of domestic life provoked feelings of profound uncertainty among economic and culturally marginal groups. The linguistic and public policy shift was in the words of Gertrude Himmelfarb fraught with moral implications that were to have "grave material and social consequences." [17] Its consequences continue to haunt America to this day.

Yet when it seemed as if the stage had been set for the final blow to fall, the merits of the conventional family were rediscovered. They were rediscovered not only by those who had stayed loyal to the virtues of the conventional family all through the years in the wilderness, but by official America as well.

How could such a reversal come about? For one, by the late 1970s it had become evident to many that the delegitimization of the conventional family had produced disastrous consequences for America's poor. Regardless which interpretation in the continuing debate over the causes of poverty will ultimately carry the day—with explanations from demography and structure competing with those of racism and moral isolation—a huge set of data collected by responsible social science researchers succeeded to demonstrate convincingly that a new welfare dependency had come into existence among the poor. The same data also strongly suggested that this new type of poverty—along with a host of other pressing domestic problems such as rampant youth crime and the catastrophic failure of public education—was to a large degree rooted in the erosion of the moral codes of behavior typically linked to the lifestyle of the conventional nuclear family. Statistics on separation, desertion, divorce, and illegitimacy when causally related to poverty, provided solid documentation for the proposition that the infectious collapse of the two-parent family among the poor made for a type of dependency on government resources which no amount of federal moneys and ingenuity was able to stem. Already by the mid-1980s it had become increasingly difficult to deny that the 1979 official redefinition of "the family" to "families" spelled disaster for America's poor. All available data indicated that the linguistic deconstruction of the conventional family greatly reinforced the liberalization of behavioral codes latently present in any group at any time, but in marginal groups in particular. No longer obliged to play by the social rules likely to ensure success in modern society, the 1979 official redefinition had opened the doors to the acceptance of a normative vacuum.[18] As the record shows, personal practices were condoned that drove ever larger numbers of single mothers and their children into poverty. In the face of this new-sprung reality, the continuing reluctance of public officials to the use of the term "illegitimacy" and their preference for less judgmental terms such as "alternate modes of parenting" or "nonmarital childbearing" appears more than a little puzzling. Though it has been obvious to most people for a long time that there exists a family connection in poverty, homelessness, school failure, and delinquency, it may yet take some time until this connection will be officially accepted as well.

For another reason, all through the 1960s and 1970s the cultural Right had not only been caught off guard by the countercultural revolution, it had, in fact, not yet been fused into anything resembling a social movement. With some notable exceptions, little had been heard from cultural conservatives nationally during these crucial years, though, no doubt, there must have been many who were greatly dismayed by the deluge of outlandish claims flooding over American public life.[19] Finally, in the 1970s two Supreme Court decisions—both connected with a woman's right to abortion—served to galvanize the organization of a "pro-family" movement. The Supreme Court decision of 1976 that put into law that abortion was a right of an individual woman over which neither a husband nor, in the case of a minor, a parent, had veto rights, was met with profound shock by a good number of people who until then had remained at the margin of the debates raging in the culture at large. Many found this decision to touch on the very notion of the family as an "organic" entity existing over and beyond the individual. Gaining in size and vigor as time went on, supported by the Catholic Church, but by no means limited to Catholics alone (the ever-louder voices of the growing Evangelical movement come to mind) an impassioned backlash movement was born. Such backlash reactions coalesced into a movement in defense of traditional values and the traditional family. This nascent movement was to become an important political force in the creation of the "Reagan Revolution" (the revolution of "the silent majority") of the 1980s.

While issues of abortion did not hold the same moral urgency for most Americans (at a later point, we shall have occasion to say a little more about this wrenching issue), the Right's clearly-defined pro-family agenda helped to rekindle a broadly-based national concern with family values. The growing realization spread among ordinary people that matters of the family went beyond the cultural Right's opposition to "abortion on demand" led to a much vilified backlash reaction in most Western countries, with America, as always, in the lead. Though many modern men and women refused to have their lives controlled by the rigidly applied moral codes of the past, too many of the countercultural claims were simply not acceptable to middle America.[20]

The changing national mood was reinforced by social science research findings conducted in the academies. Already by the 1980s the research of scholars who by no stretch of the imagination could be seen to make common cause with the cultural Right, could confirm growing public apprehensions about the validity of a good number of countercultural claims and arguments. Mary Jo Bane's *Here to Stay: The American Family in the Twentieth Century*, deserves special mention in this context. [21] Her meticulously conducted large-scale research showed that family structure and family commitments had not changed significantly in the past one hundred years: most families continued to take care of their children, even in some cases against all the odds; marriage was still a strong enterprise; child-parent bonds rather than weakened had become prolonged and intensified; married men and women were generally happier than unmarried ones; aging family members were still cared for by their families; and the much lamented isolation of the nuclear family had been greatly exaggerated. Other publications, as well, introduced perspectives on the conventional family that stood in stark contrast to those propagated by radical feminists and the countercultural Left. So for instance, Selma Fraiberg's *Every Child's Birth Right* presented a defense of traditional mothering, the Left-leaning psycho-historian Christopher Lasch published an impassioned attack on willful academic misinterpretations of the family with his *Haven in a Heartless World*, and Brigitte and Peter Berger tried to cut through a mass of confusing contemporary claims in their *The War over the Family: Capturing the Middle Ground*.[22]

By the end of the 1980s the backlash against radical feminist and countercultural visions had gained sufficient momentum for a more reasoned feminism to emerge. With the Equal Rights Amendment removed from the public agenda, the feminist movement itself developed into two directions. While radical feminists sought to reframe the public discourse in terms of violence against women, more mainstream feminists represented by the National Organization of Women set out to focus their agenda on issues important to working mothers. On occasion the two branches continued to make common cause on particular issues, such as the comparable worth in earnings and the defense of abused and battered women.

Since the middle of the 1980s the evidence on the staying power of the family had become so irrefutable and the protests against attempts to undermine the family so strong that organized feminism found it increasingly difficult to deny either. Like many Americans, feminists, too, discovered that two decades of strident and often acrimonious battle for the Equal Rights Amendment had been of symbolic value, in the main, primarily reflecting the narrow cognitive universe of a relatively small segment of highly-educated women of middle-class provenance. Putting the more extreme concerns of radical feminists on the back burner, the National Organization for Women, the chief organ of mainstream feminism, shifted gears to take up the cause of working mothers in their need for affordable childcare. This revised feminist agenda served to lure sizable portions of American feminists back from the wilder shores of madness. At the same time, it succeeded in recruiting new support for feminist causes from women who heretofore had remained rather aloof to radical feminist pursuits.

In this connection Sylvia Ann Hewlett's *A Lesser Life, The Myth of Women's Liberation*, a book that in no small measure contributed to the split in the feminist agenda, deserves to be mentioned. Hewlett faulted the feminist movement for its preoccupation with formal, legal issues of equality between the sexes, abortion rights, and lesbian rights, while woefully neglecting the concerns of modern women in their dual roles as mothers and wage earners. Hewlett's heart went out to the new breed of women who tried to combine careers in the public sphere with the traditional woman's concerns to be a good mother to her children. Examining the family policies of comparable European countries she argued that European feminists had been significantly more pragmatic and family-oriented than their American counterparts and she concluded that in contrast to England, France, Germany, and Italy, for instance, the major problem for American women was that the U.S. government had failed to provide a system of family allowances, federally guaranteed parental leaves, assured options of part-time work or flexible schedules, and federally supported child-care facilities. [23] At the same time, she faulted mainstream America and conservatives for holding women to unrealistic standards of mothering and clinging to an ideal of ultra-domesticity. While critics of the book were quick to point to the flaws in Hewlett's somewhat rash claim that women in comparable European societies were better off than their American sisters, her policy proposals, at first blush, appeared to make good sense to people with a pro-family orientation. They certainly were sufficiently plausible to a feminist leadership in search for an objective that had the potential to revitalize the faltering movement. Hence it did not come as a surprise that the National Organization for Women adopted the Hewlett policy agenda more or less unchanged. Even Betty Friedan, the godmother of America's new feminism, concurred that family allowances, parental leave, and federally-supported childcare should be the movement's central focus in the national debate. As we shall see in Chapter 6, to this day these topics have helped to frame the public debate on the family.

At the same time, we also can observe the emergence of a distinctly more moderate, pro-family feminism whose positions are distinguishable both from those of NOW's mainstream feminism as well as from those of the cultural Right proper. In contrast to the followers of the NOW agenda this group, small in size but strategically located, coalesced around the conviction that it was of some importance to keep the state out of family matters as much as possible. At the same time, the members of this group took some care not to become overly identified with the anti-abortion and anti-gay legislation that remain the driving forces of the cultural Right. Though making common cause at times with the intellectual firebrands of the political Right (Gary Bauer, Ralph Reed, and Allan Carlson come to mind) writers such as David Blankenhorn, Jean Betge Elshtain, Elizabeth Fox-Genovese, David Popenoe, Barbara Whitehead, Christina Hoff Sommers, and Danielle Crittenden (just to mention a few), are active in forging a pro-family position that seeks to capture the political middle ground. Along with the mobilization against anti-family cultural attitudes, this group was and continues to be particularly preoccupied with organizing public sentiments against special-interest-group attempts to use the intrusive powers of the law and government that result, unintentionally perhaps, in the further destabilization of the family in its more conventional mode. So for instance, with research conducted under the aegis of the Institute on American Values on issues of divorce, the decline in parental responsibilities, the importance of fathers, the public disregard of parental rights, the defense of marriage, and so forth, a growing group of researchers located at the political center are today in the process of forging a pro-family political agenda that seeks to reflect more realistically the sentiments and values of mainstream America.[24]

Lifestyle Still a Matter of Choice

To conclude our brief survey of the fall and unpredicted resurrection of the public standing of the conventional nuclear family we may observe that after three decades of lifestyle experimentations on a grand scale and greatly sobered by its fallout, we have witnessed a rediscovery of the singular importance of the family in its conventional form. Politicians in hot pursuit of votes appear to be ready to sing its praises once again and even the political elite seem to be more or less willing to acknowledge that the expansion of the welfare state is by no means able to solve all the ills of modern social life. Past experiences have painfully documented that despite massive governmental efforts all too many individuals remain trapped in poverty and for some identifiable social groups conditions have gotten even measurably worse. Like a bad echo from the nineteenth century, stories about the numbers of children growing up in poverty and ignorance today jolt the conscience of many.

Clearly the more radical versions of the counterculture's vision of political and social life appear to appeal to a dwindling number of people. The shrill headlines that flaunted from every newsstand only two decades ago seem to be neither fashionable nor marketable in today's more sober political climate and all surveys indicate that the great majority of ordinary men and women continue to profess to values revolving around the conventional family. Yet despite these shifts, visions of doom continue to issue forth from the organs of the immense apparatus of persuasion that rules the public sphere today. It does not come as a surprise then that there exists in the public at large a notable uncertainty about how people ought to organize their private lives in the future. In a rapidly changing social order most ordinary men and women are faced with the question to what degree it is possible to adhere to the practices typical of traditional family life or whether their very contemporary needs that propel them to explore new lifestyle options are harmful to themselves and their children. By the same token, social analysts and commentators across the political divide ask to what degree the well-being of individuals and society alike requires an adherence to the clearly-defined behavioral and ethical principles associated with the conventional family. Could it be, some ask, that the post-modern order rushing toward us requires the adoption of a situational ethic determined by the utility of the moment on questions relating to gender, marriage, divorce, the socialization of children, and the many knotty aspects of welfare reform. While the present ambiguity toward the conventional family may be an improvement on the past, it still relativizes the importance of this type of family and distorts its nature and mission. Though the war against the family is for all intents and purposes over, the conventional family itself remains one among several lifestyle choices in the public debate. As the subsequent chapters of the book will show, this need not be so.

Notes

1. The best known of these compilations can be found in the famous Yale Area File collected under the leadership of George P. Murdock. For an early summary see George Peter Murdock, "World Ethnographic Sample," *American Anthropologist* 59, no. 4, 1957 and for a subsequent detailed discussion of these findings see William N. Stephens *The Family in Cross-Cultural Perspective* (New York: University Press of America, 1963). The famous "Yale Area Files" that seek to inventorize the great variety of existing cultural patterns, list by now a much larger number.
2. David Schneider, *American Kinship: A Cultural Account* (Englewood Cliffs, N.J.: Prentice Hall, 1968).
3. Of the many studies conducted at the time, those by Louis Wirth, *The Ghetto*,1938, Robert E. Park and Ernest W. Burgess, *The City*,1925, Frederick Thrasher, *The Gang,* 1927, and Harvey Zorbaugh, *The Gold Coast and the Slum*, 1929, deserve to be especially mentioned.
4. See for instance the widely-read book by Francis F. Piven and Richard A. Cloward, *Regulating the Poor: The Functions of Public Welfare* (New York: Pantheon, 1971).
5. William Ryan, *Blaming the Victim* (New York: Random House, 1971).
6. Benjamin B. Barber, *Liberating Feminism* (New York: Seabury Press, 1975).
7. See for instance, Arlene Skolnik, *The Intimate Environment: Exploring Marriage and the Family* (Boston: Little Brown, 1973).
8. Bob Dylan
   > Come mothers and fathers
   > Throughout the land
   > And don't criticize
   > What you can't understand
   > Your sons and your daughters
   > Are beyond your command
   > Your old road is
   > Rapidly agin'
   > Please get out of the new one
   > If you can't lend your hand
   > For the times they are a-changin'
9. Betty Friedan, *The Feminine Mystique* (New York: Norton, 1963).
10. The pathbreaking biological research for this proposition has been conducted with great care by June Reinisch of the Kinsey Center at the University of Indiana. My

comments on Jane Sherfey's book should not be taken as a criticism of Reinisch's work.

11.   Mary Jane Sherfey, *The Nature and Evolution of Female Sexuality* (New York: Random House, 1972).

12.   Elizabeth Badinter, *L'Amour En Plus: Histoier de l'Amour Maternel* (Paris: Flammarion, 1980).

13.   David C. Cooper, *The Death of the Family* (New York: Pantheon Books, 1971) and Ronald D. Laing, *The Politics of Experience* (New York: Pantheon Books, 1967).

14.   David C. Cooper, op.cit.

15.   Emmanuel Le Roy Ladurie, *Montaillou: Cathars and Catholics in a French Village 1294–1324* (New York: Viking, 1979) and Steven Ozment, *The Buergermeister's Daughter: Scandal in a Sixteenth Century German Town* (Cambridge: Harvard University Press, 1996). Steven Ozment's most recent book *The Loving Family in Old Europe* (Cambridge: Harvard University Press, 2001) should also be mentioned in this context.

16.   Shulamite Firestone, *The Dialectic of Sex: The Case for a Feminist Revolution* (New York: William Morrow, 1970).

17.   Gertrude Himmelfarb, *Poverty and Compassion* (New York: Alfred A. Knopf, 1991).

18.   See for instance, Nicholas Lemann, *The Promised Land: The Great Black Migration and How It Changed America* (New York: Alfred A. Knopf, 1991), and Daniel Patrick Moynihan, *The Politics of a Guaranteed Income* (New York: Random House, 1976). See also Charles Murray, *Losing Ground: American Social Policy 1950–1980* (New York: Basic Books, 1984).

19.   Among the exceptions George Gilder's *Sexual Suicide* (New York: Quadrangle Books, The New York Times Company, 1975) stands out most notably.

20.   Among the Right-wing organization in defense of the traditional family that came into existence at the time only three are mentioned here: Phyllis Schlaefly's "Eagle Forum" organized to defeat the Equal Rights momentum of the seventies; *The Human Life Review*, an anti-abortion magazine, and The Rockford Institute of Rockford, Illinois dedicated to the advocacy of traditional family life. In subsequent years Gary Bauer's and Reverend Dobson's "Focus on the Family" Institute and its various organs became a central rallying point for conservatives.

21.   Mary Jo Bane, *Here to Stay: The American Family in the Twentieth Century* (New York: Basic Books, 1978).

22.   Selma Fraiberg, *Every Child's Birthright: In Defense of Mothering* (New York: Basic Books, 1977); Christopher Lasch, *Haven in a Heartless World: The Family Besieged* (New York: Basic Books, 1977); and Brigitte and Peter Berger, *The War over the Family Capturing the Middle Ground* (New York: Doubleday & Co, 1983).

23.   Sylvia Ann Hewlett, *A Lesser Life: The Myth of Women's Liberation in America* (New York: William Morrow and Company, Inc. 1986).

24.   Under the leadership of David Blankenhorn, The Institute for American Values, located in New York City, has become a central point of reference for this group.

2

Modernization and the Family:
Theorists on the Road to Postmodernism

Postmodernism is post-Vietnam, post-New Left, post-hippie, post-Watergate. History was ruptured, passions have been expanded, belief has become difficult; heroes have died and have been replaced by celebrities. Old verities crumbled, but new ones have not settled in. . . . It reflects an experience that takes for granted not only television but suburbs, shopping malls, recreational (not religious or transcendent) drugs, and the towering abstraction of money. To grow-up post-1960s is to experience the aftermath, privatization, weightlessness: everything has apparently been done. Therefore culture is a process of recycling: everything is juxtaposable to everything else because nothing matters.

Todd Gitlin, "Post-Modernism: Roots and Politics"

In the preceding chapter we had repeated occasion to be impressed by the degree to which ideological notions of all sorts have been instrumental in shaping the contemporary debate on the family. However unsecured, problematic, and at times even blatantly slanted, some of these notions have had the capacity to cast a lasting spell on the way we look at the family. Since the days of Plato and Aristotle successive generations of social philosophers have presented us with drastically different views of the role of the family in individual and social life and history. Though one particular set of notions may replace that of another in popularity, none ever seems to disappear completely and may be re-evoked without too much difficulty when needed. At times, starkly contesting visions manage to exist side by side and the resulting tensions lead to sharp ideational confrontations in the political arena.

Ours is one of those periods in history in which divergent understandings of the family formulated in different contexts and for different purposes have been rekindled with a vengeance. Claims to the contrary not withstanding, even so-called scientific approaches with their reliance on the collection of vast quantities of empirical data have not done an awful lot to improve on the ideological wars of the past. Most contemporary theoretical approaches to the study of the institution of the conventional nuclear family in the modern era are in many ways connected to earlier theoretical attempts to understand the revolutionary changes that have engulfed the societies of the West with cataclysmic speed during the past three centuries or so. From the beginning of what Karl Polanyi has aptly called the "great transformation," theorists of modernization have been preoccupied with the analysis of the economic and political forces that served not only to transform the working and living conditions of ever larger numbers of people but that also equipped men, women, and children with rights and a degree of liberty unknown to history. Obviously, changes of this scale did not come without cost. The costs appear to manifest themselves most dramatically in the life of the family and hence it should not come as a surprise that theorists today, as in the past, are inclined to use the institution of the family as a handy theoretical tool to determine the advantages and disadvantages of modernization.

From the onset of modernization much has been written about how the twin forces of industrialization and democracy served to undermine an older social order anchored in kinship, community, and religion and how these forces continue to churn on relentlessly and indefinitely. Hence, theorists found it difficult from the start to decide whether this was a good thing or a bad thing. Despite the fact that in all democratic industrial societies ordinary people—and not the elite alone—today live longer and healthier than ever before and enjoy a degree of comfort and freedom their ancestors could only dream of, theorists to this day are in sharp disagreement over what to make of the changes modernization has brought. Influenced by earlier, often contradictory, interpretational attempts, theorists of the modern era strained hard to fit their observations into plausible analytical schemas. As a result theoretical camps have emerged that run the whole gamut of ideologies, ranging from the radical to the conservative, and many gradations in between. Already differing sharply in their identification of the causes that made for industrialization and the rise of democracy, theorists tend to disagree even more pointedly about what could and should be done about their consequences for the organization of domestic life. When the nineteenth century opened, clear ideological lines had already been drawn and by the time it ended, the theoretical gulf between the opposing camps appeared to have become irreconcilable.

These early theoretical formulations, in turn, have cast a long shadow over subsequent efforts to understand the nature of modernity and its implications for the family. At times, they actually even influenced the organization of domestic and social life itself. Even though some twentieth-century theorists, like those of the structural functionalist school of thought, self-consciously tried to sidestep the ideological entanglements of their predecessors by means of the construction of a methodology they hoped to be non-ideological, they too failed to achieve their goal to put an "end to ideology." Highly abstract theoretically, and largely unable to account for the depth and dynamics of human experience, all too many left themselves open to attacks from opposing camps. When the seismic shocks of the 1960s countercultural revolution began to rock the self-understanding—and the confidence—of Western societies, the theoretical shortcomings of supposedly non-ideological theoretical attempts served to play into the hands of those who used ideological interpretational schemes indiscriminately. The inability of mainstream structuralists to defend themselves theoretically was instrumental in the venomous reemergence of older, and more radical, perspectives. The triumph of the radical perspectives in the academy in the 1960s and 1970s, and the infiltration of their catchy formulations into the public discourse elicited, in turn, two predictable responses: on the one hand they caused considerable theoretical disarray among "mainstream" structuralists, and, on the other hand, they served to rekindle conservative perceptions that had been crowded out of the public discourse for close to a century.

Today, as the twentieth century has come to a close, one may observe the copresence of a variety of theoretical perspectives on the nature and the future of the modern family as it has evolved in the West. All are distinctly hostile toward one another, all are battling for "the hearts and minds" of the wider public. For conveniences sake these perspective may be categorized into four distinct camps: First there is the *radical perspective of the family*, which, after a brief triumph, has begun to lose its attractiveness outside, though not inside, the academy. Second, there is the *conservative perspective of the family,* which, after having been more or less dormant for some time, has gained renewed credence outside, though not inside, the academy. Third, there continues to be the *mainstream perspective*, mostly held by structuralists and old-fashioned political liberals, which, though greatly weakened in comparison to its earlier dominance, tries to retain its credibility by closing itself off from attacks from both the Left and the Right by means of an almost exclusive reliance on the same "scientific method" that has been its Achilles' heel in the first place. And finally, there is the new kid on the theoretical block, the *perspective of the postmodernists*, a conglomerate of diverse analytical approaches that is held together by an intellectual bias against all the institutional arrangements characteristic of modernity.

Modernization and the Institution of the Family

As pointed out already, the ideological battles of the past century and a half were greatly fueled by questions over the evaluation of the role and place of the modern nuclear family, that is to say that type of family peculiar to the Northwestern part of Europe whose structure and ethos was carried by immigrants to other parts of the world, the United States, Canada, and Australia. Over the decades, the battle lines drawn early have assumed a life of their own so that by now we seem to be no longer able to look at the family without falling prey to the cliched visions constructed by the warring theoretical camps of a more distant past. Down to our own days they echo the same theoretical disagreements accorded to the modern family from the beginning of the debates. Today, as in the past, those informed by classical liberal principles (political centrists, neoliberals, neoconservatives, and conservatives), are inclined to assign a positive role to the conventional family and those of the Left (a motley assemblage of Marxists, neo-Marxists, feminists, and, of late, also multiculturalists) tend to perceive it in mostly negative terms. While mainstream structuralists in the academy continue to oscillate between the two opposing perspectives, pinning their position on whatever the last measured empirical data appear to reveal, the theoretically powerful postmodernist camp is in the process of projecting the to date most devastating perspective on the modern family and its future.

It is of some importance to note that their disagreements not withstanding, most theorists of the family are in rare agreement that the forces of modernization have been destructive of the conventional nuclear family. While few would deny the singular importance of the family in pre-modern society, regardless of their political bent the majority of theorists tend to concur that once industrialism and mass democracy was ensconced, fundamentally new and highly-problematic realities emerged. With the macro-institutions of the economy and the state gaining preeminence in the public sphere, the private worlds of family and community are argued to have been turned into epiphenomena of the first. Or to put it differently, the structural changes produced by the forces of modernization are to-day largely understood to have turned the conventional nuclear family into a helpless pawn subject to pressures that have their origin in the economy and the political arena. Reinforced by major shifts in societal norms, a situation is argued to have emerged that is characterized by normative uncertainty and behavioral drift. Though the combined forces of structural and normative shifts are held to have weakened all the institutions of modern society, nowhere are they said to have left a more indelible mark than on the institution of the conventional family. Marxists, conservatives, mainstream structural functionalists, and postmodernists alike are united by this under-standing of the effects of modernization and they are convinced that perpetual changes in the macro-institutional order will continue to run their self-determined course in the postmodern order and be-yond as well. With the spread of the postindustrial order, it is claimed that perpetual macrostructural changes create an increasingly unset-tling degree of fluidity that puts the continued utility of the conven-tional modern family into question. Bereft of both the capacity and the resources to respond to the needs of individuals and society alike, the conventional nuclear family is claimed to have been reduced to a sad little and embattled community.

Since it is one of the major tasks of this volume to refute this taken-for-granted understanding of the future of the modern family, we shall have to take a closer look at the presuppositions upon which the divergent theoretical visions of the modern family rest. Only when one grasps the shaky foundations on which they are built can one begin to entertain urgently needed different perspective of the nature and future of the institution of the conventional family.

The Marxist Vision

No other theoretical paradigm has had a more lasting impact on the perception of modern life than that associated with Karl Marx and his collaborator Friedrich Engels. An only cursory look at *The Communist Manifesto* already reveals the single-minded economic determinism of this peculiar mixture of sweeping analysis and prophecy. Though Marx and his followers have consistently sought to integrate the political, social, and cultural dimensions of the emergent modern order in a single theoretical construct, they adamantly remain wedded to their chief proposition that economic factors determine all of social life. Hence in the Marxist paradigm, the family is viewed as a social entity entirely dependent upon economic factors, which, in the modern era, flow from an economy organized under the principles of the market. It is for this reason that capitalism was and remains the chief target of any Marxist critique of modernity, and it is for this reason as well that the conventional bourgeois family as the carrier of the market remains a thorn in the eyes of every practicing Marxist.

Three key concepts characterize the Marxist approach to the family: the notion of the *privatization* of family life, the concept of the *bourgeois family,* and the proposition of the *matriarchal origin* of the family. The argument, in short, runs as follows: while economic production in pre-industrial Europe was integrated into the household, with men, women, and children working in tandem, industrial capitalism with its corresponding system of ownership and progressive division of labor served to undermine this balance. It took males out of the household and turned them into industrial wage earners ever more dependent upon their bosses. As the family household lost its once central economic function, it became "privatized" and women were confined to wageless domestic work and made increasingly subservient to men. Since one's location in the economic production order is held to determine the assignment of social status, a profound and growing inequality is argued to have entered into the relationship between men and women.[1]

This deplorable state of affairs is said to have found its clearest expression in the "bourgeois family," that is to say that type of family that most distinctively reflects the Marxist preoccupation with social class, both as a manifestation of the ownership of the tools of production under capitalism as well as a symptom of inequality and oppression. The bourgeois family, in this view, reached its apotheosis with the Industrial Revolution, which served to concentrate ownership and control over the tools of production in the hands of merchants, producers, and professionals—that is the rising social class of the bourgeoisie. The bourgeois family itself is seen to be based on capital, "on private gain," in which marriage becomes a "marriage of convenience," arranged on a primarily financial basis, and in which love and sexuality are turned into commodities traded in the market. Within the bourgeois family the husband dominates. His position of power derives from the capitalist organization of social life, which provides power and economic advantages to males. The chief villain in the Marxist scheme of things then is the bourgeois male who is free to exploit those subject to him, women and children, and, of course, powerless proletarian workers as well. This state of affairs is argued to last as long as the capitalist economic structure remains in place.

When one turns to "the matriarchal origin of the family," as developed by Friedrich Engels, one encounters the claim that marriage, that is the institutionalized form to enter into the state of matrimony, has continuously evolved under the influence of economic changes. Following the anthropology of the American ethnologist Lewis Henry Morgan, Engels argued that somewhere in the dim past of pre-class human history there existed an original state of matriarchy in which women dominated and sexual relationships were free and unencumbered (with various forms of "group" sexuality being the norm). The development of private property made for the rise of monogamous forms of marriage that favored males and subjugated women and, in succeeding stages, ushered in a patriarchal order. The intermediate stage, the "pairing stage," that had supplanted the original "primitive or original stage" was ultimately driven out by the rise of patriarchy which found its most prominent expression under bourgeois capitalism. The following quote may render the flavor of Engel's argument: "The overthrow of mother right was the *world historical defeat of the female sex*. The man took command in the home also; the woman was degraded and reduced to servitude; she became the slave of his lust and a mere instrument for the production of children."[2]

There exist too many versions and nuances of the basic Marxist argument that make a more detailed discussion here impossible. It will have to suffice to note that the Marxist vision, presciently perceptive at times and blatantly wrong all too often, has enduringly influenced the way in which subsequent generations of theorists have looked at the nuclear family. It most decidedly influenced the countercultural movement of the 1960s. Beyond that, it irreparably shaped the ways in which the contemporary feminist leadership looks at the family as well as at the relationship between the sexes. In fact, the spell cast by the Marxist vision has been so powerful that it has become very difficult, indeed, to ignore it. Even contemporary social scientists who pride themselves on their hard-nosed reliance on empirical data have not been immune to its lure. When one looks as their entire theoretical edifice one cannot fail but be impressed by the enduring Marxist faith in their dogma's redemptive promise that a socialist revolution will put an end to repression and all the miseries of human existence.[3]

Enter the Conservatives

Yet Marxists were not the only theorists who took a critical view of the social consequences of industrialization and the arrival of a new political order. As Marxists hammered out their basic paradigm, conservative thinkers, such as the French reformer Frederic Le Play, were equally impressed by the inexorable march of economic and political forces and the immense social disorganization they appeared to produce.[4] To this day Le Play's scalding critique of the atomizing effect of industrial technology and democratic politics on the family, the community, and the church remains the single most important conservative theoretical foil for critics of modernization from the political right.

In all of Le Play's writings the family is central to communal life. It is understood to be in many ways intertwined with other institutional structures such as religion, government, education, and the economy. All traditional institutions, including that of the family, are held to have been put under siege by industrialism and the arrival of mass democracy. With the use of many detailed studies Le Play aimed to show that the ever-expanding industrial system worked against family cohesion. Not only was work removed out of the household—and thus the household lost its central economic function—but also ever larger numbers of people were propelled to take up urban forms of life. At the same time, he argued that growing liberal tendencies based on the rights of the individual in legal and social thought had the effect to gradually replace a traditional political philosophy based on family, community, and religion.

On the level of everyday life Le Play provided a great deal of empirical evidence for his thesis that the family loses it ties to broader kinship groupings with advancing industrialism. He was also able to show that the newly emergent nuclear and individualistic family form was no longer able to exercise control over its members to the same degree it did in the past. Moreover, already at this early phase was he able to predict that the industrial system's progressing division of labor would make for the growth of specialized human activities which, without fail, would come to compete with the family in all its basic functions. Hence, Le Play argued, once the destructive forces of secularism and individualism had been unchained, the patriarchal or extended family (the ideal family form in his mind) was robbed of the integrative power it once held. Having lost its interconnectedness with the extended kin group and no longer able to control its individual members, the emergent nuclear family was thus postulated to be responsible for the rising tide of destructive social behaviors such as desertion, divorce, crime, a surge of pauperism, and an increased dependency of the individual upon public relief.

We need not concern ourselves overly much with the details of the conservative vision outlined by Frederic Le Play. A good number of his basic assumptions are clearly wrong (such as the assumption that the nuclear family is a consequence of the Industrial Revolution) and his critique of the industrial democratic system itself is overwrought and ultimately slanted. Subsequent efforts to either support or update Le Play's conceptualization of the inevitable demise of the modern nuclear family (such as the one presented by Carle C. Zimmerman in the 1950s) tried hard to guard against his gravest misperceptions.[5] While theoretically interesting, they too suffer from similar limitations and assumptions that in light of the available evidence are difficult to substantiate. Though the conservative esteem of the family in its patriarchal form came into public disrepute during the watershed years of the 1960s, the traditional sentiments expressed in this conservative approach continue to linger on, if not among academic theorists, then in conservative think tanks and publications, and certainly in the public at large.

A quite different fate awaited Henry Sumner Maine's theoretical propositions about the patriarchal origin of the family as presented in his magisterial book *Ancient Law*.[6] By limiting his analysis of ancient law to classical antiquity, this pioneering scholar of comparative law documented that—contrary to the matriarchal thesis of Lewis Henry Morgan and Friedrich Engels—the origin of the Western family was patrilocal, patrilineal, and formally or informally polygamous. Making use of Hebrew, Greek, and Roman history and tracing changes in the law related to the patriarchal family through the centuries, he was able to establish that an earlier patriarchal stage in which kinship provided the basic principle of social organization gave gradually way to developmental stages in which individuals achieved a greater degree of freedom. While in the ancient world an individual's status was derived from his membership in a particular tribal community, in progressively developing societies the movement was one from "status to contract." This movement, Maine argued, provided families and individuals with a substantially higher degree of freedom. Despite the preference he accorded to the patriarchal family, Maine's famous dictum "from status to contract" has remained a useful formulation in the interpretation of modern trends. Unchallenged to this day is the documentation of his central argument that with the loss of their legality, traditional institutions like the family, religion, and the community are in danger of losing their once taken-for-granted function to mediate between individuals and the rising megastructures of modern society. Modernity, in Henry Sumner Maine's exposition, implies that the game of society is increasingly played out between isolated individuals, on the one hand, and the megastructures of the law, on the other.

Looking back at the work of classical social theorists who decisively influenced the way we look at the modern family, our earlier observation about the pronouncedly critical flavor of their theoretical schemas gains credence. Regardless whether formulated in a radical or a conservative mode, early theoretical attempts posited what may be called a "Fall from the Garden of Eden" theory of social change. For Marxists, capitalism and the bourgeois family are the chief villains responsible for this fall, for conservatives, industrialism and mass democracy. Greatly influenced by evolutionary notions, early theorists, radicals, and conservatives alike saw their particular moment as a transitory stage in the history of the industrial world. Marxists wanted to leave the unjust and unacceptable present behind and regain the paradise that was lost by moving to a higher stage in human and social development; conservatives, for their part, longed to return to a largely mythical past in which things were held to have been better and life more natural. The new Eden, for Marxists, could only be reached by means of violent revolution and the subsequent radical reorganization of the tools of production under socialism; what mattered for conservatives was the reorganization of communal life along familistic and traditional lines. Although modern research and experience may have superseded both of these opposing visions in many ways, their antithetical conceptualizations have remained fairly intact down to our own times.

The Freudian Legacy

The psychoanalytical approach associated with Sigmund Freud and his followers is yet one more theoretical claim that had a profoundly negative impact on the twentieth-century view of the modern nuclear family. In their search for the causes of adult neuroses the Freudians diagnosed the modern family to be a cauldron of pathology. The middle-class family and its restrictive demands, in particular, was seen to provide a teeming source for depressions, alienation, and assorted dysfunctions of adulthood. Though after initial skepticism, Freud himself concluded that most of the psychosexual incidents reported by his patients were fantasy and that adult neuroses resulted from inevitable psychological traumas of sexual maturation which tended to be compounded by parental error, the vanguard of today's theorists working in the psychoanalytical tradition claim these fantasies to be based on reality. Already by the middle of the twentieth century it had become customary on all levels of the rapidly expanding therapeutic empire to fault parental shortcomings for virtually all miseries of personal adult lives. The fusion between psychoanalytical approaches and "vulgar" Marxist assertions on the omnipotency of economic power invested in the capitalist system that carried the day with the rise of the countercultural revolution left the conventional family as the primary culprit of everything that was held to be wrong and pernicious in the modern world. The melodramatic vision of the earlier-mentioned radical psychiatrist R. D. Laing whose memorable phrase that "the initial act of brutality against the average child is the mother's first kiss," reflects the potent mix of New Left and psychoanalytic perceptions. Even happy families where nobody has openly broken down, Laing averted, conceal the existence of terror and oppression. In the bourgeois family, in particular, there is an inherent tendency to turn people into things, into mere pieces of private property. Women and children were argued to be the ultimate victims of this sorry state of affairs. In short, New-Left theorists, working in the Freudian mode, understood the conventional family to be a kind of political incubator in which power rather than affection is organized and through which the need to dominate and be dominated is nurtured implicitly. For some, like Christopher Lasch, children were seen to be victimized by their intrusive mothers and absent fathers, while for others, like Richard Sennet, the conventional family was reasoned to be an instrument of socialization that conditions the young to accept the illegitimate authority of the marketplace.[7]

Regardless of the degree of their animosity against the conventional nuclear family, theorists and analysts working in the neo-Freudian tradition recognized that the modern individual requires an emotional and spiritual "home." Some tried to locate it in "sisterhood" and "fraternity," others hoped this need could be met by encounter groups, support groups, and similar forms of assemblages individuals tend to join and leave of their own free will. Yet while such modern forms of sociation undoubtedly offer individuals liberated from the bonds of the family a wide variety of options, they ultimately remain provisional, open-ended, and impermanent in nature. Thus it is hard to imagine how they can ever become more than a surrogate to the family, and a diluted and fickle one at that.

The Structural Functionalists and Recent Shifts in "Mainstream" Theory

Preoccupied with tracing the broad contours of the consequences of modernization's transformatory shifts, structural functionalist theorists came into academic prominence during the first part of the twentieth century. Politically liberal, intellectually leery of applying evolutionist claims to society, and methodologically adverse to all historical schemes proceeding on a grand scale, they were predisposed to relate shifts in the technical and political structures to changes in other spheres of society. Despite their tendency to accord primacy to the role of technology in the modernization process, they generally argued that the institutional shifts in all spheres of social life occurred more or less in tandem. When pressed, they were willing to grant that the equilibrium of a modernizing society could be thrown off balance, at least for a while, but in the end society would achieve a new equilibrium. The mere fact that a particular social institution persisted despite massive systemic changes was held to be proof that it met the needs of that system. That is to say, although a given institution could experience considerable changes, the very fact that it continued to exist was seen to provide evidence to the argument that the institution continued to meet the functions of the system and had the capacity to adapt itself to ongoing changes.

True to their underlying theoretical premises, structural functionalist theorists emphasized the fit between the nuclear family and the modern industrial system. From the beginning, they were impressed by those features of the institutionalized form of the nuclear family system that made it uniquely fit to meet the requirements of the modern industrial order. Based on their theoretical assumptions, they concluded that alone among the many family forms potentially available only the nuclear–conjugal family had the capacity to adapt itself to the ever-changing needs of the industrial system. Consequently, influential sociological theorists such as Talcott Parsons proposed that many of the manifest weaknesses and problems of the nuclear family should be seen more as symptoms of short-term disorganization rather than as expressions of discontinuity or even family breakdown. [8]

To the degree that the mainstream structuralist approach is based on the interdependence of the various segmented spheres of the larger social system, it further assumes that shifts in one structure, primarily in the economy, necessitates shifts in other structures as well. The ongoing adaptation of all institutions in the maintenance of the social system holds equally true for the institution of the nuclear family.

In a widely discussed book, *World Revolution and Family Patterns*, the sociologist W. J. Goode used the term "functional fit" to describe the interdependence between the industrial system and the institution of the conventional family in its nuclear and conjugal Western form.[9] Inasmuch as this family type emphasizes the importance of free choice in the selection of mates, the welfare of individuals rather than the interests of the larger family unit, and the establishment of independent households, this type of family is argued to have given birth to an ideology of individualism and equality that fits well with the needs and the ideology of the industrial system. The industrial system, in turn, weakened the power of the extended family, furthered individualism, and gave rise to conjugal relationships based on the equality of the sexes. After an examination of massive amounts of comparative materials, both historical and cross-cultural, Goode went on to argue that the ideology of the conjugal nuclear family system and that of the modern industrial system complement each other—are in equilibrium, if you wish—through the sharing of common ideas and values intrinsic to both. What is more, he hypothesized, that as the industrial system expands worldwide, it is reasonable to expect a worldwide "revolution in family patterns" in the direction of the type of the West. Although it became fashionable in the second part of the twentieth century to challenge the particulars of this interpretational scheme, many social scientists remained for long in tacit agreement with the core structuralist propositions of the existence of a "functional fit" between the nuclear family and the industrial system and the simultaneous diffusion of both. Whatever disarray in the family might exist was held to be temporary only. Further advances in the technological system would return the family system into balance in due course so that the entire system of modernity could attain a new equilibrium.

Inasmuch as the viability of the industrial system was seen to be dependent on continuously progressing processes of the division of labor and specialization, structural functionalists were faced with the question of where to locate the source of the modern family's vital social functions in an era where its traditional economic, political, and social functions had been replaced by specialists and professionals located outside of the family. For Talcott Parsons himself the evidence was clear: the primary function of the nuclear family in the modern era rests on its ability to provide emotional support to its members. Moreover, he argued that it was the genius of this type of family to ensure the formation of a personality type that holds the capacity to adapt itself to unforeseen contingencies, to experiment, and innovate. Hence Parsons and his followers postulated that modern individuals had not only the capacity to adapt to the requirements of the continuously changing industrial order, but that they were also inspired by desires to construct meaningful lives for themselves. Above all, they maintained that the modern family's capacity to maximize the twentieth-century dictates of equality and individualism within its institutionalized way of living endowed it with new vigor and strength. Hence, theorists working within this particular theoretical perspective were convinced that all the turmoil created by industrialization and shifts in values would be temporary only. To be sure, the conventional family had changed economically from "a unit of production" to "a unit of consumption," and politically from a unit determined by "patriarchal principles" to a unit determined by "principles of equality and individuality," and many of its traditional functions had been replaced by specialized out-of-home services. Yet modernization was nonetheless held to have a mostly positive effect upon the family, for it permitted the family to "come into its own" at last. Stripped from its many erstwhile duties in the public sphere, the family could now concentrate on its core functions: the provision of companionship and emotional support.

As structural functionalist theory evolved into what has come to be known as the "mainstream" academic approach to the family, more philosophically-inclined theorists had a somewhat more negative take on modernization's effect on the culture at large. Sociologists like David Riesman, for instance, set out to identify the processes that made for the expansion of a normative vacuum and a general drift in behavioral standards. In his widely-read *The Lonely Crowd*, Riesman drew public attention to the rise of modern massman for whom neither tradition nor timeless ethical principles were any longer of particular relevance. Denuded of any inner principles, an all-powerful identification with peers was argued to replace the influence of the conventional family and its ethos.[10] Modern men and women—"other-directed" and unprincipled—ultimately signaled the triumph of the masses.

By the same token, ever larger numbers of moral philosophers and theologians expressed their misgivings for the realities modernization had wrought. As the twentieth century progressed, many of the concerns about modernity's destructive fall-out that had been floating about in a more or less discombobulated manner for some time already gained in strength and velocity. They, no doubt, contributed greatly to a growing discontent with modernity. In time, the divergent theoretical perspectives coalesced to produce a high degree of theoretical doubt about the plausibility of the mainstream interpretation of the functional fit between the modern nuclear family and the requirements of the modern industrial world. The resultant theoretical uncertainty, in turn, served to influence social norms as well as actual human behavior.

In this situation as in any other, one is left to conclude that where ideas about rules governing individual behavior are held to be no longer applicable while new ones have not yet emerged, behavioral and normative drift are sure to follow. It was not difficult to find empirical documentation for such behavioral consequences to have occurred. The interactive dynamic between normative drift and actual behavior manifested itself most conspicuously in the organization of human sexuality. Already by the middle of the twentieth century it had become evident that sexuality was increasingly viewed to be separate from normatively prescribed rules of marriage, that illegitimacy, once condemned and stigmatized, had started to lose its opprobrium, and that divorce, once held to be a measure of the last resort, had come to be seen as a socially acceptable way to end an unsatisfactory domestic situation. The theoretical uncertainty helped to legitimate a gradual relaxation in the established moral code that in short order led to the establishment of a publicly-endorsed "new morality." With the passage of time, the softening of the public moral code in turn came to act back on the structure of the conventional family in that it produced catapulting rates of nonmarital sex, illegitimacy, and divorce. Taken together, these shifts made it increasingly difficult for mainstream theorists to reconcile the contradictions between their long-held modernization model that posited a close "functional fit" between the institutions of modernity and the nuclear conjugal family. Within a short span of time their research focus began to shift to what may be called a "dysfunctional system" model. It required that special public attention be accorded to groups exhibiting "dysfunctional" behavior. With this theoretical modification it became possible for critical theorists to argue that "the label" of dysfunctionality affixed by structuralist theorists was the consequence of prejudices inherent in their theoretical model. The once unquestioned normative requirements of the conventional family thus became ever more suspect to academic observers.

As this brief synopsis of the mainstream theoretical approach to the family shows, long before the middle of the 1960s the stage had been set for the onslaught against the conventional family that soon was to burst onto the public scene. A tendency had come to prevail among intellectuals and political elite in all Western democracies (and in some sooner than in others) to attribute individual and social deficiencies to the incapacity of the conventional family to respond adequately to the pressures flowing from the industrial system when organized in the capitalist mode. As a result, they hypothesized that left to itself the conventional family had neither the capacity or the resources to stem the growing isolation of individuals nor had it the normative power to control behavioral drift.

As pointed out in the preceding chapter, such grim academic prognoses helped to prod the political elite into action. As it was held that only a centralized government had the kind of resources at its disposal to make provisions for an array of supplementary family support programs, it did not take long for a conviction to spread among those who prided themselves of their realism and compassion that at this critical moment in American history it had become inevitable for the federal government to get more directly involved in the affairs of families.[11] As such an involvement had existed in comparable European countries for some time already, activist academics never ceased to hold the European model up for emulation.

At the same time, it was also taken for granted that only the knowledge generated by social science research had the capacity to design and deliver policy mechanisms that could effectively counterbalance manifest symptoms of family disorganization and failure. Small wonder then that as the assault against the family gained momentum, mainstream theorists began to doubt the adequacy of the theoretical pillars upon which their social policy model of the family rested. To many it now appeared that the ever-changing needs of an evolving postindustrial system required different theoretical models altogether.

The Resurgence of Radical and Conservative Perspectives on the Family and the Slide toward Postmodernism

While mainstream social theorists and moral philosophers were preoccupied with adjusting their interpretational schemas to emergent new social realities, a vision of a very different sort was forged in many academies of the West. For some time traditionally Left-leaning theorists had been faced with the theoretical problem of how to reconcile the Marxist prophecy of the inevitable corrosion of capitalism and the progressive immiseration of the working classes with empirical manifestations that the opposite was occurring in social reality. If anything, capitalism had proven to become stronger and more productive as time went on, and instead of the rise of a huge impoverished working class, the twentieth century had witnessed an unprecedented expansion of the middle classes and a undeniable improvement in the lot of the actual living conditions of the poor. Such unpredicted developments compelled post-World War II Marxists to cast about for new intellectual themes to defend their steadfast adherence to a theoretical paradigm conceived in a Leftist mode. Enraptured with the imaginative quality of Freudianism, many set out to accomplish this task by means of the construction of intellectually-seductive interpretational schemes that combined classical Marxian notions with a medley of psychoanalytical presuppositions. The resultant heady theoretical brew frequently provided insights into the nature of modernity which, at the time, appeared to be spectacular, though, in hindsight, rather problematic. Based on a self-contained research methodology, growing bands of young and hungry theorists—men and women alike—attempted to substantiate empirically what they had set out to proof. In sharply-formulated arguments they postulated that the advanced industrial societies of the West had for some time been moving toward a future in which it becomes increasingly difficult to reconcile the principles of modernity with the very dynamics engendered by the modern system itself. Jarring social problems had begun to pile up in virtually all areas of modern life and hence they could no longer be understood to be the result of the inability of some individuals to adapt to the changing system. Rather, they argued, these problems must be understood as an expression of the failure of "the system" itself. Data on the phenomenal increase in drug addiction, crime, and family breakup on the personal level and the growth of income differences and the unequal distribution of power on the systemic level, were routinely trotted out to attest to the need for new theoretical formulations. In the writings of this new band of theorists can thus be found the origin of the popular notion of "blaming the victim" we already encountered in the preceding chapter.

In a long line of theorists spanning from Karl Marx in the nineteenth century to Juergen Habermas in our own time, much has been written about "the inner contradictions of capitalism." Alain Touraine, a French theorist of some note, coined the phrase "the modernization of modernization." It served to expand the postulate of the inner contradictions in that it conveyed the paradox that once the forces constitutive of modernization were unleashed and propelled on their protean path, they tended to undermine the very institutions distinctive of modernity itself. It was further argued that if twentieth-century social realities were indeed the product of the capitalist system, then the "root causes" of all problems plaguing industrial capitalist society had to be located in the malfunctioning of the system itself. Rather than "blaming the victim," many claimed, governmental efforts should not merely be stepped up and expanded but they had to be radically redirected. With ever-increasing insistence vocal advocates soon radicalized such demands by arguing that if flaws inherent in the system must be held responsible for the malfunctioning of a growing number of individuals, if not whole segments of society, justice required that the system itself had to be transformed.

Based on this line of reasoning it took not much to argue that the institution of the nuclear conventional family was a chief culprit in the unfolding of the destructive dynamism inherent in modern capitalism. To the degree that this type of family can be held to be an integral part of the modernization process, the need for its destruction stood high on the revolutionary agenda. Already by the late 1950s, the social theorist Barrington Moore predicted that "One after another of society's traditional institutions have fallen before the forces of modernization. The fate of the family as a social institution will not differ in its essentials from that which has befallen others."[12] Infused with psychoanalytic proposition about the "terrors" of the conventional family and supported by frightening statistics on symptoms of social disorganization, neo-Marxist theoretical expositions closely dovetailed with the sentiments of the counterculture and the *Zeitgeist* of the period.

In the preceding chapter we had occasion to describe in some detail how countercultural arguments on the family received not only a public hearing but came to undermine public policy itself. We saw how the revival of the chief Marxist notions of the "privatization of family life," the pejorative evaluation of the "bourgeois family," and the "matriarchal origin of the family" came to invade the language of the public discourse and how the new politics of the family officially signaled the termination of the special place that had been accorded to the conventional family for so long. Yet we also had occasion to see how the triumph of a psychologized Marxian vision called forth a powerful political backlash that greatly served to rekindle more conservative visions of family and communal life.

By the middle of the 1980s, when it had become an established fact that the public at large had refused to abandon the ideals of a conventional family life, at least not to the degree its foes had argued, even radical theorists ensconced in the academy could no longer deny this fact. Once more they were compelled to take stock of the explanatory power of their theoretical models. While intellectuals inclined toward classical liberalism found it relatively easy to return to conceptualizations of the family in a somewhat modified mainstream mode, the once revolutionary Left seemed to have a much harder time to make theoretical concessions that went beyond theoretical propositions consisting of a mixture of structuralist, psychologistic, and watered-down Marxist postulates.[13] To this day the family remains a theoretically embattled topic.

This intellectual lack of nerve has given carte blanche to theorists of postmodernism who with their nihilism and extreme anti-institutionalism hold the potential to create considerable mischief. Before we can turn to take a closer look at the postmodernist propositions, however, it may be useful to briefly summarize the legacy of the thirty-year theoretical war against the conventional family.

The Legacy of the Sixties as Preamble to the Postmodern Theoretical Vision

It is of great importance to understand that despite the rediscovery of the importance of the two-parent or nuclear family and the conventional lifestyle associated with it, anti-family theoretical views have managed to prevail more or less unchanged. The significance of their influence becomes evident when one looks at three primary dimensions of social life: the political, the individual, and the cultural.

On the *political level* it is important to recognize that as the twentieth century progressed the state and its agencies gained an evermore towering role in matters pertaining to the organization of private life in virtually every society of the West. The growth of state power neither occurred by design nor by the force of necessity, but almost by default. Since theorists and the intellectual elite became progressively convinced that the forces of modernity had weakened the institution of family, they felt compelled to shore up the modern family in many of the tasks it had carried out in the past as a matter of course. This conviction brought into existence a public climate that led the state to intrude into what was held to be a practical and moral vacuum. On the road toward the post-modern order there developed thus a taken-for-granted understanding that the state was the preeminent resource and the ultimate arbiter. This general trend was greatly reinforced, if not accelerated, by the countercultural revolution of the 1960s and by radical feminists waging battle against the real as well as perceived oppression of women. A situation was subsequently reached in which a fractious public expects the state to intervene, legislate, police, and punish in matters pertaining to personal and familial life. Regardless whether one thinks this to be a good thing or a bad thing, one is bound to take note of the fact that across the political spectrum the state is expected to play the defining role in issues pertaining to private life. The conservative demand for state action in matters of protecting the life of the unborn or on behalf of traditional cultural values is no exception to this trend.

At the same time it is also important to face up to the fact that most state efforts continue to be informed by visions of the legitimacy of alternative lifestyles as they have emerged during the past three decades. In other words, the conservative backlash of recent years has been largely powerless to infiltrate into the political culture, its vehement argumentation not withstanding. This political trend has severely undermined the traditional reliance on the family for the care and socialization of the nation's children. What is more, even anti-state interventionist efforts tend to solicit the power of the state for this purpose.

On the *level of the individual*, it has to be observed that the same shifts that deprived individuals of the traditional support of their families and communities also made for the establishment of a huge social-service sector—educational, therapeutic, and otherwise—designed to serve as a surrogate to the family. Yet the effectiveness of the newly-established public measures to provide sustenance and support to individuals and integrate them into wider society has turned out to be disappointing. Feelings of loneliness and loss of purpose among members of targeted groups appear to be on the increase. In all too many cases the shift away from the family has led to the emergence of anomic, self-seeking, and hedonistic individuals who are now compelled to enter into surrogate communal arrangements ultimately condemned to be fleeting and unsatisfactory. This trend had the paradoxical effect that bereft of traditional networks able to provide anchorage and support, individuals have more than ever been turned into pawns of the very same forces the mushrooming service sector had set out to counterbalance.

On the *cultural level* the identified shifts made for parallel shifts in the moral code that served to structure the normative order of democratic industrial societies since the beginning of "the great transformation." The moral and behavioral patterns of the conventional family, once the publicly-acclaimed ideal and the unquestioned measure of individual behavior, have lost their supremacy today. What is more, it is hard to imagine how their legitimacy can be restored in an open democratic society. The reign of confusion is astounding. No one seems to be able to agree on what modern culture is nor to know how the autonomous individual is linked to the megastructures of the public sphere.

This brief summary of the consequences of the shift in theoretical thought on the practice of social life takes us to our next task, namely to look at what contemporary theorists of postmodernism have to say about the modern family and its future. We shall undertake this exploration in some detail since postmodernists claim to be the guardians of our future and profess to be the only ones who have the key to an appropriate understanding of the dynamics of modern culture. Judging by the career of past theories, the postmodernist theoretical paradigm is unlikely to remain without consequence. If nothing else, the reader of these pages may find it instructive to reflect about the degree to which postmodernist notions have already entered into the current public debate.

The Family and the Theorists of Postmodernism

Postmodernism, it has frequently been said, is more of a mood than a unified theory. Hence it appeals to vague sentiments rather than reason and holds the potential for creating considerable confusion. Postmodernist theorists are mainly located in the academy. Their chief concern is with the *deconstruction* of every aspect of social and intellectual life, including that of the family. Among their numbers one finds former Marxists, radical feminists, radical Freudian psychologists, and a new breed of multiculturalists, in short, all manner of dissenters from the Western epistemological rationalism that has informed modern life since the Enlightenment. Along with a deep-seated, often personal, enmity against the meanings and interpretations with which human actions have been endowed for some time, their diverse analytical approaches are held together by a strong intellectual bias against the institutions distinctive of modernity: the market economy, the law, traditional education, modern medicine, and, of course, the conventional family. Postmodernists, such as Michel Foucault, have directed their attention to experiences of fragmentation, disorder, and pluralism that are not part of the staple of the modernist paradigm.[14] From there they go on to argue that if modernity, and hence modern concepts of reason and progress, have in some sense failed, then presumably a very different set of principles must be at work in the world.

Like Marxist theorists before them, postmodernists posit that the broad societal shifts occurring today are propelled by the dictates of an ever-changing amoral technology organized under the principles of a rapacious and fundamentally immoral market economy. They hold everything to be in a state of flux, nothing can be taken as given or certain. Yet they are theoretically distinguished from modernization theorists by the proposition that a distinctive postmodern culture has come to replace Marx's economic infrastructure as the crucial generative force. Whereas the modernizing world was organized around the production, the manipulation, the exchange, and the consumption of manufactured goods, postmodern society, in contrast, is argued to be characterized by its (dis)organization around the quasi-autonomous and uncontrolled production, manipulation, and consumption of images, symbols, signs, and simulations. Hence postmodernists argue that the institutions of modernity have reached their end. With this the legitimizations used "to terrorize" modern individuals into meeting the pernicious requirements of modern reality have come to an end as well. In the words of one proponent "We are now in the process of wakening from the nightmare of modernity, with its manipulative reason and fetish of the totality."[15] In its place postmodernists seek to put a "total acceptance of ephemerality, fragmentation, discontinuity, and the chaotic."[16]

The empirical proof for this line of argumentation is based on the manifestations of symptoms that are held to reveal that the private life of modern individuals has become increasingly fragmented and disorganized. Therefore, postmodern theorists propose that a general rethinking of the nature of the family and what they like to call "the sex/gender role system" is in order. In facilitating such a rethinking, they like to regard themselves as midwifes to the postmodern social order. In short, postmodernists see it as their solemn historical mission to help postmodern men and women to overcome the outmoded modes of thought and behavior they allege to stand in the way of the emerging new.

As expected, the deconstruction of the modern family in its conventional form fits well into this theoretical agenda as postmodernists are convinced that this type of family presents a particularly obdurate hurdle on the way to the realization of the new social order. The conventional family, they argue, is the linchpin of the "imperialism of the patriarchal Western tradition," the emblem and carrier of a dominant power structure preoccupied with vulgar commerce and lucre, indifferent to the lot of women and the downtrodden. In short, they see the conventional family to be at the root of all contemporary ills and evil.[17]

Despite some differences, three discreet, though interconnected themes inform the post-modernist view of the family. First, on the economic level it is argued that structural shifts have replaced classical notions of production with the consumption of images. Second, on the psychological level the same shifts are claimed to have made for the rise of a postmodern self, that is to say, a self that lags in unity because changes in the dispositions and ways in which individuals approach the world can no longer be integrated. And third, on the societal level the unifying themes of modernity need to be replaced by a yet to be defined multiculturalism in which all modes of thought and living together are equally acceptable.

The Modern Family and the Formation of New Images of Consumption

As pointed out earlier, postmodernists are given to the argument that shifts in economic industrial production have given way to the dominance of language and communication. Those social forms that are anchored in the political institutions, economic structures, moral norms, and social practices typical of industrial modernity are no longer applicable. Hence "new social forms, new ways of acting and thinking, new attitudes, a reshuffling of the cards of 'fate' and 'nature' and social 'reality'" are awaiting to be given form."[18]

It is for reasons of this sort that postmodernist theorists attribute great importance to the mass media. As guardians of the future, they see it as their task to keep a close watch over the ways in which meanings produced by the media penetrate into all corners of contemporary life, but particularly those revolving around the family. They are particularly leery of what they call "television-set family myths," such as those portrayed in soap operas and situation comedies, which they hold to be out of touch with the family realities that have emerged in recent decades. The media does not portray real families, they are what Baudrillard calls "hyperreal."[19] Contemporary mass-mediated images of the family have to be monitored and attacked as they are argued to be "cultural fantasies" which do not provide practical—or "politically correct," if one prefers—guidelines for how to live today.[20]

As may be expected, such hyperreal, mediated fantasies are of particular interest to radical feminist theorists. The soap operas and sitcoms of television in particular are held to be primary sites for the ideological construction of male-dominated heterosexual couple relationships. Hence, they revile the main staple of the mass media with their recurrent themes of love and fear, submission and autonomy, sexual desire and asexual caregiving that revolve around scenes of everyday family life. Arguing that it is "gender instability and identity confusion" that characterizes life in postmodern society, they insist that the media's traditional ideological representations provide an illusory and unacceptable resolution of the contradictions inherent in postmodern life. They maintain that today's early childhood socialization is typically carried out in front of the television set and in daycare settings that reinforce conventional modes of thought and attitudes. For that reason they demand a close monitoring of mass-media offerings as well as the content of educational programs and the pedagogical approaches of public education. By the same token, they demand that family practices guided by more conventional modes of socialization carried out in the privacy of the home need to be exposed and delegitimized.

This anti-conventional family agenda has entered the public arena with considerable fanfare. In some school districts in the United States this agenda has been adopted lock, stock, and barrel, though conservative forces, on occasion, have been quite successful politically in making their counterclaims stick. There can be little doubt that the ideological battles over the content of public school curricula and library holdings have in no small measure increased the ferocity

of the cultural wars of today. And there is no telling whose vision
will ultimately win out.

The Rise of the Fragmented Postmodern Self

A postmodern society needs postmodern individuals. In his influential essay, "Postmodern Man," Vytautas Kavolis proposed as early
as 1970 that the rapid pace of the forces leading to the arrival of
postmodern society makes not only for the obsolescence of social
institutions in their present form, it also makes it impossible to command the emotional, intellectual, cultural, and biographical commitments of modern men and women.[21] Individuals living in conditions of uncertainty are said to find it futile, if not even absurd, to
conduct and limit their life and sense of self along lines informed by
outmoded institutional norms. Inasmuch as conventional mores and
expectations have become increasingly irrelevant, it cannot be reasonably expected that they will endure in the future. Unconstrained
in their expressions and unable or unwilling to be located within the
social institutions that have traditionally shaped and limited them,
modern men and women are now compelled to achieve their essential selves "in the expanding peripheries," or what Kavolis calls "the
vanishing horizons of experience." The postmodern self thus manifests its essence through "static fragmentations" or "dynamic
occasionalism." [22] The conditions of the postmodern order encourage individuals to focus on the immediate present as the only tangible context within which they are able to experience their sense of
authenticity or being.

This early conceptualization of the postmodern self echoes through
the entire postmodernist discussion. In an earlier phase it echoes
through the writings of modern social theorists like Christopher Lash
(*The Rise of Narcissism*) and Robert Bellah (*The Habits of the Heart*)
who cannot be easily located in this camp. While different writers
have emphasized different aspects, and variable takes on the theme
have yielded different results, viewed as a whole, the conceptual emphasis of this approach suggests the rise of a new human nature. Modern sentiments and dispositions, in this view, evoke different aspects
of the self that eventually lead to profound changes in the old "bourgeois" self formed in the conventional "bourgeois" family setting. While
remnants of the older self may continue to linger on, the disappearance of this older self is held to be merely a question of time.

Additionally, postmodern emotional dispositions coming to the fore today are described in terms of "blankness," "pessimism," "affectlessness," "cynicism," and a general "passionlessness." They are held to have dissolved feelings and commitments into irony and flatness. To some it appears that the slew of studies on the emotional socialization of "postmodern" children in contemporary daycare facilities bear out the empirical validity of such observations. While these posited consequences have caused much public concern in recent years, postmodernist theorists persist in calling for the abandonment of older and tested patterns of socialization. Though unable to provide persuasive alternative models of socialization and childcare, they continue to flaunt their vague and distinctly utopian messages of the creation of a postmodern world in which family values and aspirations are replaced by values of genderlessness and the celebration of universal brotherhood and sisterhood. Frequently reduced to platitudes, such amorphous arguments have received a favorable hearing in opinion-making circles. In a later chapter we shall have occasion to see how pop psychologists, refusing to be outdistanced by postmodernism's prominence, have already taken their often arcane speculations into distinctly anti-family directions. Striking, though somewhat bizarre, claims that "parents are bad for their children" are floated in a seemingly never-ending line of bestsellers.[23]

With the exception of a small upper-middle-class group of voracious consumers of childcare literature, ordinary men and women, for their part, appear not to be impressed by many of the claims in favor of new forms of socialization and the celebration of alternative lifestyles. To the dismay of postmodernist theorists, the vast majority of American men and women have remained loyal to the ideals of the conventional family in matters concerning their children. According to a 1996 census report most American families are still headed by married couples (78 percent to be precise), marital bonds are still seen as binding (98 percent think marital infidelity to be wrong according to a 1996 University of Chicago sex survey), and, like parents all over the world, most American parents are passionately committed to their children and claim to be guided by conventional principles in the socialization of their children.

Yet postmodern socialization theories and their approach to the formation of the modern self have not been without consequences.

It remains a fact that many people have lost confidence in their own judgment about how best to organize their private lives and decide which methods of socialization are likely to do no harm to their children. Adrift in a sea of contradictory expert notions and advice, they have become increasingly uncertain about what precisely is good for them. The juxtaposition between invalidated old models of socialization and the lack of available new ones has led to a situation in which modern parents who know a lot about children and child development still feel at a loss about what to do. They eagerly listen to the advice of experts, but soon discover that they often prove to be unreliable and unworkable. One year they hear that children absolutely must eat at regular times, the next year they must be allowed to eat whenever they feel hungry. One year the children must have as much freedom as possible, the next year strict rules of behavior must be enforced. Nobody seems to be able to give hard and fast advice, the know-how changes just as quickly as a child's development itself.

The Rise of Multiculturalism

The deconstruction of modernity—in thought as well as in practice—involves the deconstruction of the epistemology that has served to undergird the worldview of Western civilization. The epistemology of the West, and the way in which knowledge has been defined, acquired, tested, accumulated, and disseminated over time, postmodernists find to be no longer valid and in need of a fundamental reconstruction. What precisely this epistemology consists of is rarely made explicit. It is argued to operate tacitly beneath the surface of everyday Western existence and its content and cognitive style is no longer sustainable in a rapidly changing world.

Conveniently ignored is the fact that it took a long time for this epistemology to evolve and that its history is in essence the product of complex contestations and interpenetrations of the civilizational themes associated with classical antiquity, the Judeo-Christian tradition, and the Enlightenment on both sides of the Atlantic. It is an epistemology shaped by particularistic philosophical, religious, and aesthetic insights into the nature of man and community, as well as by a shared understanding about the human condition. In short, this epistemology can be argued to be a remarkably multiperspectived and multiethnic worldview that, in the words of one of its advocates, "is both breathtakingly expansive and prohibitively inclusive—and, because of its respect for truth tested and tried, appreciably traditionalist and orderly." [24] The multicultural origin of the epistemology of modernity, as we shall see in a subsequent chapter, is interwoven with the institution of the modern family in complex ways. It inspired in individuals a way of thinking that made it possible to transcend the interests of the immediate family and allowed for the emergence of a "civil society" and with its emphasis upon the individual it had the capacity to incorporate the most diverse groups imaginable into the emerging civilizational order of the West.

The theorists of postmodernism, and many academics along with them, however, have a radically different view of this tradition. They argue it to be oppressive to the core, embedded in sexist, racist, classist, heterosexist language and literary presuppositions that privilege white European males, and hence they see in it the source of much that is wrong with modern life. The Western tradition, they claim, revels in a perilous individualism that penalizes and ostracizes whole groups of people such as nonwhites, non-Westerners, women, homosexuals, and so forth. In its place they seek to put a new kind of ethnic tribalism based on gender, race, or tribe, in which individual personhood is merged into newly-constituted stereotyped collectivist group-identities. On the political level the new tribalism expands to discover ever-new numbers of epistemologically victimized minorities. As agents of the new multiculturalism, postmodern theorists call epistemological minorities to action and throw off the shackles of the dominant theoretical paradigm that held them captive in their underprivileged position for so long.

The deconstruction of the modern paradigm has been remarkably successful to date in the area of public education. In assigning pupils and students to some demographically-derived, ethno-gender category, the theorists and agents of the new multiculturalism were able to marshal political forces behind all sorts of propositions that reinforce the notion that individualism is a bad thing and that there is no personhood based on universally valid values. Their efforts have already gone a long way to undermine the ethos of the America's educational enterprise that was traditionally based on notions of individual effort and merit. In a recent article in *American Scholar*, Diane Ravitch, the prominent educator, describes how under the banner of multiculturalism, public elementary and secondary schools have become increasingly politicized and forced to respond to the narrow epistemological interests of "Europhobic" activist groups. Across the country, school systems have begun to inaugurate explicitly ethnocentric and gender-specific curricula, and reforms like "ethno-mathematics" have been initiated for the purpose of liberating this seemingly innocent science of the taint of "Eurocentrism."[25]

Perhaps nowhere there exists a greater potential for the new multiculturalism to create havoc than in the affairs of a family system based on personal responsibility and individual achievement. The distinctly unique ethos of the modern nuclear family steadfastly maintains that achievement is possible only by way of self-discipline, hard work, persistency, frugality, accountability, and a capacity to delay gratification. Upward mobility—"making it"—is viewed as both desirable and attainable and very much the result of individual effort. To be sure, there was always an illusory quality about the mobility expectations of many people and, in terms of actual mobility, America was never quite the "open society" it was proclaimed to have been in the popular mind. Nonetheless, as history has shown, the values and behavior patterns fostered by the conventional family's ethos, more often than not, turned out to be decisive

Thus is the power of the postmodernist lure that even social scientists who cannot be readily placed in this theoretical camp argue that the ethos and structural requirements of the conventional modern family no longer applies to life in the postmodern world. While most resist the temptation to see the family of the future exemplified in the "single-parent family, headed by a teenage mother, who may be drawn to drug abuse and alcoholism . . . liv(ing) in a household that is prone to be violent," [26] many are inclined to argue that it is a good thing that the old codes of behavior have given way to more pluralistic ways of conduct which accepts no one single ethic as binding for all. Since old verities have crumbled and nothing seems to matter any longer, everything is possible and equally acceptable. To suggest otherwise, that is, not to be politically correct in the new multicultural sense, is morally offensive if not worse.

Toward a Different Theoretical Understanding of the Nature and Role of the Modern Family

This brief synopsis of the various theoretical approaches to the family was guided by the effort to provide a fair presentation of the core assumptions of each theoretical camp. This was a difficult task in more ways than one as the historical record not only reveals the intellectual poverty of some of the theoretical approaches but the weakness of the presuppositions upon which they rest. Hence it was not possible to make some critical comments on each. With the exception of W. S. Goode, few of the theorists discussed found it theoretically necessary to distinguish between modern consciousness and modern institutions and all—Marxists, conservatives, and mainstream functionalists alike—found it sufficient to focus their research on the primacy of the structural dimensions of modern society. Though Goode, following Parsons, made that important distinction, he showed himself strangely resistant to follow-up on the theoretical implications posed by the discrete, though parallel, processes of changes in structure and the processes of change (or non-change) in consciousness. Across the political spectrum theorists take it for granted that changes in consciousness and values are the product of preceding changes in structure and they find it hard to reconcile structural shifts with the persistence of values and ideals.

The same shortcomings apply to those postmodernists whose theoretical constructs must be seen as a combination of structuralist and Marxist core assumptions to which something akin to a fixation on the overpowering influence of quasi-autonomous images and symbols mediated by modern forms of communication has been added. Inasmuch as all theorists of the conventional family are united by their conviction that it is changes in the realm of technology and its economic organization that determine changes in all social institutions, their rock-bottom theoretical assumption has made for the preponderance of a one-dimensional theoretical model of the family. What is left out is the possibility that ideas, cognition, values, and the like may also be shaped by nonmaterial and nonstructural factors. This theoretical omission had dire consequences for the institution of the conventional nuclear family and, by extension, for the health of modern society as well.

It is of some importance to keep in mind that modernization is a process that goes beyond technological and economic development. When properly used the concept of modernization refers not only to changes in the economic, political, and social structures of society but also to changes in the structure of the consciousness of individuals—their ideas, values, and norms. While it can be plausibly argued that the onset of industrial production dramatically transformed all aspects of social life, including consciousness, it is hard to maintain that this particular form of production appeared suddenly out of nowhere. Moreover, it is one thing to argue for the interrelationship between the macro- and micro-levels of modern society—which undoubtedly exists—it is a different thing altogether to argue that changes in the latter are preceded by changes in the first in a more or less mechanical fashion. The relationship between these two spheres is decidedly more complex and less predictable than either of the theoretical camps assumes. To the same degree that it can be shown that historically the structures of modern consciousness and corresponding behavior patterns frequently antedate their realization in modern institutions, it is also not difficult to point to substantial empirical evidence that leads us to believe that modern ways of thinking and behaving continue to produce considerable pressures on the larger institutional order. But most importantly, in the midst of all these changes, turmoil, and debates, there can be little doubt that the modern family in its conventional form continues to hold the loyalty of today's men and women. Contrary to theoretical claims and predictions the family is more than a lifestyle choice. The exploration of why that is so is the task of the next two chapters.

Notes

1. Friedrich Engles, *The Origin of the Family, Private Property and the State* (New York: Pathfinders Press, 1972, originally published in German in 1884).
2. Ibid. p. 110.
3. A very readable refutation of key Marxist notions can be found in Ferdinand Mount, *The Subversive Family* (London: Jonathan Cape, 1982).
4. Frederic Le Play, *Les Ouvrier Europeans (The European Workers)* (Paris: Hachette, 1855). For a synopsis in English see C.C. Zimmerman and M.E. Frampton, *Family and Society* (Princeton, N.J.: Van Nostrand,1935).
5. Carle C. Zimmerman, *The Family of Tomorrow: The Cultural Crisis and the Way Out,* (New York: Harper & Bros, 1949).
6. Henry Sumner Maine, *Ancient Law* (New York: J.M. Dent & Sons, 1960, originally published 1861).
7. Christopher Lasch, *The Culture of Narcissism: American Life in an Age of Diminishing Expectations* (New York: W.W. Norton and Company, 1979) and Richard Sennet, *Authority* (New York: Alfred A. Knopf, 1980).
8. Talcott Parsons et al., *Family: Socialization and Interaction Process* (New York: The Free Press, 1955) and Ernest W. Burgess and Harvey J. Locke, *The Family from Institution to Companionship* (New York: Academic Book, 1945).
9. William J. Goode, *World Revolution and Family Patterns* (New York: Free Press, 1963).

10.   David Riesman et al., *The Lonely Crowd* (New York: Doubleday Anchor, 1960; first published in 1950).

11.   The most succinct summary of this line of thinking can be found in Ernest W. Burgess and Harvey J. Locke's influential book *The Family from Institution to Companionship* (New York: American Books, 1945).

12.   Barrington Moore, *Social Theory and Social Power* (Boston: Beacon Press, 1958).

13.   Randall Collins, *The Sociology of Marriage & the Family* (Chicago: Nelson Hall, 1985).

14.   Michel Foucault, *Discipline and Punish: The Birth of the Prison* (New York: Vintage Books, 1977) and Michel Foucault, *The History of Sexuality: An Introduction* (New York: Pantheon, Vol. 1, 1978).

15.   David Harvey, *The Condition of Postmodernity* (London: Basil Blackwell 1989, p. 9).

16.   Ibid., p. 44.

17.   The following books and articles may be helpful in getting a first notion what this diffuse camp is about in general:

pro postmodernism: Juergen Habermas, "Modernity Versus Postmodernity," *New German Critique*, 22, no.3 (winter 1981); Jean Baudrillard, *Fatal Strategies* (New York: Semiotext(e) 1990); Steven Connor, *Postmodernist Culture: An Introduction to Theories of the Contemporary* (New York: Basil Blackwell, 1989), and in particular the 1988 special issue of *Theory, Culture & Society*, 5:217–37.

against: George Steiner, *Real Presences* (Chicago: University of Chicago Press, 1989); John M. Ellis, *Against Deconstruction* (Princeton, N.J. : Princeton University Press, 1989).

There exists a large variety of books on the deconstruction of the family, most are associated with the writings of academic feminist theory such as Sandra Harding and Dorothy Smith. Among sociologists David Cheal and Norman Denzin stand out and Todd Gitlin, "Postmodernism Defined, at last!," *Utne Reader,* (July-August 1990): 52–63 deserves special mention.

18.   Michael Ryan, "Postmodern Politics" in *Theory, Culture & Society*, 5:559–76, 1989, p.561.

19.   Jean Baudrillard, op.cit.

20.   Norman K. Denzin, "Postmodern Children," *Society,* 24, no. 3 (March-April 1987): 32–35.

21.   Vytautas Kavolis, "Postmodern Man: Psychocultural Responses to Social Trends," *Social Problems*, 17-4 (spring 1970): 435–48.

22.   Ibid., p. 439.

23.   Barbara Defoe Whitehead, "Are Parents Bad for their Children?," *Commentary*, April, 1991.

24.   Bruce Edwards, "Deconstruction in Academia," The Heritage Lecture, The Heritage Foundation, Washington, D. C., 1990.

25.   Diane Ravitch, "Multiculturalism: E Pluribus Plures," *American Scholar*, 59, no. 3 (summer 1990): 337–54.

26.   Norman Denzin, op. cit., 1987, p. 33.

Part 2

The Modern Family:
Its Nature and History

3

The Family: The Primary Institution of Individual and Social Life

> The family is, as far as we know, the toughest
> institution we have. It is, in fact, the institution
> to which we owe our humanity.
> —Margaret Mead

In the preceding chapters we saw how the once taken-for-granted institution of the family sustained a massive erosion in confidence in the course of a few fateful decades. Among the decision-making elite a view had come to dominate that the fallout from the modernization process had irrevocably exhausted the family's capacity to provide individuals with the sustenance and resources modern social life requires. At the same time we learned that ever more social science data continue to reveal that the family has shown a remarkable staying power in the face of predictions of doom. The evidence strongly indicates that the vast majority of ordinary men and women—in all walks of life and from the most varied ethnic backgrounds imaginable—appear to hold on to their unwavering conviction that the family is the single most important thing in their lives. Neither the pressures emanating from a rapidly-changing industrial order nor the radical criticism produced in academic isolation seem to have been able to devalidate the ideal of a life which in structure and style revolves around the nuclear family in its more or less conventional form.

The curious discrepancy between elite perceptions and the actual way ordinary people behave underscores the need for looking at the institution of the family through an analytical lens different from the one customarily used. In what follows the attempt will be made to show why the various factions participating in the public debate over the family today—postmodern visionaries as well as their traditionalist counterparts and all gradations of views in between—who stress family discontinuity, if not worse, argue from theoretical postulates that stand on unsecured intellectual grounds. Regardless whether one faction foresees impending catastrophe if the powers of the state fail to return a seemingly recalcitrant population to the strictures of the family life of an earlier age, as conservatives do, or whether more liberal factions are more inclined to support postmodernist projections of the flourishing of a plethora of lifestyles unencumbered by any such strictures, all camps party to the debate today appear to be in danger of overinterpreting the signs of decline and hence they needlessly project a vision of the future in which life promises to become an increasingly wretched affair.

While it is hardly the task of this book to acquaint the reader with the finer points of academic theorizing, it is necessary to say a little more about the theoretical perspective that allows us to take a different look at the modern family and its future. It is a perspective that makes use of a large quantity of empirical as well as historical and cross-cultural materials collected in different academic disciplines. Theoretically it is based on two distinctive analytical traditions: that of philosophical anthropology as it relates to the role of social institutions and that of the "interpretative" approach in sociology associated with the name of Max Weber (the latter approach is supplemented by aspects of phenomenology and the sociology of knowledge). Though it is impossible to provide a thoroughgoing commentary on either of these theoretical approaches, their usefulness will become evident fairly quickly as the argument progresses. By the time we come to take a closer look at the central themes dominating the current public discourse in a later chapter, the reader will thus be in a better position to judge the validity of the many and often contradictory policy propositions championed by either of the factions active in the public arena today. Moreover, the distinctive approach to the family advocated here is able to avoid many of the theoretical pitfalls that have plagued the analysis of the family for so long. In making use of an institutional approach to the modern family the following explications are able to provide a bridge between contending theoretical camps.

On Human Nature and the Institutional Dimensions
of the Family

The family, it has often been argued, is the product of the most elementary and most virulent emotions of human nature—love, hate, sex, hunger, sacrifice, punishment, loneliness, and so on. At the same time, wherever one turns, the family also provides the basic locale in which human production and reproduction takes place. Hence the family has a dual function: to organize and give purpose to human emotions and to ensure the continuity of a given social group.

The ways in which both emotions and activities becomes routinized, habituated, and, ultimately, institutionalized, however, differ greatly from place to place. Over time, the patterns, or ways, in which these properties of human nature and human existence interact and reinforce one another lead to the formation of an almost inexhaustible variety of distinctive family cultures, close to two thousand by the count of anthropologists. So, for instance, it is reported that there were societies in the past where it was the main purpose of the family to guarantee the continuity of the family line, as was the case in traditional China, or where there existed a strong objection to love marriages, as in traditional India, where romantic love was held to have the potential to prevent the male householder from meeting pressing family obligations and duties. And then in large parts of the African continent one encounters family systems that recognized neither private property nor monogamy in the past, just as there continue to exist family systems in the Islamic world today that seek to relegate women to a life exclusively spent in the confines of the household. Examples of this type abound and it would not be difficult to fill a lengthy book describing the many ways in which human propensities and behavior have been shaped and become institutionalized. From there one could go on to show how these distinctive family systems, in turn, came to provide the foundations from which vastly different cultures and civilizations arose. However interesting and perhaps even necessary such a quest might be, a full treatment of this topic would take us into directions far removed from the major themes of a book that seeks to fathom the fate of the modern family in the modern order.

It also has to be kept in mind that this book is not designed to provide a treatise on human nature. Although there is a good deal of truth to the often-voiced argument that every theory of the family implicitly contains a set of assumptions about human nature, what interests us at this point in the argument is the question of why the institution of the family arises from interlocking needs built into human nature itself and why among all the human groupings known to us the family better than any another conceivable mechanism available is peculiarly well-suited for setting the boundaries for the expression of human propensities.

Let us then tackle a question that, at first blush, sounds deceptively simple: what is it in human nature that makes institutions necessary? The academic literature on institutions is replete with learned treatises on the nature and functions of institutions. Since no particular purpose would be served to recapitulate the major arguments, we shall let ourselves be guided by propositions on human nature derived from the pioneering work of human biologists working in the tradition of Adolf Portmann in Switzerland and F. Buytendijk in Holland, and the application of their findings to the social sciences by Arnold Gehlen, the German philosophical anthropologist.[1] This approach permits us to glean the reasons why institutions in general, and the institution of the family in particular, are an indelible part of all forms of sociation.

Unlike other animals, these scholars argue, human beings do not dispose over an instinctual arsenal that provides them with a reliable guide for most of their actions. Gehlen, in fact, goes to some length to show that humans are "instinctually deprived" and hence are, by necessity, compelled to create their own guidance. And this precisely is what social institutions do for them. If it were not for institutions, the world would have to be reinvented every day anew—surely an impossible idea! This can be illustrated by a simple example: If a man and a woman, mutually attracted to each other, had not recourse to institutional patterns in their efforts to act on the basis of the attraction, they would have before them a vast number of imaginable options. To be sure, this would give them a great deal of freedom, could fill an awful lot of time, and, perhaps, could also be very exciting, at least for a while. As a permanent state of affairs, however, it would be quite impossible for there would be neither energy nor time left to do much else. To imagine the whole human race existing in this fashion would be to imagine a very short-lived species, indeed. Even if individuals could spend their entire lives reinventing the world on a daily basis, it would be well nigh impossible to socialize and adequately prepare children for the future in such a situation. To the same degree, it would also be impossible to establish any ordered and predictable political and economic life.

This view of human nature circumvents a discussion of the great variety of theories that seek to identify the many properties of human nature just as it abstains from rendering an appraisal of modern-day arguments on the relative importance of external factors flowing from the environment—including economic and political factors—on the concrete manifestation of human behavior. Though rooted in human biology, the argument set forth here strenuously avoids any biological determinism (as sociobiologists and those working in the tradition of Desmond Morris and Edmund Wilson are prone to do) and accepts the possibility that human propensities, lacking in stability because of the instinctual deprivation of humans, are open to being shaped by external factors. This perspective leads to an analytical mode that recognizes the importance of biological as well as cultural factors and hence it is able to return a modicum of common sense to many of today's hotly-contested issues. While it is reluctant to provide an unqualified endorsement for biologically-based arguments that hold that the vast complex of instincts are an unmodifiable part of the human being's biological heritage (and hence remains beyond human control), this perspective is equally leery of propositions which aver that every aspect of human behavior—sexuality, gender, mothering, and so forth—is little more than a cultural or social construct. On the one hand, the sheer weight of accumulated historical and cross-cultural evidence makes it abundantly clear that the way in which instincts become manifest varies greatly from culture to culture. But the same evidence also strongly indicates that there exist limitations to a free-floating construction of behavior patterns at will and wish. Rather, the empirical evidence suggests that because of their instinctual deprivation at birth, human beings are dependent upon external structures or institutions that allow for the unfolding of everything we associate with the meaning of being human.

Of course, this insight in itself is not new. Already the philosophers of classical antiquity argued in favor of particular institutional forms in the conduct of political life. In the modern era Thomas Hobbes, in particular, drew our attention to their importance when he argued that in the absence of institutions people would be living in "a state of nature" in which everyone would be engaged in a permanent war against everyone else and "the life of man (would be) solitary, poore, nasty, brutish, and short."[2] While some of Hobbes' arguments on the potential consequences of an assumed "state of nature" may resonate well with many readers today, his social contract theory in favor of the elevation of the state and its legal arms to sole authority in the conduct of human affairs strikes many modern-day social analysts as decidedly naive. Though the Hobbesian view has greatly influenced contemporary thinking about the role of the state in the affairs of familial and social life, the experiences of the past century have taught us that a total reliance on the state as the final source and arbiter of all aspects of social life is oddly optimistic. A much better argument can be made that this view has taken us a long way down a perilous path from which we find it exceedingly difficult to extricate ourselves today.

The institutional perspective derived from the field of human biology allows us to see why human beings are by nature dependent upon the availability of socially-constructed institutions; for it is social institutions that permit them to conduct their lives in a more or less consistent and predictable manner. Though John Locke's notion of the human mind as a "clean slate," a *tabula rasa*, at birth has to be put into question in the light of modern research, there can be little doubt that individual traits are malleable—within limits, to be sure—and in need of institutional guidance. The view that human nature is unfinished at birth, incidentally, finds today strong support from research conducted in the biological sciences. One can only hope that in the future more systematic thought will be given to the proposition that human beings are in need of institutional guidance.

The "Visible" Consequences of "Invisible" Social Institutions

Any attempt to understand social institutions is complicated by the fact that institutions are not visible to the human eye. They arise out of the interaction between human beings in response to universal and recurrent problems. The process whereby responses to similar situations and challenges become habituated, routinized, and eventually "institutionalized" is a question that cannot be pursued here. For our purposes it is important to understand that once institutionalized patterns of behavior have come into existence, they tend to take on a dynamics of their own. They now provide the basis for normatively approved ways for regulating the behavior of future generations when confronted with similar challenges. Emile Durkheim, one of the founding fathers of sociology, has provided us with the classical description of how social institutions organize social life.[3] Social institutions (or in Durkheim's terms "social facts") are external to the individual (i.e., they are there whether the individual wishes it or not); have the quality of objectivity (i.e., individuals cannot determine their characteristics in accordance with their subjective preferences or idiosyncratic perceptions, but must come to terms with the way in which any particular institution is collectively understood and "acted out"); have coercive powers (i.e., if individuals decide to ignore or resist a genuine institution, sanctions are available against them and any number of more or less unpleasant things may happen to them); and finally, they have moral authority and historicity. By this he implied that an institution—though not visible to the human eye in that it arises out of interaction between human beings—exists not only as a fact that is real and must be treated as such, but almost invariably is justified as having a right to exist. Individuals, therefore, are supposed to adhere to institutionally appropriate conduct not only because they fear the sanctions, but because they acknowledge an institution's moral authority. What is more, every genuine social institution is experienced by the individual as a historical phenomenon: that is to say, it was there before he or she were born, and it is likely to outlast the individual's own life.

One does not have to be a professional social scientist to appreciate that in this classical understanding of social institutions each of the features characteristic of the family is exemplified in a particularly striking manner. The social institution of the family not only brings order and structure to the infinite possibilities open to human beings for acting out their biologically-given endowments, it also provides purpose and meaning to their life. The first is achieved by means of clearly-established social rules—such as the taming of sexuality by means of relegating it to some socially sanctioned form (typically marriage)—and the second is accomplished by assigning social roles to individual behavior that specify how individuals are expected to behave in particular situations. So, for instance, the social roles a particular society assigns to husbands and wives, or to parents and children, tell them how they *ought* to perform their respective marital or parental obligations. By the same token, they instruct individuals of their rights to each other and vis-à-vis the unit of the family as a whole. Regardless of its culture-specific form, the institution of the family acquires moral authority as well as coercive powers in this way. In our type of society, for example, the father's role traditionally required the man to provide for his family, to protect it, and to represent it to the outside world; while the role of the mother charged the wife with taking care of the inner life of the family, with the nurture and socialization of small children, and with being responsible for the running of the family household. As we have seen in earlier chapters, these traditional role requirements and the normative aura surrounding them have in recent decades led to much discontent and protest in the societies of the West. Yet regardless which side in the battle over socially-prescribed roles one ultimately is inclined to come out on, our very human nature, as Arnold Gehlen has shown, entraps us into accepting the existence of institutionalized roles. As argued earlier, if such institutionalized roles were not available to individuals, which allow them to act out the ordinary tasks of daily life in a quasi-automatic fashion, they would have no energies left to engage in tasks that are out of the ordinary. Like Sisyphus in Greek mythology they would be condemned to reinvent every human act time and again. To be sure, in times of transition, like the one we are experiencing today, the confusion created by role ambivalence and a general lack of normative guidance causes considerable stress to individuals and society alike. Yet even if the present family system could be completely abolished, a new institutionalized substitute would arise. Although role expectations may change over time and the adaptation of social roles to newly-emerging social realities is an ongoing and never-ending process in every known society, the fact remains that there simply is no escape from institutions!

It is of great importance to appreciate that every social institution is expressed by means of a system of social norms. Social norms, in sociological parlance, are the rules whereby society informs its members about the accepted ways of doing things. Growing up in a society means learning its norms. Social norms themselves arise in a complicated fashion out of human interaction and the need of human beings to give purpose and meaning to everything they do, think, and feel. It is at this point that religion and religiously-constructed meaning systems come to play a central, if not indispensable, role, for religion endows ordinary actions with a higher meaning that transcends the actions of the individual. Once established, a normative system influences and, in turn, controls the conduct of the individual. In their influential book, *The Social Construction of Reality*, Peter L. Berger and Thomas Luckmann have set forth in some theoretical detail the constitutive elements of this dialectical process.[4] For our purposes, we shall simply argue that the normative aspects of particular institutions vary from society to society just as they may change within a given society over the course of time.

Let me illustrate the normative dimension of the institution of the family with the following examples: in the family, any family that is, there exist norms that specify which persons are eligible to marry, how many spouses they may have, where and how they should live, what the division of labor in the household should be, what the proper attitudes toward children and the old are, and so forth. Such norms may range from the formal (each person by custom and law may have only one spouse) to the informal (letting father have the largest piece of meat, mother does not take out the garbage). What is more, both informal as well as formal norms may change over time. So, for instance, sexual relationships once restricted by marriage may at a later period occur outside of marriage without the customary social opprobrium that was the stuff of Victorian fiction. Or take another example, the old adage that children should be seen but not be heard may at a different point in time change to the requirement that the happy home is a home filled with the laughter and noise of children. In sum, the examples used here allow us to see that institutions are defined not only by complex patterns of norms, but also the way they are defined provides them with purpose and power. What is more, the social power of particular norms may change in the course of time.

Regardless of the processes whereby the "institutionalization" of human behavior occurs, taken together the basic institutions of society compose not only "the social structure" of every known society, they also are interrelated with each other in a multiplicity of ways. There is no reason to expect that this will, or even can, ever change. Hence we may conclude that the human capacity for living together is dependent upon the availability of social institutions. Even the most ferocious form of anti-institutionalism may become an institutionalized pattern of behavior, at least for a short while. In other word, institutions and society are synonymous.[5]

As pointed out previously, the manner in which particular institutions come into existence is an exceedingly complicated process in which a multitude of factors play a role. Yet it is important to understand that this process is primarily a social process in which the interactions of individuals with one another as well as between individuals and their larger social world are decisive. The theoretical parameters for the detailed processes whereby interactions between particular individuals and the institutionalized ways of doing things come to interpenetrate one another were developed by George Herbert Mead and Charles Horton Cooley, both of whom taught at the University of Chicago during the early part of the twentieth century. To this day scholars—particularly those working in the field of early childhood socialization—are indebted to their pioneering work.[6] Regrettably space does not permit elaboration on their important contributions here a little more as it would take the argument before us into a different direction.

The foregoing theoretical considerations allow us to conclude with considerable confidence that it is not difficult to show why the institutionalization of human propensities and behavior is an a priori requirement both for human existence as well as for the maintenance of any human society. It is also not difficult to see why the institution of the family plays the first and foremost role in this process. It is within the family that the child experiences the social world for the first time and is within the confines of the family that most of us experience life at its most intense and profound. In view of these realities one is tempted to argue that if the institution of the family would not exist, it would have to be invented. At the same time, it must be pointed out that to recognize the universality and power of social institutions does not imply that institutions and the social roles connected to them cannot change or should not change. Indeed, institutions change all the time. They must change, almost by definition, because institutions are nothing but the inevitably tenuous products of innumerable individuals "throwing out" meanings into the world. Yet it is important to realize that such changes cannot be designed and superimposed from above, either by groups, agendas, or governments. For changes in human behavior to become real, they must be rooted in changes occurring in the interactive and communicative process of people actually living together. It is a process that takes a long, often a very long, period of time. For changes to last, they must not only be anchored in experience, they also have to respond to deeper levels of human life and must be sustained in an ongoing fashion on that level as well. So for instance, for decades the communist government of the People's Republic of China, the PRC, was determined to destroy "the sib-fetters of kin" that have permeated the whole of Chinese social and political life as long as Chinese history remembers. This determination was based on the conviction that powerful family ties have in the past prevented the Chinese state to modernize and develop economically. Despite the Maoist regime's often draconian measures, the record shows that sweeping national programs to replace the traditional Chinese family with new allegiances to communes and other state-organized collectivities have failed miserably. Whatever other factors may have been responsible for this failure, surely none were more important than the regime's decision to work against the institution of the family rather than with and through it—as overseas Chinese in other parts of the world have done to their great benefit.

To take a different view on the question of changes in the institution of the family let us construct a hypothetical, though extremely unlikely, case: If all Americans should decide to have children without being married, then marriage, that is to say the institutionalized process for the establishment of a family, would disappear. Yet this change would also require the creation of new boundaries, rules, and provisions—such as who is responsible for the daily care of children, who nurtures and guides them, who pays for their needs, etc., etc. In other words, all the new practices that would result from the removal of marriage as a social institution would now have to be routinized and stabilized. Eventually they would result in the formation of new institutional structures. The new institution—perhaps called the y-generation lifestyle—would be characterized by its own distinctive features and practices. It would require new legitimations to explain why these, and no other practices, serve the needs of children, adults, and the existing social order better than other alternatives do. Undoubtedly this effort would have to be validated by some theory of human nature, which in the new social order—post-postmodern, if you will—would keep legions of academics and pundits employed for generations to come. Any novelist blessed with only a modicum of imagination could think up scenarios that could entertain, titillate, and inspire awe. To translate such imagined scenarios into social reality, however, is a different matter altogether. It would require that ordinary individuals would by nature be predisposed to take up in practice modes of existence theoretically devised by individuals in pursuit of a life free of institutional constrains. Surely an impossibility!

The Family: The Shaper of Order and Meaning

As we have seen, the human being enters the world with a repertoire of specialized drives and propensities. Since they are biologically denied the ordering mechanisms with which other animals are endowed, humans are compelled to impose their own order upon experience. In other words, human beings must make a world for themselves and they achieve this task by means of creating institutions. This is an arduous, never-ending, and, by definition, a collective enterprise. Yet while human beings together shape tools, invent language, adhere to values, build institutions, and create culture, this culturally-constructed world is inherently unstable, precarious, and open to change. This quality of human life manifests itself to a particular degree in modern societies where it produces a profound sense of homelessness and anxiety in individuals, who by nature are dependent upon constancy and security.

It is here where the family plays an indispensable role. For the family, more than any other institution, has the capacity to reconcile the fact that life is perpetually in a state of flux with the human need for order and stability. It is in the institution of the family where the most basic dimensions of human life intersect and sustain each other—the biological with the social, the material with the normative, the symbolic with the transcendental, and so forth—and it is in the family where institutions are continuously produced, reproduced, and passed on from one generation to the next. It is for this reason that the family is the institution-creating entity par excellence.

This potential of the family becomes unmistakably evident when one looks at the ways whereby the routines of everyday life are given shape and meaning. In organizing routine activities and objectivating them through institutionalization, the family creates order out of the infinite number of possibilities potentially available to humans. In the rich anthropological literature on the subject, the writings of Mary Douglas, the British anthropologist, stand out for their poignant description of the culture-specific manner in which institutions operate. [7] Like other social anthropologists, she describes how despite otherwise vast cultural differences one encounters in all cultures not only a distinction between the sacred and the mundane but also distinctive spatial and temporal divisions in the organization of the routine activities of everyday life in terms of private and public. In all cultures there exist divisions between publicly and privately appropriate behavior in activities relating to eating, sleeping, working, and the performance of bodily functions. Yet they are expressed to an extreme degree in activities relating to excretion, sexuality, and, to a lesser degree, ingestion. So for instance, defecation is a private matter in most cultures and it is typically relegated to a special space set aside for this purpose. We know of no culture to date in which people defecate in public or in the company of others. Similar proprieties govern sexual activities and the evidence shows that the practice of group sex in societies argued to live "closer to nature" is more a figment of fevered imaginations than a reality. Even in so-called extended families (like those of Rahjahstan) where adult sons, their wives, and their many children live in communal households with little or no privacy available, sexual intercourse and defecation are frequently found to be organized in ways that may strike the Western mind as distinctly prudish. Similar boundaries rule activities related to eating and drinking, as, for instance, the requirements for men and women to eat separately in traditional Hindu, Muslim, and some African cultures indicate. Even in the societies of the modern West the activity of eating is organized in more or less distinctive ways. Telling evidence for this can be found in the availability of an extensive literature on social manners that sets forth the rules on "proper" table behavior, how to be a "good" host, what to eat at what time, and so forth.

There exists a yet further dimension to the institution-building role of the family. To the degrree that typical, recurring, situations need repetitive behavior, institutions hold the potential of becoming solidified in rituals. In doing so, new social forms are born that transcend individual experience. So, for instance, there exists not only a tendency in all societies to ritualize basic household activities—the "washing on Monday, ironing on Tuesday, sewing on Wednesday, baking on Thursday, cleaning on Friday, shopping on Saturday, and worshipping on Sunday" syndrome typical of traditional Western cultures—but the elaborate rituals that have been developed for purposes of recognizing important events in an individual's biography—marriage, birth, maturation, and death—permit us to see how in all societies known to us individual experiences are transformed into social experiences. The social ritual, Peter Berger has argued, transforms the individual event into a typical case, just as it transforms individual biography into an episode in the history of society.[8] As a consequence of this transformation process the individual now can be seen as having been born, living and suffering, and eventually dying, as his ancestors have done before him and as his children, in all likelihood, will do after him. In other words, rituals, frequently endowed with religious meanings, not only serve to firm up and substantiate the mundane forms of behavior in everyday life, but in providing meaning for individuals and other participants alike, a special social bond is created between them that takes on its own dynamics. It is in this transformation of the personal to the social that a quality of constancy is introduced which protects the individual from an otherwise unbearable anomie and meaninglessness lurking behind every corner. It is through the erection of institutions and rituals that the potent and alien forces of chaos can be kept at bay, as the example of the old and persisting Irish ritual of "the wake" shows. "The wake," as the evidence shows, serves to make death into a bearable event confirming life and community. Beyond that it is yet one more testimony to the fact that the great majority of rituals relate to family and communal life.

Institutions and Social Roles

In the everyday world of the household institutions are represented by social roles that serve to motivate and control individuals to behave in role-specific manners. So, for instance, we find roles determined by factors of gender and age, just as we find more broadly-defined roles such as the role of the "dutiful daughter," the "caring parent," or the "loving child" that have developed gradually over the course of many centuries. At the danger of gross oversimplification, we may understand social roles as emerging out of typical reactions to typical expectations in typical situations that have become ensconced as more or less fixed and recurring patterns of conduct over time. In this social roles may be seen to serve as a further stabilization of human experience to which socially-constructed meanings have been added. Roles, as George Herbert has argued, allow individuals to act out the requirements of specific situations in a taken-for-granted manner. They help them to perform the routine tasks of everyday life without further ado and relieve them of the need to contemplate time and again the appropriateness of every action to be taken. In this sense it can be said that social roles serve as some form of crutch for individuals who are now free to devote their attention and energies to other matters.

In the modern world there has been a proliferation of situations for which specific roles have not yet been institutionalized. This lack has frequently been a source of considerable stress to individuals and society alike. The modern social category of "the adolescent" or teenager, may serve as an example. In contrast to traditional societies which simply differentiated between childhood and adulthood, the term "adolescence" refers to that stage in modern life where the comforts of childhood are in the process of disappearing and the rewards of adulthood are slow in making themselves available. Inasmuch as adolescence as a separate period of life is a recent invention, it is as of yet unclear when adolescence begins and when it ends, what dividing lines separate the stages of biology and which "rites of passage" mark the thresholds between clearly-defined stages in the individual's progress through life. Nevertheless, young people in modern society are frequently exhorted to "act their age," while, at the same time, society is very ambiguous as to what this actually means. The absence of a clearly-defined and institutionalized adolescent role explains why it is not easy to be a teenager today.

Social roles, it is important to keep in mind, are not carved in stone. They can be acted out differently by different individuals and they are open to change. If and when social roles change, one can expect that this change will be accompanied by much controversy and strife. In later chapters we shall have occasion to talk more about the precariousness of social roles and the confusion that reigns over the definition of such social roles as the "good mother," the "loyal husband," and so forth in an age where men, women, and children are faced with a bewildering variety of contradictory demands. For the time being, we shall simply observe that just as there can be no social life without institutions and rituals, social life without social roles is equally unthinkable.

Institutions and the Question of Freedom and Constraint

Already Aristotle argued that man is *zoon politicon*. He was convinced that a human being outside of society is an unknown quantity, "either a beast or a god," and that it takes social life to make human beings out of biological entities. Few today would contest this basic proposition. For human beings to develop their essential human qualities, it is necessary that their most basic natural endowments are tamed and shaped. As we have seen, the process of shaping the natural endowment occurs in intensive interaction with other human beings, which starts in the family and the home. It begins in early childhood and continues as the individual passes through the various phases of his or her lifecycle, ending with that ultimate stage, dying. It is a process that involves the learning of ever-new social roles at different stages of life and is a process that is in many ways connected to the family. Inasmuch as every new situation and every new stage of life requires individuals to adapt themselves continuously, all organized forms of living together involve dimensions of control if not coercion. As we have seen, the existence of predetermined social roles that enable individuals to perform adequately in a given situation provides them with the freedom to devote their energies and imagination to a great variety of tasks that otherwise would have to be left undone. One is almost tempted to argue that without the availability of institutionalized roles that have the capacity to organize everyday occurrences in efficient ways, social existence would be a chaotic affair indeed.

At the heart of the family then lies a theoretical paradox: it constrains as it sets free. There can be little doubt that there exist pronounced dimensions of control in every family system. Such controls are perhaps most harshly expressed in traditional societies, where deviations from traditionally-prescribed norms are likely to provoke severe personal consequences. As we shall see in the next chapter, the history of the modern age reveals that it took the modern family considerable time to realize its inherent potential to liberate individuals from the tyranny of traditions. This revolutionary achievement of the modern family, incidentally, is a story that tends to be largely forgotten today.

Although one encounters perennial human yearnings for freedom—freedom from want, from oppression, and from danger—

wherever one turns in history, in our own times, these yearnings have expanded to powerful cravings for freedom from all boundaries and structures, for a life that allows individuals to soar—like angels without a body and a care—above the reality of a life that, by definition, must contain dimensions of control. Many modern individuals are inclined to perceive all forms of control, be this now by individuals, families, groups, traditions, or governments, as violations of their basic human rights and they have become increasingly resistant to endeavors in this direction.

Among the many outcries over the progressive loss of freedom in modern society the writings of Michel Foucault stand out for their haunting message. Provocatively formulated and widely read, they reflect the growing discontent with the controlling consequences of modern social institutions. Although Foucault failed to pay particular attention to the family and rarely used the term "social control," he formulated a general theory about how the agents of modern society came to dragoon, or discipline, its members into behavior acceptable by the officially standardized norms of modern society. He tried to trace impulses to control back to the eighteenth century, when the belief spread that individuals should become better soldiers, better workers, and better subjects and all in the service of an illusory notion of progress. From that time on, he contended, institutions such as the army, the school, the factory, the asylum, and so on, strove hard to standardize thinking and behavior, that is, to discipline and correct "that which does not measure up to the rule." Moreover, Foucault and his followers suggest that the rise of the new professions—educators, engineers, social reformers, doctors, and psychiatrists—served to extend the control over body and mind of modern individuals ever since that period.[9]

While there is a lot of truth to many of the historical examples Foucault cited in support of his argument, they also reveal a basic misunderstanding of the dual nature of modern social institutions. This applies in particular to the institution of the modern family. What Foucault and his followers refuse to see is that it is not that modern individuals are progressively subjected to experiences of social control (to be a member of any social entity implies by definition, as we have seen, some elements of control), but that it is our notions of freedom from control that have expanded. The critics of the modern family who work in the Foucaultean tradition focus in the main on the family's controlling dimensions at the expense of individual freedom. In doing so they have fundamentally failed to apprehend the dual nature of all social institutions. During the past fifty years much has been made of the first and very little of the second. The literature abounds with accounts about how the humdrum quality of family life stifles individual creativity and authenticity, how it oppresses and deforms human potentials. Yet we read little about the protean quality of the modern family that induces individuals to connect to other individuals in new ways and provides them with a stable basis from which larger social entities can emerge. Though all human beings acquire their essential human qualities and capacities for living together through the mediation of the family, any family at that, the modern family alone is uniquely suited for the development of those human qualities that are capable of transcending not only our biological nature but also customs and traditions that served to oppress individuals in the past. What is more, many fail to understand that the modern family alone among the many family systems available is able to provide a fortuitous balance between institutional constraints and individual freedom.

On the one end of the ideological debate today then stand those social engineers who profess an unalterable faith in the power and ubiquity of science and technology to provide modern individuals with interminable quantities of liberty. Their assumptions have provoked a whole generation of men and women to expect that all boundaries and structures can be overcome, if not by design, then by political maneuver. On the other end stand Foucault and his followers who are inclined to think that life outside of the boundaries and structures of modern society would be more natural and more humane. Both sets of utopian tendencies frequently, though illogically, merge with each other in contemporary debates. They have induced many moderns to forget—for a while at least—the basic truth about human life and social existence, namely that one cannot have freedom without constraint, that the one is productive of the other. Both sets of ideas are chimeras, and perilous ones at that.

On the Timeless Quality of the Institution of the Family

Family and culture are intimately connected. Like the family, culture must be continuously produced and reproduced and passed on from one generation to the next. Like culture, the family is perpetually in a state of flux, inherently unstable and open to change. This juxtaposition manifests itself in many ways, two of which deserve special mention here. On the individual level, there exists in every society a basic need for a stable social order in which children are allowed to develop and adults can persevere and prosper. The always present danger that forces external to the family can effectively undermine, if not even derail, the world of the family, posits one of its gravest challenges. Today as in the past, men and women all over the world make great efforts to secure an environment that allows them to pursue goals connected to the welfare of their families. And on the political level history has shown that whenever the family and the traditions it represents are held to be endangered, powerful social reactions tend to follow. In the case of China under Mao-tse-tung, the family went underground. In the Muslim case grave fears about the future of the traditional Muslim family and Islamic communal traditions contributed substantially to the rise of politically-potent fundamentalist backlash movements from the Maghreb on the Mediterranean to Iran, Afghanistan, and points beyond in Central and Southeast Asia.

When it comes to the Western case, it is not difficult to argue that here too the family was central in all spheres of social life in the past—after all the clan, the tribe, the "gens" of antiquity, and even the communities of the feudal ages, were originally based on extended family groupings. Yet it is considerably more difficult to maintain that the Western family continues to exercise this pivotal role in the modern age. As we have seen in the preceding chapter, nineteenth-century writers from Karl Marx, Henry Maine, and Ferdinand Toennies down to the legions of subsequent generations of political philosophers and those speculating on the rise of the postmodern order today, claimed that the family is progressively losing its public significance and increasingly relegated to primarily assuming private functions. These theorists typically tended to base their arguments on the phenomenal rise of modern economic and political structures and the concomitant inclination to think in largely contractual and functional-rational terms. Shifts in structure and thought, they argued, tend to blanket out older forms of action, association, sentiments, and thinking. Since these early formulations, life in modern society has been held to be dominated by large, impersonal, bureaucratic structures and impersonal "functional rational" ways of doing things that have few linkages to the personalistic dynamics distinctive of the family. And even here in the private sphere, modern theorists conclude, the contemporary family, sad, fragile little community that it has become, appears to progressively lose its once vital functions.

These assumptions are patently false. To be sure, the public institutions of modern society are substantially driven by guiding principles that appear to be diametrically opposed to the more personalistic rationality of the family and family life. Yet empirically and theoretically, the inner dynamics of the family are bound to shape individual behavior and values today in the same basic ways they did when the world was younger and things appeared to have been more transparent. Why that is so can best be illustrated by example of the inherent needs of individuals, children as well as adults, today and in the postmodern world looming on the horizon.

The Importance of the Conventional Family in the Postmodern Order

Socialization, in every society, is a long and often shaky process in which the socially accepted and rewarded ways of doing things need to be internalized—perhaps even "imprinted" if one takes the proposition that human beings lack instincts at birth seriously. Once acquired, habits and norms must be maintained in the face of the never-ending disturbances that domestic and external events inject into this process. In other words, what is needed is a home in which routines and procedures have been established that provide stability and continuity and that have the capacity to mitigate against the worst from happening. This process is a universal process, regardless whether it occurs in traditional communities in the highlands of New Guinea or in the urban centers of the highly-modernized societies of Asia, America, and Europe. No matter where one turns, throughout human history this process occurred on the level of everyday experiences, in the spatial setting, or locale, of the family household and the way in which it was carried out served to define the formation of basic patterns of behavior and thought. As we already have seen, once a basic matrix of consciousness has been established, every subsequent experience will be filtered through that matrix to the same degree that basic behavior patterns once formed will determine the actualization of future actions. It may be unnecessary to add that it would take an inordinate amount of effort to change such basic patterns once they have taken hold. There can be little doubt then that the ways in which a household is organized and the ways in which interaction between husbands and wives, parents and children, family members and outsiders, is conducted and viewed, will leave an indelible imprint on both processes. It is for reasons like this that psychologists and sociologists alike view early childhood experiences as pivotal, though the first place greater attention on the earliest interaction between mother and child and the second view this process more in its totality, stretching over a longer period of time and placing greater emphasis on issues of stability and continuity.

Perhaps even more than in the past, modern children living in highly-industrialized societies need a special world to grow up in. In the modern era more is at stake than simply meeting such basic physical requirements as the protection from outside dangers, the capacity to provide food, the prevention and treatment of illnesses, and so on. What precisely children need continues to be an issue of some contention. Yet there can be little doubt that these needs include the early acquisition of those habits and competencies that will allow the modern child to function well in school and in life beyond. Modern society requires individuals to develop a distinctive sense of time and space, a capacity for self-reliance, motivation, achievement, collaboration and sharing, habits of trust and inquisitiveness, just to mention some of the behavioral ingredients important for individuals to function in the complex networks of the modern world. Yet these cognitive and behavioral capacities do not come natural to human beings, that is to say, they are not part of our instinctual makeup. They must be elicited and honed in a persistent and ongoing fashion during the long years of early childhood socialization. In sum, modern criteria of good childcare make it necessary that more than ever before an extraordinary amount of attention and involvement on the part of caregivers is available, and then for a much longer period of time than earlier generations were either able or willing to provide.

It is frequently argued that we know today a lot more about child development than we did, say, fifty years ago. We certainly have today a much better knowledge about the physical requirements that make for good health in infancy and early childhood in terms of prenatal and postnatal care, hygiene, nutrition, and the like. Beyond that, child psychologists have acquired very reliable knowledge about the details of the development process—such as the amazing variety of communication processes going on between infants and adults (smiles, "eye language," the acquisition of symbolic communication, the stages of language learning, and so forth). They have also drawn our attention to the processes whereby infants begin to relate first to one "significant" adult (most typically the mother) and subsequently to others. Moreover, we have learned that not all children are born with the same capacities either for learning or for forming relationships, and it has become clear to many that biological heritage and temperamental dispositions make for vast differences in the ways in which children develop, adapt, and learn.

Yet aside from the research findings on specific aspects of child development, ordinary people are often hard put what to make of the conflicting information dispensed in the immense advice literature that has become available in recent decades. An often-cited case in point is that of toilet training, where more authoritarian methods clash with those advocating permissiveness and either method alleges the other to scar the child for life.[10] Other issues, such as those connected to weaning, punishment, play, self-determination, and a myriad more, whose pros and cons have given rise to heated debate among experts, leave caretakers at a loss as well about which information and advice to follow. *Nolens volens*, caring parents have been reduced to solving particular dilemmas of childrearing by relying on their own commonsense and what they hope is likely to work best in a given situation. And this may all be for the good. To decide which advice to follow requires an intimate knowledge of a child's propensities, a lot of patience, persistence, and, above all, the kind of love only parents are likely to muster and give generously. It is not surprising then that in recent years we also find a new appreciation of parents in the professional literature. Such well-established child development experts as Uri Bronfenbrenner have made it clear that in addition to a stable physical and congenial social environment, the presence of adults who can provide care, a fair amount of interaction, communication, and stimulation, a child's well-being and healthy growth requires above all love.[11]

These identified requirements make good sense from the perspective of this chapter, which emphasizes the persisting significance of institutionalized, conventional interaction patterns in the emerging postmodern world. The question of where adults can be found who have the capacity and the willingness to create an environment in which the arduous, time-consuming, and prolonged care modern childrearing requires has become particularly critical today. It used to be taken for granted that there exists a built-in mechanism in human nature that makes parents want to perform these needed functions as a natural part of family life. An earlier generation of scholars steadfastly maintained that parenthood is natural—that is to say, that there exists a symbiotic relationship between the needs of the infant and innate parental sentiments. It was widely accepted that infants require consistent loving care just as most mothers (and to a lesser degree perhaps fathers as well) need contact with them. In other words, it was an unquestioned maxim that the child's interests and those of the mother coincided fortuitously. Commonsense and history supported this view for a long time. The countercultural deluge that swept over the Western world attacked precisely such commonsense views of human nature.

In the first chapter of this book we already had occasion to see how the countercultural attack against the existence of a "maternal instinct" resulted in seeing parenthood as a social construct without deeper ties and meaning. As the biological connection between child and parent came to be put into question and "baby gurus," from John Bowlby to Penelope Leach to Barry Brazelton to Dr. Spock, were accused of suppressing, like an evil force, the freedoms of women, limiting their options and burdening them with guilt, a wedge was driven into the relationship between parents and children. The tendency to view children as entities separate from the family ultimately gained credence in public policy, though not in the popular mind. This new tendency was to have grave consequences for the legitimacy of the conventional family. It soon was manifested in the quasi-official conviction that anyone who had the proper qualifications (acquired by means of credentials) was able to carry out the demanding tasks associated with the care and socialization of children, perhaps even better than parents themselves could. Two sharply contrasting positions on childcare emerged during the past decades. The radical childrearing model argued for the acceptance of a bewildering number of newly "liberated" childrearing approaches, while the much larger, and politically more powerful, group of policy experts favored the establishment of vast programs of academically-credentialed early childhood education. The first radical model opened the gates to all sorts of at times even bizarre, experimentations in socialization, and the second led to the professionalization of childcare. Taken together, both approaches strongly reinforced existing anti-conventional childrearing and anti-conventional family sentiments. It can thus be said that the current politics of childcare is in more ways than one the product of a fusion between countercultural dreams of a life unencumbered by constraints and the more practically-oriented, though frequently misconceived, attempts to meet the fallout of the modernization process. Both factions clamor for the establishment of professionalized childcare services, out of the home and paid for by the state.

Although the attacks against the childrearing patterns of the conventional nuclear family have notably deescalated in recent years,[12] the separation of a child's needs from those of its biological parents has given rise to considerable confusion in the public at large. It drove a wedge between parents and their children and created a misplaced confidence in the expertise of often ill-prepared (and underpaid) care-providers. While it is one thing to claim that there exist a great variety of ways in which the tasks of childrearing may be met, it is an altogether different thing to aver that there are no natural bonds that tie families together or that such bonds are insignificant. Moreover, the professionalization of childcare has failed to address the not unimportant question of where individuals are to be found who have the capacity and the wish to perform lovingly and persistently the arduous tasks of childrearing for a long period of time. The willful way in which this question has been glossed over reveals a serious misunderstanding of the human condition and places demands on professionals that they are, almost by definition, unable to meet.

In view of such contradictions floating about it does not come as a surprise that the rational and experimentally-inclined science of child psychology has rediscovered in recent years what ordinary human beings have taken for granted for a very long time: namely that it takes two individuals—a father and a mother—united by a mutual commitment to provide love, care, and a stable household for their children to develop and grow up in. Despite the existence of a seemingly endless variety of forms, both family and household are indelibly intertwined and both remain as important today as in the past. While the anthropological evidence strongly suggests that the precise form of the family does not matter as long as the structure is stable and parents care for their children and command a certain level of competence, it also suggests that it is preferable that both parents have an intensive—though not necessarily identical—interactive relationship with the child. This is particularly the case in modern societies where a child's well-being and future depends to a much larger degree upon intensive parental efforts. Whether we like it or not, today as in the future, there simply are no good parenting substitutes available. Only loving and devoted parents are ready and willing to go into voluntary slavery for many years to come, to forgo payment, respite vacations, and personal luxuries.

The cross-cultural and historical evidence furthermore suggests that interaction in an infant's early stage of development is typically tied to the mother in all known cultures. The absence of the biological mother, however, does not necessarily spell disaster for a child's future, provided that some "mother figure" can take over this role consistently, lovingly, and for a long period of time. This evidence can be accepted regardless whether one agrees, or fails to agree, with the notion of the existence of a "maternal instinct" in the human species. It also leaves open the possibility that a man can perform a "mothering role" (though one wonders why this has not been tried before in any of the varieties of family forms known to human history). In sum, personal ambitions and economic circumstances may differ from culture to culture, and between different groups within a given culture, yet there appear to exist some minimal basic requirements for the successful upbringing of children wherever one turns. Regardless whether one looks at the world of a little girl growing up in a Moroccan harem, a boy born into a Punjabi farming household in India, or that of an infant opening its eyes for the first time in the protected environment of middle-class suburban America, the basic needs of children are universal. On the most basic level of human existence vastly different cultures appear to have met these requirements in fairly similar ways. It is a world in which committed, caring parents have the desire and the capacity to meet the needs of their offspring and no substitute arrangement—and be it yet ever so carefully planned and professionally organized—is better equipped to meet these demands. It is hard to imagine that conditions could be so radically different in the societies of the future, modern, postmodern, or whatever label one may wish to use—that they could invalidate this imperative.

As the child grows older the imperatives for direct and intensive care begins to be less acute. Gradually, he or she is able to adapt to strangers and develop relationships outside the family with peers and other adults. The details of the process in which this growth occurs differs from child to child and from culture to culture. Yet to forge positive and successful relationships outside of the family in modern urban and suburban environments the help and guidance of parents, both of fathers and mothers, are required. It needs wise and dedicated parents to guide their growing children through all sorts of potentially problematic situations ranging from rules of conduct and peer-group pressures, to issues such as the respect for rules of the law, tolerance, religion, equality, and liberty, in short, all those values and behaviors that hold our kind of culture together. The inculcation and honing of the prerequisites for responsible citizenship requires competent parenting. Neither school nor any other learning mechanism or effort at value clarification can compete or replace the role of parents in this important task. Though parents, conventional and liberal alike, may differ greatly on the particular values they wish to pass on to their children, the thought of their children's future compels them to think carefully about the consequences of the values they hold and in this sense it may be argued that children hold parents captive to history. Though the socialization of their children may appear to be a never-ending and at times harrowing experience, the one thing modern parents have learned after decades of listening to all sorts of admonitions and expert advice is that there are no cookbook recipes and no shortcuts.

It is an undeniable fact then that parents all over the world, regardless of race, ethnicity, religion, and social class, are concerned with the well-being and progress of their children. No other social concern activates and, at times, even enrages people more than this. Across all cultures and throughout history parents have gone to great and extraordinary length to search for what they deem to be optimal, or at least, tolerable situations for their children to grow up and prosper in. No matter which aspect in the socialization cycle one looks at—behavior development, character formation, social and academic learning—it is hard to think of any other persons or agency who has more a child's best interests at heart than its parents. It comes close to folly to assume that the coming of the postmodern order could change this basic fact. As the evidence shows, in no other family system do children play a more central role than in that of the conventional nuclear family. In fact, the whole complicated and demanding edifice of the conventional lifestyle revolves in one way or another around the real or assumed needs of children. Though the maintenance of a child-oriented lifestyle frequently requires considerable personal and financial sacrifices on the part of modern men and women, there exist few indications to date that give reasons to assume that responsible and loving parents, when given the choice, would wish it any other way.

The Conventional Family and the Life of Adults

When one turns to the life of adults, large sets of data available today document as well that despite all their problems and tedium, the institutions of marriage and family are still the best thing we have. The good news is that both men and women are healthier, happier, more productive, and live longer when married. This is particularly the case when the marriage is stable. The bad news is that many are not aware of this linkage and consequently a propensity has come into existence among the married and unmarried alike, to expect that the grass is greener on the other side of the fence. Yet despite this tendency the data also indicate that by and large marriage continues to be extremely popular. Although middle-class couples have fewer children than in the past, they do have children nonetheless. Despite the sexual revolution of the sixties and despite the enormous expansion of freedom in the choice of lifestyles in Western democracies, the hunger for an exclusive sexual relationship remains to be as strong, if not stronger, today as during the Victorian era a hundred years ago. In fact, when sorting through the mountains of relevant literature, one comes to the conclusion that exclusivity in sexual relationships is more important today than at any other time in history. Moreover, if we are to trust the findings of recent research, there is much less philandering in marriage going on than sensationalist media reports have led us to believe.[13] If couples divorce—and we should remember that in large parts of the world this is still a relatively rare occurrence—it appears that both men and women spend an awful lot of time and effort in getting married again. Dr. Johnson's lapidary finding that remarriage constitutes the triumph of hope over experience appears to be as valid today as it was some two hundred years ago. The question of why there should be a prevailing tendency among those who have just escaped the reportedly oppressive prison of one marriage to voluntarily return to the confines of another in an age of unprecedented personal freedom still begs for an answer.

While any particular marriage may be said to reflect merely the capacities and inadequacies of particular partners, the reasons why the institution of marriage remains fairly unchanged rests on different grounds when viewed within the institutional framework of this volume. They suggest that they must be located in the perennial need of individuals for structure, stability, and meaning, rather than in a societally superimposed harness that deforms and destroys. This is particularly the case in democratic industrial societies where the dynamism of change compels individuals to search for a tolerable balance between brightly-burning visions of personal freedom and a resting place for their hearts and souls.[14]

What Have We Learned

Let us then sum up the argument of this chapter: the foregoing elaborations have made it evident that society and social institutions are synonymous. One cannot have society without social institutions. To achieve their essential humanity, by their very nature, human beings are in need of institutionalized guidance. As long as recorded history remembers, the institution of the family has performed this monumental task not only in a taken-for-granted manner, but also in culturally specific ways. Since the days of Plato and Aristotle, successive generations of social philosophers down to our own conflicted times have asked the questions whether other institutional arrangements could perform this mission equally well or even better. To date no one has come up with a plausible alternative. It is in the family that the most basic dimensions of human life intersect and sustain each other in a multiplicity of ways—the biological with the social, the material with the normative, the symbolic with the transcendent, and so forth—and it is hard to imagine any other institutional arrangement that could replicate or improve the many functions the family performs.

At the same time we have also learned that the institution of the conventional nuclear family remains not only central to the well-being of individuals in modern society, but that despite great efforts on the part of contemporary groupings and policymakers alike, no plausible alternatives have emerged that could serve as a substitute for the many functions this type of family performs in our increasingly complex world. The household of the conventional family provides the single best locale for the responsible socialization of modern individuals and despite the tedium of married life, the family in its conventional form remains central to the values and wishes of modern individuals.

The meaningful question today then is not whether there will be an institution of the family in the future, but rather, to what degree the family of the future will resemble that of the nuclear family in its conventional form. To answer that question we will have to now take a closer look at the constitutive elements of this type of family, its history, and its permutations and explore to what degree the fate of the conventional family and the fate of modern society are intertwined, if not inseparable. The next chapter is dedicated to showing not only how the conventional family alone among the many family systems available was able to engender those social forces that made for the rise of the modern world but also how it provided the modern world with its unique notions of individual freedom and equality.

Notes

1.   Arnold Gehlen, *Der Mensch,seine Natur und seine seine Stellung in der Welt* (Frankfurt: Vittorio Klostermann, 1980); A shorter English version of this book was published under the title *Man in the Age of Technology* (New York: Columbia University Press, 1980); Adolf Portmann, *Zoologie und das neue Bild vom Menschen* (Hamburg: Rowohlt, 1961); and F. J. J.Buytendijk, *Mensch und Tier* (Hamburg: Rowohlt, 1958).

2.   Thomas Hobbes, *Leviathan* (ed. and introd. by C. B. Macpherson) (Harmondsworth: Penguin, 1958, p.189).

3.   Emile Durkheim, *The Rules of Sociological Method* (New York: Free Press, 1950—English translation of the French original published in 1895).

4.   Peter L. Berger and Thomas Luckmann, *The Social Construction of Reality* (New York: Doubleday, 1964).

5.   See George P. Murdock, "World Ethnographic Sample," *American Anthropologist,* 59 (August 1957): 664–87.

6.   George Herbert Mead, *Mind Self and Society* (Chicago: University of Chicago Press, 1943). Charles Horton Cooley, *Human Nature and the Social Order* (Glencoe: The Free Press, 1956).

7.   Mary Douglas, *Purity and Danger* (London: Routledge & Kegan Paul, 1966) and Mary Douglas, *Natural Symbols* (London: Barrie & Rockliffe, 1970).

8.   Peter Berger, *Invitation to Sociology* (New York, Doubleday Anchor, 1963).
9.   Michael Foucault, *Discipline and Punish: The Birth of the Prison* (New York: Vintage Books 1977), and Michael Foucault, *The History of Sexuality: An Introduction* (New York: Pantheon, 1978).
10.   See Christina Hardyment, *Dream Babies: Three Centuries of Good Advice on Child Care* (New York: Harper and Row, 1983).
11.   Among the many publications on child development, the many writings of Uri Bronfenbrenner stand out for their clear and detailed descriptions of the optimal requirements for a child to grow up and develop. Beginning with his early work on class differences in childhood socialization—see Uri Bronfenbrenner, "Socialization and social class through time and space" in Eleanor E. Maccoby et al. (eds.), *Readings in Social Psychology* (New York: Holl, 1985)—over the decades Bronfenbrenner has kept tabs on changes in socialization in America, Russia, and China that are still interesting to read today.
12.   The various publications of the Council on American Families (located at the Institute for American Values in New York) and the writings of William J. Bennet of the Hudson Institute reflect the revived appreciation of the importance of the nuclear family and its conventional ethos.
13.   Edward Lauman, John Gagnon, and Gina Kolata, *The Social Construction of Sexuality* (Chicago: University of Chicago Press, 1994).
14.   A good source about the importance of marriage in the contemporary world can be found in David Popenoe, Jean Bethge Ellshtain, and David Blankenhorn, *Promises to Keep: Decline and Renewal of Marriage in America* (Boston: Rowman & Littlefield, 1996).

4

The Conventional Nuclear Family and the Rise of the Modern World

> We do not understand ourselves because we do not know what we have been, and hence what we may be becoming.—Peter Laslett

It has become customary today to attribute all sorts of predicaments to modern existence. Life is said to have become too materialistic, too hectic, too superficial, too fragmented, too lonely, and so on ad infinitum. Yet there can be little doubt that the vast majority of people who have the good luck to live in the highly-industrialized democratic societies of Europe, Asia, and America live today longer, safer, healthier, freer, and in a degree of comfort their predecessors could never have imagined. It is hard for moderns to picture how difficult life was in the traditional societies of the past or, for that matter, continues to be in large parts of the world today. For most people there was nothing very picturesque nor edifying about life in the past and it is well neigh impossible to draw any philosophical conclusions about its superiority either economically, politically, or socially. For millennia human existence was united by what the Dutch historian Jan Romain has called "the common human pattern" and its transformation into the modern way of life must be understood as one of the most remarkable revolutionary events in history.

For some time now economic historians and philosophers have tried to identify the factors that made for a social revolution of this magnitude. Some, like Adam Smith, saw the rationality flowing from the market as the causal force in the transformation of an obdurate medieval feudal society to a perpetually changing and ever-expanding industrial order. Others, following in the footsteps of the philosopher Georg Friedrich Hegel, attributed the triumph of freedom and prosperity to the growth of rationality in human thought. The question whether economic rationalization was productive of political liberty or vice versa, however, remains an unresolved question down to our own time. Although the classical "mind over matter" versus "matter over mind" disagreement continues to occupy the academic mind to this day, all analysts are in agreement that both transformations made their first appearance in the northwestern part of Europe in the early modern period and most tend to agree with Alexis de Tocqueville that the rise of the modern world is the consequence of peculiar institutional developments which found their clearest expression in the capitalist economy, political democracy, and individual liberty. What is more, most contemporary analysts take it for granted that the institutions constitutive of modern society are "functionally" interrelated and dependent upon each other. What precisely these linkages are and the ways in which they are anchored in society, however, remains elusive and the subject of much debate.

If one looks at the rise of the democratic industrial order through the prism of the family, one cannot fail but become impressed by the protean role the nuclear family played in the great transformatory process. This impression is supported by a formidable body of research collected by social demographers such as the Cambridge historians around Peter Laslett, Anthony Wrigley, and Alan Macfarlane in England, Jean Flandrin in France, Helmut Conze in Germany as well as a good number of others on the European continent. This band of scholars can document with a fair degree of certainty that the nuclear family—called the "proto-industrial" family in the relevant literature—was instrumental in the modernization process.[1] In being able to trace the existence of the proto-industrial family as far back as the thirteenth century, they succeeded to "nullify" the widespread assumption that the nuclear family is a product of industrialization. To the contrary, their studies unmistakably indicate that this type of family unleashed the very social forces conducive to the formation of modern economic and political institutions. A wealth of detailed historical community studies furthermore permits us to observe how the inner dynamics peculiar to the nuclear family fostered those patterns of behavior and relationships that were to have far-reaching consequences.[2] Reinforced by a very distinctive ethos, the unique demographic, structural, and affective characteristics of the nuclear family produced the "new manner of life" (to use Max Weber's suggestive term) upon which the modern social order rests.

The nuclear family's historical role in the "great transformation" must thus be viewed to have been one of the great, though unrecognized, accomplishments of history.

As observed earlier, the institution of the family, any family that is, is not only the product of the most basic elements of human nature, it is also the basic locale in which human production and reproduction takes place, becomes routinized, habituated, and, ultimately institutionalized. The ways in which the properties of human nature and existence interact and reinforce one another, it was argued in the preceding chapter, led to the formation of a great variety of family systems, which, in turn, provided the foundations from which vastly different cultures and civilizations arose. This culture-creating potential of the institution of the family applies to the case of the nuclear family as well. Its institutional arrangements stand not only in close affinity to the market economy and the formation of modern democratic institutions, but its ethos can be said to be the ethos of modernity par excellence.

What Made the Nuclear Family So Special?

Since the present chapter seeks to explore the factors that endowed the nuclear family with its modern civilization-building ability we have to look at its inner dynamics, which not only enabled it to throw off the shackles of stifling traditions when the opportunity presented itself, but which also allowed it reinvent itself time and again once the modernization process unfolded its transformatory powers. At focus then are those core elements of the nuclear family that have made for its strength and success in establishing and maintaining new social realities in which the search for liberty, justice, and equality figures prominently.

Let us begin this exploration with questions about what made the Western nuclear, or if one prefers, the "proto-industrial," family so special. Peter Laslett has provided us with detailed descriptive documentations of its outstanding structural features among which three, in particular, stand out: *the sanctity of private property* and an inheritance system based on primogeniture; *a marriage system dependent upon individual choice* and based on a *contractual* relationship; and *the requirement to establish and provide for one's own conjugal household*. In an age of scarcity and insecurity these three features required individuals to rely on their own hard work and ingenuity. It was a system that worked in favor of the first born, pushed out the later born, and prevented a good number of individuals from marrying altogether. Taken together, these requirements made for late marriage and responsible procreation. Since it was impossible to establish one's own conjugal household without the necessary resources, it encouraged parsimony and habits of saving. The central social norms of the proto-industrial family forced individuals to be responsible for themselves, inspired intellectual curiosity and restlessness, and made them eager to acquire competencies and knowledge that could ensure measurable personal economic and social advancement.

Beyond that, the practice to marry late limited the number of births to any married couple. It made for the demographic fact that families, already small in size because of high infant mortality rates, became even smaller. The ever-present fact of early death in adulthood often led men and women to enter into two or three marriages in the course of their life. The stark realities of life in pre-modern European societies made for what has been called the "hybrid" nature of the nuclear family, with children and stepchildren of one or even both spouses co-present in many households.[3]

Two further peculiarities played an important role. First, there existed an apprenticeship system that compelled parents to farm out *all* their children—boys as well as girls, the rich as well as the poor—from the parental household at an early age. This practice undoubtedly must have had an effect upon familial relationships (though it would be wrong to conclude that the practice reflects an absence of love and concern, as some historians have been inclined to do). And second, there existed a rigid hierarchical social order that placed every individual in a ranked series of classes with proscriptive as well as prescriptive consequences. These two dominating features had undoubtedly a particularly debilitating effect upon the existence and life chances of the vast rural population and they may well explain why the poor and disenfranchised embraced the coming of the industrial system despite often harsh consequences in dislocation and hardship. The industrial way of life not only allowed families to stay and live together (which clearly was a primary value for many) but it also provided individuals with fervently desired personal freedoms and new opportunities to improve their lot.

Although the new manner of life called forth a kind of individualism the world had not yet seen, it is important to appreciate the degree to which sentiments of family and family well-being motivated individuals to take advantage of the possibilities to change their life when such opportunities offered themselves. The close connection between family sentiments and family progress becomes abundantly clear when one reads a number of detailed English and continental studies, among which Rudolf Braun's demographic transformation study of the Kanton of Zurich in the early nineteenth century stands out for its clarity in formulation. [4]

As Braun and others have shown, during the second part of the eighteenth, and even more so during the first part of the nineteenth century, new forms of work became available in the "putting out" cottage work system that was not only typically connected to the emergent textile industry of the time, but also to the expanding demands for a great variety of objects for everyday use produced by myriads of household-based small artisan enterprises. The increasing availability of new forms of work served to galvanize deeply-rooted habits and norms that had been available in the nuclear family for long but failed to flourish under circumstances confined by the limits of rural production. For the first time in history new opportunities to earn an independent living were thus opened up for large numbers of individuals mired in the rural subsistence economy. Barely managing to eke out a living and fated to live the life of merely-tolerated retainers, the flotsam and jetsam of the period were offered novel opportunities to marry and to establish their own independent households. All that was needed was a good measure of self-reliance, hard work, persistence, planning, frugality, prudence, and the willingness to take rationally-calculated risks. Since these behavior patterns had already been firmly established aspects of the proto-industrial way of life and since the creation of one's own family, one's own "little world," was the desired way of life for most, it did not take much to encourage individuals and their families to avail themselves of the opportunities offered by the nascent industrial system. The newly-energized patterns of behavior and the new forms of work together rendered tangible material results fairly quickly and it did not take long for the new manner of life to be emulated by many.

The strength of the core features of the nuclear family manifested itself time and again during the various phases of the Industrial Revolution. As production shifted from the putting-out cottage industry to urban-based factory work, and consequently from the manufacture to the administration, sale, and promotion of products, it was the genius of the conventional nuclear family to motivate its members to adapt and instill in them those behavior patterns that allowed them to take up new opportunities for individual advancement. It not only provided them with a haven during periods of economic fluctuations and political unrest, but also with a launching pad to venture out from and improve their economic prospects and social standing. In the first phase it motivated the rural poor to make the switch from agricultural to industrial work, and in the second phase the class of artisans and craftsmen, who had limited opportunities for advancement in the feudal system, were now able to use the available normative behavior patterns of the conventional family to their economic, political, and social advantage. Through skill, frugality, and sheer hard work they managed to move up the socioeconomic ladder and in doing so they changed in time the face of their society. In the third phase the nuclear family reinvented itself once more by seeking to promote and hone skills and knowledge necessary to succeed in a technologically and administratively ever more sophisticated industrial system. To be sure, technological innovations making for shifts in economic production and new legislations played an important role in opening up new avenues for men, and later for women as well. Yet none of these factors can measure in significance and effect with the resources and flexibility offered by the conventional family. They provided the indispensable precondition from which the industrial system rose and reinvents itself time and again.

The Protestant Ethic Connection

These structurally-produced behavior patterns stood in close affinity to a public ethos that came to exercise its power and influence as the modernization process progressed. Much has been written about the Puritan or Calvinist ethic in the creation of the modern world. A full discussion of the much debated "Protestant Ethic" thesis made famous by Max Weber is beyond the scope of the present argument and readers interested in the intricate relationship between demographic, economic, and ideational factors may wish to turn to Alan Macfarlane's brilliantly argued books on the role of English individualism in the creation of the culture of capitalism.[5] For our purposes, it will have to suffice to observe that this religiously-inspired ethic with its doctrine of predestination and this-worldly ethical orientation not only served to give shape and meaning to the structurally available forms of behavior, but it also served to greatly reinforce already existing individualistic tendencies in the population at large.

Equally importantly, this distinctive ethic bolstered and legitimated those specifically modern forms of cognition that emphasize rationality, empiricity, and makeability. In a round about rather than direct way, religiously-informed ideas and ideals enjoined individuals to aspire toward empirically realizable goals and infused their daily activities with a higher moral purpose. Though the harsh grandeur of the original Calvinist doctrine came to be "vulgarized" in the course of time (in fact, a good argument can be made that by the turn of the eighteenth century, Puritanism had already turned into utilitarianism), the Protestant ethic, even in its vulgarized form, served to further strengthen the existing cultural tendencies of long standing. [6]

The consideration of the role of the family in the rise of "a new manner of life" is alien to most social historians, including Weber. Yet when one looks at the rise of the modern world from the perspective of this book it may well be observed that the Protestant ethic, albeit weakened in its original religious content, is the ethic of the nuclear Western family par excellence. While Weber, and others working in this tradition, clearly saw that the newly-emergent ethos took older and deeper tendencies rooted in long-held cultural practices into new directions, he failed to see that these tendencies themselves had their origin in the nuclear family. The affinity between the injunctions and ideals of the Protestant ethic and the norms and values of the nuclear family created a potent social force when the Industrial Revolution made new opportunities available. Slowly yet progressively, and further enriched by ideas and reflections derived from a variety of philosophical traditions, the new ethos transcended the private sphere of the family. Patterns of behavior and values that had their origin in the nuclear family coalesced over time into an ethos that made itself increasingly felt in the expanding public spheres of politics and the economy. The once private ethos now turned into a new public ethos that has become the hallmark of Western civil society.

In the rich literature on the West's rise to prominence and power much has been written about factors of geography, and the economic, political, and historical circumstances and ideational constellations that are held to have favored this part of the world.[7] Many of these arguments make good sense. There surely existed a combination of forces that helped to transform the medieval European economy and polity into a productive modern democratic system. Yet neither geographical location, historical circumstances, nor the Protestant ethic alone could have produced the modern world. Without the social foundation provided by the nuclear family, the modern world could not have come into existence.

Equally significant from a civilization-building perspective, a large body of literature reveals that Protestantism was able to inspire new forms of trust and responsibility, both on the individual as well as on the social level. It compelled individuals to transcend the limitations of the "amoral familism" (the "me and my family first and the rest of the world be damned" syndrome) that has ruled much of social life for as long as history remembers. It shows that on the level of the individual the new social ethos served to provide a felicitous balance between desires for individual autonomy and self-advancement, on the one hand, and social responsibility, on the other. On the social level it inspired the kind of public trust and civic cooperation every expanding industrial democratic system must depend upon by necessity. [8] That is to say, crass egoism and base greed, those perennial features deeply ingrained in the human psyche, were kept more or less at bay by religiously informed commands of personal accountability and responsibility in all matters pertaining to daily life including all dealings with people and organizations.

The "Other" Protestant Ethic—The Romantic Ethic

The dominating public ethos that solidified ever more as time went on proved to be beneficial to the economic advancement of individuals and their families in the expanding economies of the early industrial age. As argued, it allowed many to improve their lot in life, move up in the social hierarchy, and become economically affluent. Yet once prosperous and socially established, many started to consume in a distinctly unpuritanical manner. The historical record shows that as the nineteenth century progressed it was precisely that segment of the population which had traditionally espoused an ethic of asceticism and industry while condemning idleness, luxury, and indulgence which now became avid consumers of all sorts of objects, symbols, and economically nonproductive activities. In a recently published book, *The Romantic Ethic and the Spirit of Modern Consumerism*, Colin Campbell, the noted British sociologist, set out to explore this intriguing historical puzzle.[9] Taking the reader on a fascinating journey through competing arguments, discarding the methodological individualism of economists and building on the insights of others, Campbell arrives at the conclusion that there coexisted side-by-side two, and not only one, powerful cultural traditions of thought. Both, according to him, developed out of eighteenth- and nineteenth-century Puritanism. The first with its contempt for pleasure and comfort and emphasis upon rationality, instrumentality, industry, and achievement, corresponds to Weber's Protestant ethic. The second—a more "optimistic," "emotionalist" version—developed into a full-fledged sentimentalism and romanticism by the middle of the nineteenth century. The Romantic ethic, as Campbell calls it, values self-expression, imagination, and the search for a higher, nonconformist, morality. The two competing ethics, the rational utilitarian tradition Max Weber wrote about and the one that fosters romantic, at times even utopian, values, are thus argued to have not only common origins, they also have stayed with us over time. The two sets of antithetical components central to the modern way of life appear to have been productive of each other. What is more, Campbell holds, the competing impulses served to produce a peculiar tension in the minds of modern individuals. It made for a high degree of restlessness, activism, self-examination, and guilt. It may well be argued that this tension peculiar to modernity has remained with us to this very day.

Though there are no reasons to assume that the Romantic ethic Campbell writes about is intrinsically anti-family in orientation (in fact, the next chapter will develop the opposite argument), the available documentation needs to be carefully examined before clear conclusions on the Campbell thesis can be reached. There already exists a body of literature that provides us with some insights into the multifaceted origin of modern thought. So for instance, in her much-noted book, *The Feminization of American Culture,* Ann Douglas, the Columbia University professor of English, presents us with a body of materials that documents the civilization-building role of nineteenth-century women. Many manifestations of contemporary cultural life, she argues, must be understood as products of an alliance forged between highly-literate, middle-class women and the clergy of the period. [10] Their collaboration fostered a cultural milieu that favored the flourishing of what she calls the more refined "feminine" sentiments of art and literature—as opposed to the more "masculine" and cruder sentiments of politics and the market, the domain traditionally dominated by males. Feminine sentiments, Douglas argues, brought dimensions to modern life that added a new richness and sophistication to an otherwise utilitarian, rationalistic modern culture. Economic affluence provided the talented women of the bourgeoisie with the leisure to pursue their interests and vocation just as new understandings of personal liberty allowed them to express themselves in novel ways. Sheltered by their families and freed from the necessity to work, these middle-class women contributed greatly to a new appreciation of individual merit that made suspect the privileges bestowed by birth and social origin. The women of the rising bourgeoisie also became major exponents and chroniclers of shifts in sentiments and values that have spread through Western societies in the modern age. At the same time, middle-class women and their allies in the clergy were not only concerned with the "finer" things of life, they also were the trailblazers of new concerns for the poor, the homeless, the workless, orphans, and widows. Their relentless dedication to help those who cannot help themselves encouraged the development of a revolution in social consciousness and their tireless activism changed the ways in which societies look at social welfare.

The feminization of culture is a progressively expanding process. Rather than remaining confined to the domain of literature, art, and welfare, it appears that it has expanded to encompass the transformation of the culture of corporations and organizations today. With its dual roots in the past, its expansion today seems to be driven by the changing role of women and, most recently, it has been the cause of much debate and some consternation. Though many of the questions that have been asked are still awaiting an answer, the most intriguing one from the perspective of this book is an old one. It revolves around the issue of to what degree industrialization and modernization inevitably leads to a weakening of family ties. And it is to this issue, that has occupied the minds of intellectuals and ordinary people alike for some time, that we shall turn our attention now.

Industrialism and the Ties that Bind the Family Together

When the dominant mode of production shifted increasingly from agricultural work to industrial work in the course of the nineteenth century, the role of the family changed as well. With the relocation of the work place from the household into the factory, the family ceased to be the basic "unit of production" and economically it was reduced to a "unit of consumption." This shift, as we have seen in the chapter discussing theorists of the family, appeared at first blush to imply that the family had no longer the same integrative function it had in earlier times. Hence many analysts concluded that with the loss of its once vital economic function the overall function of the family was fundamentally diminished, if not irretrievably lost.

There is, of course, some truth to this argument. Yet it is not the whole truth, nonetheless. Though economic factors explain a lot, they cannot explain why ever-larger numbers of people were willing, if not eager, to adapt themselves to the rigors of industrial work and the type of constraints the urban way of life requires. When one looks at the growing interplay between the different spheres of social life—the economic, political, structural, cultural, and ethical—it becomes evident once more that the conventional family continued to play the same pivotal role. While social historians appear to be caught up in debates over the degree to which the ruthless interests of early capitalists forces brought unspeakable misery to a hapless population during the great industrial transformation—as reflected in studies on the land "enclosure" system that compelled the English rural poor to search for means of survival in the "satanic mills" and grubby mines of the rising industrial order—there can be little doubt that many, if not the majority, of the industrial workers were also motivated by burning desires to acquire the wherewithal for a domestic life that revolved around the family and the family home. In fact, the historical record shows that by the middle of the nineteenth century a new culture of domesticity had spread like wildfire from one end of Victorian England to the other. It was a culture that permeated all levels of English society, engulfing even those living in slums and dire straits. As Edward Shorter put it:

Home, however, poor, was the focus of all his love and interests, a sure fortress against a hostile world. Songs about its beauties were ever on people's lips. "Home Sweet Home" first heard in the 1870s, had become almost a national anthem by the turn of the century.[11]

Though family values and family ideals had been the distinguishing characteristics of the nuclear family for long, for many the love of family and one's own conjugal home could only be fully realized with the arrival of industrialism. The progressive expansion of industrial production provided large-scale opportunities for the realization of these family-centered values. Similar processes appear to have occurred in all the countries of northwestern Europe. Simon Schama, for instance, describes in eloquent terms how the modern Dutch identity was largely a consequence of earlier cultural tendencies revolving around family and home. When one contemplates the paintings of Dutch family life in the early modern period reproduced in Schama's *The Embarrassment of Riches,* one gets the overwhelming impression that Dutch life was a celebration of nuclear family life in all its forms. Though this celebration existed long before the onset of the Industrial Revolution, its arrival seemed not to have changed it in the least.[12] By the same token, early nineteenth-century Swiss and German literature supplies us with moving testimonies in praise of a new and expanding domestic way of life. Contrary to the often-voiced claim that industrial capitalism loosened the ties that bind families together, the evidence available today leads us to conclude that the new forms of work and the accompanying relocation in urban settings more often than not served to strengthen both family ties and the institution of the family itself. For the first time in history the poor were no longer compelled to send their daughters into domestic service and their sons away from home to work on another man's farm or toil in another man's trade. To be sure, in the early phases of industrialization it was mostly men who benefited from new opportunities to make an independent living, yet already by the end of the nineteenth century we can also see an ever-increasing number of females entering into industrial work on both sides of the Atlantic. Though the women's struggle for full partnership was a long and difficult one, Western-style industrialism offered women paid work and made for an independence that was coveted by their sisters in other parts of the world.

The "great transformation" was by no means easy. As the literature shows, it was frequently accompanied by harsh dislocations and upheavals. Yet the protective haven of the conventional family provided the striving poor with the strength to persevere just as it equipped the ambitious and frugal with behavior patterns that allowed them to advance in the expanding industrial order. By the same token its revolutionizing sentiments made for new concerns for individual rights, including those of women and children. When during the early nineteenth century the practice to use cheap child labor flourished for a brief period in the weaving and mining industry, the increasingly child-centered European middle classes became enraged to a degree that by the middle of that century protective legislation was enacted in all northwest European countries. Since then the protection of children has been one of the chief missions of Western middle classes. Today it reaches into the far corners of the under-industrialized world.

By the same token, it would be a serious mistake to assume that the fortress of the family and its accompanying domestic style of life was an act of defense or despair. When compared to the life most people were compelled to live in earlier times, where sizable numbers of the rural poor were obliged to remain unmarried, homeless, and die alone in often wretched poverty, any opportunity to marry and establish one's own household, and be it yet so humble, was deemed to be preferable by most. One does not have to go far to find support for this choice. So, for instance, when one applies the prism of the family to the first chapters of E. P. Thompson's poignant record of life in a Lancashire milltown at the turn of the nineteenth century in his celebrated *The Making of the English Working Class*, one soon begins to realize that the gritty tenacity of the rural migrants working in the mills was fed by their unwavering determination to have a family and to keep that family together come hell or high water.[13] In *The Subversive Family*, Ferdinand Mount, the British historian, presents us with a brilliant summary of the interaction between family sentiments and the new opportunities offered by industrialism. His analysis succeeds in exposing as a sham those deepest myths held by modern intellectuals that the past was a time when all people were part of one supposedly harmonious community, living in bliss and plenty. Since in rural preindustrial England marriage was the prerogative of those who had the resources to support their own household, a substantial number of the poor remained unmarried. Based on the painstakingly careful research of Peter Laslett and his associate, Mount convincingly shows that a genuine freedom to marry came to many only after having moved to the city. By the same token, industrialism allowed the poor to keep their children at home for a considerably longer period of time. The fact that young people were sent out to work at an early age and that their earnings, however meager, were used to contribute toward the common household expenses, Mount argues, should not be confused with a pervasive abuse of the children's economic power. The practice should rather be understood as a desire of parents and children to stay together as long as it was expedient and work together for the family's upward move in the economic hierarchy. The data cited by Mount indicate a startling increase in the practice of married couples to live in one common household with their aging parents. This notable shift was made possible by the young couple's capacity to earn enough to feed the grandparents, who, in return, could act as child minders and perform a few odd jobs at the same time as well. And again, rather than viewing such practices as a consequence of strictly economic hardship, as conventional wisdom has it, the great majority of the rising working classes welcomed them as they led to material advancement and an improved family life.[14] By the same token, the records unearthed by Peter Laslett also show that illegitimacy, the scourge of an earlier age, was always higher in rural areas than in the industrial city (in fact, in many European countries—Austria, Belgium, Denmark, Germany, the Netherlands, Sweden, and Switzerland—the rate of illegitimacy actually fell, often quite sharply, throughout the period of maximum industrialization.) Mount goes on to argue that contrary to the automatic assumptions of novelists (such as Charles Dickens and Benjamin Disraeli) and social commentators (Karl Marx and Friedrich Engels, for instance), there is no evidence for the assumption that migration to industrial cities implied either an erosion of family life or a new laxity in sexual mores. "Marx may have had a child by his maid, Engels may have seduced the girls in his father's mill," Mount finds, " but the great majority of urban courtships and pregnancies ended in marriage between young people of equal social status."[15]

When it became evident that behavior patterns emphasizing individual productivity, initiative, and achievement led to tangible results, the striving families of the assenting working and lower middle classes went a long way to foster corresponding behavior patterns in their children and hone those productive skills they hoped would make for their success in the changing industrial order. And again, it would be a mistake to assume such socialization practices to have been invariably abusive of the rights and proclivities of individuals. The newly-established and expanding public educational regime fused long-existing cultural forms with the requirements of the industrial system and the family continued to be the link between the two.[16]

The effects of the growing utility of family sentiments can be observed on the economic level as well. The desire for one's own home unleashed not only existing productive work patterns, but it also created demands for consumer goods on a large scale. As Neil McKendrick recently articulated:

> Who bought the cottons, woolens, linens and silks of the burgeoning British textile industries? Who consumed the massive increases in beer production? Who bought the crockery which poured from the Staffordshire potteries? Who bought the buckles, the buttons, the pins and all the minor metal products on which Birmingham fortunes were built? Who bought the Sheffield cutlery, the books from the booming publishers, the women's journals, the children's toys, the products of the nurserymen? Which families purchased the products of the early consumer industries?[17]

McKendrick and others argue that "the foundation of the industrial revolution was laid by the home sale of articles of everyday life to a section of the labor force which was neither very poor nor very rich." [18] While in the early phases of industrialization the consumption for home purposes was largely a middle- and lower middle-class matter—restricted to the nascent bourgeoisie of artisans, tradesmen, the more substantial farmer, engineers, and clerks—it spread to the working classes as the Industrial Revolution gained momentum. In this sense it is possible to argue that sentiments revolving around the family and the value of one's own home contributed not only to the rise of the industrial order, but to its expansion as well. To put this observation into the analytical frame of economists based on supply and demand, it is possible to conclude that growing demands for household goods that could be met by newly available technologies led in no small measure to the expansion of the manufacturing system.

As Colin Campbell and others have argued, in due course it became customary for the growing middle classes to adorn their homes and themselves and consequently the once characteristic habits of economic thrift gave way to new forms of consumption that were anything but restrained. Although such observations are based on solid documentation, it should be noted that the new consumption practices were far from reckless in most cases. To be sure, everyone consumed as much as their means and life plans allowed, yet any excessive risk-taking was frowned upon not only as an irresponsible squandering of precious capital but, first and foremost, as an action that put the family's future and its standing in the community at risk. Unlike the aristocratic elite, with its proclivity for extravagance, frivolity, and a haughty disregard of the opinions of others, the consumption culture of the rising middle classes was distinguished by its measured balance and a constant vigilance not to arouse the opprobrium of neighbors and community. True to their Puritan heritage, they tended to justify their consumption in terms of what is ethically permissible. This tendency sent them on a path of wresting with their conscience and many sought to reconcile the consumption of goods and leisure with their notions of "goodness" and "propriety." [19] This tendency took on forms of excessive other-directness, smugness, and a stultifying slavishness to form at times. Yet it also opened up the path for individuals to test the moral basis of their actions in ethical terms, often expressed in terms of "sincerity" and "righteousness." Rarely excessive, civil, mediocre, and frequently sentimentalized to a fault, the consumption behavior of the rising middle classes remained informed by conventional norms and values that had their origin in the conventional family. It was guided by an unwritten expectation that husbands, wives, and their children would abstain from all expenditures and actions that would bring disgrace or ruin to the family. In other words, in this sphere of life as well as in all others, the values of the conventional family served to "domesticate" acquisitiveness and temptations of excess in consumption. In those case where vanity, greed, cupidity, lust, pride, or crass egoism gained the upper hand, the transgression against accepted norms invariably generated a great deal of guilt in individuals and evoked the moral opprobrium of the community. Not much has changed in this respect over the entire course of the industrial system's expansion. Through periods of turmoil and change the conventional family saw it as one of its central tasks to teach its children to master the perennial temptations deeply ingrained in the human psyche. At times the narrowness and self-righteousness of the "petite bourgeois" provoked the distaste and scorn of liberal-minded intellectuals and artists and their derision of the conventional norms echoes through the generations down to our own days.

Industrialism and Gender Inequality

The art of household management provided a basic training ground for the acquisition of broader economic skills in the historical past. It was widely held that the well-managed public realm had its origin in the well-managed household and the literature of the early modern period abounds with tracts that sought to give advice on the effective management of the household and to warn against the social consequences of a disorderly home.[20] The vital tasks of household management were typically assigned to mothers, rather than fathers, and for a long time a woman's social standing among her neighbors and in the community was determined by her competence in the management of the family household. One of the puzzling features of contemporary feminist literature is its disregard of the fact that pre-modern economic life revolved around the household and the pivotal role women played in it. This omission has led to the deplorable tendency to overemphasize the unequal position of Western women in the European past.

We are told that the developing capitalist economic system perniciously subjected women to a life of drudgery and powerlessness from the start and that not much has changed since then. Marriage and the family in times past in general, but in the capitalist societies of the West in particular, are argued to be the major source of women's oppression. Though some of the available evidence reflects the existence of aspects of gender inequality in the past, it is difficult to substantiate the overall thrust of such arguments. Allan Macfarlane writing on the origin of English individualism and Eileen Power writing about the position of women in the proto-industrial era, offer a good deal of evidence that a much greater degree of equality existed between the genders in the early modern period than is commonly thought.[21] Both Ferdinand Mount and Simon Schama, two social historians who take their historical sources very seriously, present us with a considerably more complex picture about how men and women organized and conducted their married lives during the past few centuries in the northwestern part of Europe. Arguing that a distinction between public and private law was typical for medieval Europe, Ferdinand Mount, for instance, summarizes that there unmistakably existed two worlds for women: "the public world of modesty, silence, subjection and rightlessness; and the private world of responsibility for children and household, of rights to property and to a hearing at law, of authority over children and of assertiveness in commercial dealings, no less than in marital discussion and decision."[22] Considering that the economic and political life of that period was family and household based, a woman's standing must have been considerable. Similarly, Simon Schama's rich and minutely researched treatise on Dutch social life in the early modern period documents in some detail that while women were indeed excluded from public offices, they hardly were the downtrodden species that figures so prominently in present-day feminist writings. They enjoyed considerable legal protections, property rights, and a degree of freedom women in other parts of the world could not even dare to dream about. And Schama concludes that the "humanist and Protestant ethos, often taken to have imposed grimly unyielding patriarchalism, turns out, in the Netherlands, as well as in Germany and Switzerland, to have been responsible for their more generous treatment." [23]

Contrary to the assumptions of some historians of the family that there was an evolution from "patriarchal" to "companionate" styles of marriage—or as Ferdinand Mount put it, proceeded along "the well-trodden trail: the patriarchal family, the troubadours, the rise of capitalism, Engels"[24]—the historical materials collected by modern social demographers both in England and on the European continent suggest that marriage in the early modern period had already been a true partnership, with husbands and wives carrying out their respective domestic roles and duties. Both were equally committed to the creation of a domestic union characterized by affection, love, and a concern for the common good. This partnership rested upon mutual consent and clear definitions of rights and obligations, with legal and custom-sanctioned recourse available to both partners if either did not live up to these expectations. In chapter after eloquent chapter Schama, in particular, conveys a picture of Dutch domestic life which the contemporary reader will be tempted to describe as coming as close to the ideal: free from force and want, mindful of the rights of the individual, and a commitment to the welfare of the community. Insofar as this description reflects social reality, it augured well for the triumph of a liberal democratic social order.

To sum up our argument we may suggest the simple and straightforward proposition that at the cradle of the modern world stood a culture which sees the larger order of things as an extension of the little world of the nuclear family. In the course of time the power arrangements of the family were externalized and their spirit infused the power arrangements of the community and the society at large. In this manner the inner dynamics peculiar to the nuclear family found their manifestation in the political institutions of the rising democratic order, among which the equality of individuals before the law, equal treatment by the state, and the value of individual freedom—all those guiding principles of liberalism—stand out. It was on the basis of such solid cultural foundations that divisive factors of parentage, religion, and, in subsequent times, also those of gender and race, could decrease in importance. To put it differently, the egalitarian, individualistic, and achievement-oriented rules that governed the inner life of the proto-bourgeois family provided nineteenth-century liberalism with its lasting political creed. They ultimately promoted the breakdown of those stifling economic and political barriers that have been the bane of much of social life as long as human history records. Affections revolving around trust and confidence developed in the privacy of family life supplied a stable foundation from which our much-cherished "civil society" could emerge. The proto-industrial family and its successor, the conventional or bourgeois family, represented a family type that made the victory of values promoting equality, liberty, and justice for all possible.

The Modern Family's Great Educational Mission

While it may be argued that parents everywhere and at all times have loved their children and were devoted to their welfare and progress, few—if any—have shown a more abiding preoccupation with their children's success than the fathers and mothers of the conventional nuclear family. What is more, to the same degree that the Protestant ethic may be argued to have been the ethic of the proto-industrial family, it may also be argued that the ethos of Western Europe's rising middle classes reflects the essence of modern education *par excellence*. In his celebrated book *Centuries of Child-*

hood, the French historian Philippe Aries suggests that the notion of childhood as a distinctive phase of life was the invention of the rising bourgeoisie in Europe.[25] While some of Aries' inferences on the implications of this invention may be debatable, there can be little doubt that with their power growing in politics and the economy, middle-class childrearing practices and ideals gained in public credence with the progress of industrialism. As these ideals came to be institutionalized in the law and the expanding educational system, middle-class understandings of the needs of children and their education were institutionalized as well. For better or for worse—and one may well argue about either—all other educational tradition's were henceforth measured by the educational ideals of the conventional middle-class family.[26]

In the vast literature on the subject two dominating features stand out: the centrality of children in the life of the modern nuclear family and an obsession with the methods to be used in their instruction. Both features sharply differentiated middle-class thought on education from those of the aristocracy. The latter tended to think in biological terms—an individual *is* his "blood"—and aristocrats had considerable difficulties in accepting the proposition that a child's inherited make-up could be modified by either specialized attention or education, for "blood," in the end, will always win out. The bourgeoisie, by its very origins, could not aspire to be an elite of the "blood." It was an *ethical elite*—that is, its status depended on the successful cultivation of time-tested virtues, and this status, in the language of sociology, must be "achieved" rather than "ascribed." An individual's place in the community and in the society at large was thus seen to be a consequence of his or her upbringing and schooling. In other words, while the aristocracy legitimated their social standing in terms of biological inheritance, the competing bourgeoisie was inclined to conceive of the child as a blank piece of paper that needs to be "written on" (i.e., shaped and formed) by those charged with its socialization. It is for these reasons that middle-class families always placed great store in the importance of environmental factors in childrearing and middle-class parents took great efforts to secure what they held to be a congenial educational environment for their children to grow up in. [27] Though John Locke, to whom the image of the blank paper is attributed, still spoke of "innate" differences in talents and temperament, by the end of the nineteenth century middle-class pundits and educators had succeeded in almost completely pushing aside notions of innate differences in favor of the importance of the educational environment.

To this day the family household remains the basic locale for early childhood socialization. A good variety of published sources provide us with descriptions of the efforts families make to mold responsible, competent, and morally sensitive individuals, though the specific content of socialization tends to be greatly influenced by the economic and professional opportunities that are available at any one point in time. It has been frequently observed that with every shift in the industrial system the requirements for operating and managing the system itself change as well. While entrepreneurial ownership was the customary path to wealth and power in the earlier phases of industrialization, at a later phase both wealth and power could be achieved in areas related to its finance, technological innovation, and the administration and promotion of the goods produced by the industrial system. When large-scale organizations made their entrance in the twentieth century, we see a shift in favor of organizational management. And today, as the organizational world is once more transformed by the technological power of the communication revolution, emphasis shifts to the honing of new sets of cognitive potentials. In short, every shift reveals that there exists a cognitive affinity between the requirements of the industrial system and the personality structure of its carriers, men and women alike. Yet any historical review reveals that the behavior patterns and values encouraged by socialization in the conventional mode have retained their utility. With its emphasis upon motivation, individual performance, and personal responsibility, today, as in the past, the conventional family's educational regime appears to be peculiarly well equipped to provide children with a competitive edge, regardless of their social origin.

The centrality of child-raising functions also helped to transform the conventional family from *within*. As the industrial system matured, the educational mission of the conventional family expanded, at times even with a vengeance. Since *everything* parents did came to be related to the family's great educational mission, *everything* had to be organized in accordance with that mission. This task had a rationalizing effect that extended to the body as well as to the mind. Much attention was paid to factors of health, nutrition, and personal hygiene. It became customary to experiment with methods that were hoped to produce strong bodies able to resist the many childhood diseases that beset children of all social classes well into the twentieth century. So, for instance, the physical living arrangements of the family were subjected to similar rationalization processes. The separation of space for different domestic activities—sleeping, cooking, working, entertainment, bathing, etc.—became the order of the day. And along with this physical rationalization occurred what Norbert Elias has called "a rationalization of the senses."[28] In his fascinating book, *The Civilizing Process,* Elias discusses the many ways in which the rising bourgeoisie handled even the most minute aspects of daily activities—how to eat, when to eat, what to eat, where to eat, for instance—and came to be elevated to the status of "good manners" at the exclusion of others. In due time they became the only valid prescription of behavior to boot. Judging by the evidence available, ever more aspects of the child's life came to be organized and planned with this educational mission in mind: toys to stimulate the cognitive function of the small child, the reading of character-forming literature, the promotion of leisure-time activities and sports that were held to provide children with future advantages, and so on. The restructuring of the conventional middle-class family for purposes of childrearing served to foster and enhance yet further the emphasis on rationality and experimentation that had been one of its characteristic features from the beginning. Inevitably such attempts carried out in the domestic sphere were transported to other spheres of life as well, most notably in the educational system. In short order a distinctively middle-class educational ethos came to pervade the entire learning process at all stages.

The class aspect of all of this cannot be emphasized enough. For a long time the preindustrial elite of the aristocracy and gentry despised the striving ambitions of the expanding middle classes. In rejecting them as grasping, uncivil, and vulgar, they failed to fully comprehend for a long time that the new political-economic order tended to reward the socialization patterns of the middle classes. Only when the offspring of the reviled bourgeoisie began to outdistance upper-crust children in securing coveted positions of power and wealth, did the old upper classes begin to wake up to the new challenges. The same held true for those at the opposite end of the socioeconomic hierarchy. The vast segment of the population who continued to eke out an existence in the rural economy along with the new arrivals in industry whose energies were sapped by making ends meet, failed to link middle-class lifestyles and childrearing practices with economic and organizational success. It took the trumpet call of nineteenth-century sectarian religious movements to alert and convince the working classes of their importance. The introduction of universal compulsory education undoubtedly enhanced the social mobility of working-class children. Yet without the adoption of conventional nuclear family practices and norms, the working-class child's move up the socioeconomic ladder would have been significantly more difficult. Those lower-class families who, for whatever reasons, failed to recognize that childrearing and education were an increasingly serious business deprived their children of the capacity to avail themselves of the desired opportunities.

In sum, in realizing its educational mission the family of the rising middle classes became both an agent and a conduit of modernization, industrialization, and democratization. When one looks at this momentous transformatory process through the lens of cultural change, one begins to understand how the great educational mission of the conventional middle-class family was one huge and comprehensive exercise in the inculcation of the *balanced individualism* and the *rational cognitive style* that stands at the core of the modern social order. Everything parents did was motivated by the objective to prepare children to participate and succeed in the increasingly sophisticated technological and bureaucratic structures of the industrial system. This preparation required parents to instill an ethic of responsibility and civility in their children that augured well for the life of the community. The old virtues of proto-industrial family provenance had prepared its successor family forms for this task to a degree that by the turn of the twentieth century Emile Durkheim, the great French sociologist, could write about "cooperative individualism" as being the distinguishing characteristic of modernity.

Some fifty years later, the cultural revolution of the 1960s put this great cultural mission into danger. The same individualism and the same rationality that once was the hallmark of the conventional family had turned into hyper-individualism and hyper-rationality. The core elements of modernity had thus been severed from their anchorage in the family. Lost in the ensuing battle against the family was the balance the conventional family had been able to strike in the past. While there has been a return to a new appreciation of the family's role in education in recent years, it looks as if it will take some time until a full restoration of its conventional middle-class content can be achieved.

Some Theoretical Implications

The aim of this chapter was to provide a brief overview of the nature and career of the modern family. Since we have traveled a long way and looked at the family's many dimensions it may be well to summarize some of the key insights this chapter has rendered. First and foremost, it is important to appreciate that the modern nuclear family is anything but conventional. In many ways the success of this type of family had lasting revolutionary consequences. Alone among the many family systems available it had the strength and the capacity to help transform the existing social order. It was this type of family that became the carrier of a modernizing way of life and it was this type of family that provided the countries of the region—England, Holland, parts of France and Germany—with their competitive advantage for so long. [29] Reinforced by a religiously-inspired ethos and legitimated by the visible evidence of its efficacy, the lifestyle of the conventional nuclear family came to be the culturally accepted and binding standard of life in the industrializing societies of the West. In the migration of large numbers of people from the region this distinctive family-based organization of life was carried to the New World—the United States, Canada, Australia. And with this movement from one place to the other the migrants carried with them the social capital conducive to the development of democracy and industrialism. It is one of the great merits of the economic historian Thomas Sowell to have been able to persuasively trace this process of diffusion.[30] By the same token, a good number of comparative studies on urban migration indicate that under favorable circumstances social forces can be unleashed that induce migrating families to relinquish traditional behavior patterns and take up patterns that look a lot like those akin to the modernizing family of West European origin. Already in the early 1960s William J. Goode described this process in terms of a "world revolution in family patterns."[31] In the currently popular debate over the advantages and disadvantages of "globalization," scant attention has been paid to this, perhaps, most basic transformation process that is about to engulf the entire world.

This brief, perhaps all too brief, historical sketch holds a number of important theoretical insights. Two in particular deserve to be mentioned. The first may serve as a long overdue correction of theories on the rise of the industrial democratic order and its consequences, and the second may provide countries coming from different cultural traditions and historical experiences with an appreciation of the vital role the family plays in the building of a prosperous and free society.

As to the first, it may be observed that contrary to Karl Marx's theory of class conflict that holds that capitalism would lead to the economic immiseration and political enslavement of the industrial worker, the history of the proto-industrial family shows that the expanding industrial capitalist system and the concomitant rise of political liberalism offered unmatched economic and political opportunities to the poor and set them free. By the same token, the reading of the same social historical record also shows that it was the culture of the nuclear family that provided the dynamism necessary for the transformation of a basically dysfunctional feudal society to a productive industrial order. Once the occasion offered itself it was primarily the dynamism of the nuclear family rather than the rationality flowing from the market, as Adam Smith assumed, that accomplished this revolutionary feat. The same holds for Friedrich Hegel's majestic philosophical vision that attributes the triumph of freedom in the West to the progress in rationality in human thought and cognition. Without its anchorage in the everyday life and ethos of the nuclear family, human thought and ideals would have remained mere abstract entities without practical consequence.

To be sure, each of these theoretical approaches can marshal considerable support for their respective arguments. Thus it can be argued in a Marxist vein that the onset of industrial production dramatically transformed all aspects of social life, *including* consciousness. But this particular "mode of production" did not appear in history *ad novum*. It was the result of long historical processes that included far-reaching changes in human consciousness as Hegel claimed. If industrialization caused great changes in cognition, the advent of industrialization itself was in turn rooted in specific changes in consciousness (which, if Max Weber was right, may go back as far as the origins of the Judeo-Christian religious worldview). Yet both spheres of social life, the material as well as the ideational, are indelibly intertwined with the social, and here in particular with the way in which individuals organize their personal lives. The perspective of the family that undergirds the arguments of this book thus can serve as an important corrective to each of these approaches. It alerts the scholar to the fact that social change, *any* social change, is the result of the interaction between the cognition and behavior of human beings and the concrete material situation in which they occur. It further cautions the scholar not to attribute causal primacy to any one single set of factors. The empirical evidence of a particular situation, rather than some theoretical a priori, will determine which set of factors held the greater share at any one particular historical point in time. But above all, the family perspective alerts the scholar to the fact that both, the material and the ideational, are defined by a third set of factors that have their origin in the life of concrete human beings, their values and their hopes. The interplay between these three dimensions of human existence—the ideational, the material, and the family-based behavioral—has determined the course of the past and it will undoubtedly affect the future of the industrial way of life in the years ahead as well.

It was the genius of Adam Smith's argument—and our misfortune, I may add—that economists to this day have remained wedded to Smith's *idee clef* that the capitalist market economy is the "natural" way for individuals to organize and that it is the purpose of economists to understand the laws of the "natural" system. If viewed through the prism of the family, however, the way people behaved and continue to behave under capitalism is anything but "natural." Our brief excursion into the history of the conventional family has made it clear that for behavior to become purposive it must be motivated: motivated to work, to delay gratification, to save, to plan, to take rational risks, and so forth. To be sure, we may assume that human beings have always meant well by their offspring and wanted to protect them from harm. But this "natural" desire does not necessarily lead to a life of self-denial, nor does it inspire never-ending efforts to care, to build, to accumulate capital, or to restlessly search for ever-new horizons. A more "natural" attitude, I think, might be to save for a certain measure of material well-being and then say "enough is enough" and begin to enjoy the fruits of one's labor by feasting and celebrating. It may well warm the cockles of a traditionalist's heart that in many part of the world—in India, Africa, and Asia—poor and rich families alike are willing to incur immense expenses in connection with elaborate wedding celebrations (or funerals, as the case may be). Some appear to be even willing to go into hock for years to come. Yet such practices are surely not conducive to the amassing of capital for purposes of production. The saving of capital by large numbers of ordinary people, while perhaps negligible at the outset, is precisely what occurred in certain parts of Europe in the early modern period.

There can be little question then that the lived reality of individual life was basic to the momentous shifts in the transition from a feudal to a modern industrial order. As we have seen, that life was organized around the family, and a particular one to boot. The historical evidence strongly suggests that the structure and consciousness of the nuclear family had prepared the stage for the great transformation and its inner dynamics provided the engine for its expansion and progress. If one were asked to summarize this insight succinctly in one sentence it would be not at all far-fetched to observe that modernization did not produce the nuclear family, but, on the contrary, that without the assistance of the nuclear family the modern world would not have been produced.

The second insight of our brief journey into the social history of the modern family relates to the nature of the democratic capitalist order itself. The historical record strongly suggests that democratic capitalism is based on a fusion between private practices and public exigencies and that the two present just different sides of the same coin. Both are constitutive parts of a particular way of life and cannot be taken apart easily. The stark fact that the two—the private and the public—are intrinsically connected has far-reaching policy implications. Though the two realms are based on different principles and each unfolds its own distinctive dynamics, it is impossible to consider the one without the other. This suggests that it would be a fatal error to cast currently pressing social issues in economic and political terms only. It is well neigh impossible to consider issues of education, work, poverty, social mobility, health, housing, and crime, just to name a few, without taking into account the consequential effect the organization of private life has on these issues.

The Family Factor in the Emergence of the Culture of Modernity in the Developing World Today

The proposition that there exists an intrinsic linkage between private and public institutions opens up a Pandora's box of questions. As recent history shows, many contemporary countries have encountered considerable difficulties in realizing their desire to achieve an economically productive and politically stable democratic society. To date, many developing countries have failed to modernize in ways that make for self-sustained economic growth and afford their citizens the freedom they so dearly crave. After decades of shattered efforts and hopes it has become evident that issues of culture are ultimately what determines success. This is not to deny the importance of the ways in which the economy is organized and a legal-political system is in place that assures equal treatment to all. Yet to ignore the importance of factors of culture in the organization of economic and political institutions is no longer possible today.

"Culture" is an amorphous and difficult concept to handle. However defined, there can be little doubt that the family plays an important part in the creation of culture broadly understood. As we have seen in the preceding chapters it was the conventional nuclear family that permeated the creation of a distinctly modern culture, which with all its local variations continues to be an active ingredient in the maintenance of modern civilization itself.

There also can be little doubt that under specific circumstances family cultures, like cultures at large, are open to change, provided that political circumstances permit. Although the historical evidence strongly suggests that there exists a "cognitive fit" between the nuclear family and the institutions characteristic of modern capitalist democracies, there are no intrinsic reasons why cultures based on different family dynamics should be deprived for all times to come from developing those institutions that are indispensable for the formation and maintenance of a politically free and economically productive modern order. To take factors of culture seriously one does not have to go to the extreme to explain the existence of manifest differences in the potential for development solely in terms of differences in family structure as some, like Emmanuel Todd, the noted anthropologist based at the Institut National d'Etudes Demographiques in Paris, has done.[32] Culture, at its most basic level, emerges out of the ordinary, everyday activities of ordinary people, their habits, their practices, their ideas, norms, and values. Taken together these factors constitute powerful patterns of behavior which may facilitate, deflect, transmute, and, perhaps, even preclude the development of possibilities which lie in the structural arrangement of any society. At the same time, culture is not merely learned and automatically passed on from one generation to the next. Cultures have not only the potential to change, but under particular circumstances they do change. In this sense culture is also an active response of individuals and groups to external conditions and the challenges that are reproduced and enriched through daily experiences. While these processes occur in all spheres of life, they are given meaning and significance in and through the private life of individuals, which in large measure revolves around the family.

To illustrate how family-fueled dynamics play today a vital part in the transformation of cultures that differ in their basic presuppositions from the West European experience one only has to look at the migratory experience of massive numbers of people currently taking place in large parts of the world.

For purposes of space in what follows the focus will be on the experience of Latin American urban migrants.

The recent history of large parts of the world has been influenced by the movement of often desperately poor people into the sprawling shantytowns and squatter settlements of the steaming cities of Africa, Asia, and Latin America. Pushed out of rural areas by the lack of opportunities and drawn to cities by promises of economic opportunities, these migrants often found themselves without work and caught in conditions of abject poverty. Unwanted and unaided, lacking in resources and skills, without the availability of housing and basic amenities, the poorest of the world's poor were thus thrown back upon their own meager resources to find shelter, food, and work. In their struggle for survival they invariably discovered that the social norms of their rural past could no longer guide them through the labyrinthine requirements of alien cities and many experienced an acute sense of dislocation and disorientation.

A considerable number of ethnographic studies have tried to sort out the various dimensions of the migratory phenomenon. Many have focused on the inability of governments to control the flow of migration and to provide them with work and shelter. Quite a few researchers have turned their attention to the migrants' potential to organize politically. Others looked at factors of labor markets, questions of capital formation, and the expediency of the transfer of funds and technical knowledge from the industrialized to the not yet industrialized world and yet others looked at the importance of social relationships in the migrants search for work, food, and shelter. Some, though not many, even tried to focus on the family connection in their heroic struggle to survive. Although the best of these studies indicate that mass migration was by no means as destructive to human lives as many tended to believe in the past, few have found cause for optimism. Life in the vast squatter settlements and shantytowns of the developing world continues to be hard, full of strife, and privation.

Yet there exists some evidence today that it is decidedly premature to entertain visions of lasting poverty and doom. Contrary to the jeremiads of early observers, most have prevailed against all the odds and in many instances migrants have proven to be less marginal and politically more resilient.[33] Contrary to expectations, they neither have organized themselves to supply the ground troops for a revolution many predicted to be inevitable, nor does the available evidence give cause to assume that most have disappeared into an underworld of crime and corruption.

Three related developments occurring simultaneously on the economic, domestic, and spiritual level may help to explain why some migrants, though by no means all, have done so much better than predicted. For one the inability of governments to provide the migrants with work and shelter may have a lot to do with bringing to the fore unexpected capabilities and strength. In the absence of work in what economists call "the formal sector," enterprising migrants, more by necessity than inclination, were driven into the economic underground, the "informal sector," where they tried to survive by means of self-help economic activities on the smallest scale. Some turned to the production and vending of food and the supply of a great variety of services the more established urban dwellers found too ungainful or undesirable. Others were able to acquire more basic technical skills, like the repair of dilapidated cars, trucks, and appliances and subsequently succeeded in finding forms of work where the skills they learned in one area could be transferred to another without too much difficulty. Though the British social scientist Bryan Roberts documents in his extensively researched book *Cities of Peas-*

ants: The Political Economy of Urbanization in the Third World that such make-do economic activities prevented the worst from happening, in and of themselves they provided few opportunities to move ahead either economically or socially, and he explored in some detail the various economic options open to migrants.[34]

Scholars who have been actively trying to make sense of contemporary trends have argued that as a consequence of these make-shift economic activities two antithetical economies have emerged in the cities of the developing world, the "economy of firms," the official economy sponsored by the state, and what the anthropologist Clifford Geertz has called the "bazaar economy."[35] The first is based on the rationalization of production and the accumulation of capital for further investment and expansion, and the second on the logic of the household economy that makes intensive use of the labor of its members. Geertz and others hold the urban poor's reliance on the economy of the household to be not much more than a stop-gap survival measure that has led to economic "involution," rather than an evolution toward a modern way of life. On the other hand, more recently Hernando de Soto has presented a much more positive picture of the potential of the much ignored sector of the informal economy in his widely-noted book *The Other Path,* a book on the underground economy of Lima, Peru.[36] De Soto strongly argues that the misguided policies of governments, rather than the economic and social conditions prevailing in developing countries, have prevented the urban poor from developing those dynamics that would allow them to lift themselves out of their dismal situation. Consequently, he and like-minded activists advocated the removal of existing political-bureaucratic barriers that prevent the urban poor from moving into the socioeconomic mainstream of their countries.

While there is much to be said for either of these contrasting views, a closer reading of the mass of materials available today suggests a reappraisal of the migration phenomenon that differs from both. In contrast to the Geertzean perspective, the bazaar economy of developing countries holds a much greater economic potential than it is assumed, provided the political-economic system permits family dynamics to unfold their productive power. And in contrast to de Soto's straightforward assumption that a change in government policies will do the trick, the family perspective indicates that regardless of how much entrepreneurial activities may be encouraged by appropriate official policies, they are bound to fail unless they are anchored in the daily life of ordinary individuals. In other words, the focus on the family reveals not only the shortcomings of either perspective, but also suggests how the two may be reconciled.

Already some twenty years ago, Bryan Roberts, the British social anthropologist, warned that it would be a mistake to think of individuals laboring in the urban penny economy as isolated economic units and assume that their activities are profitless. Although small-scale purveyors of goods and services may appear to be desperately poor at times, it is important to see them within the context of the larger economic unit of the family household. Roberts goes on to argue that the place of these small-scale economic activities is in many ways similar to that of domestic out-work and petty commodity production characteristic of the early stages of the Industrial Revolution in England. Like there, activities that look to careless observers like exploitation and abuse are often far better than the alternative. Then, as now, life in an imagined Arcadia where happy villagers live in harmony with nature, is indeed brutish, nasty, and short. While then as now the move to the city by no means assures success in every case— the record is full of stories of failure and desperation—survival was and remains greatly facilitated if and when the migrants can rely upon the kind of cooperation only a family has to offer.

In this "if" and "when" lies a problem. A considerable body of literature on the relationship between persistent poverty and marital instability in the developing world highlights its dimensions. So for instance, a number of studies in the Caribbean and the countries of Central America suggest that men living under conditions of poverty and job insecurity are unwilling to commit themselves to the more permanent obligations of family. By the same token, women appear to be likewise unwilling to take on the liability of a permanent attachment when the man might prove to be a drunkard, a philanderer, unable to earn a living, or is prone to violence. [37] In the Latin American case a deeply entrenched culture of *machismo* where males conceive of themselves as *conquistadores* whose strength can overcome all resistance, as Don Juans whose charm no woman can resist, undoubtedly contributes to conflicted relationships that make family stability virtually impossible. In short, many of the urban poor in the developing world, (and not only those on the Latin American subcontinent) appear to be caught in a vicious cycle of behavior that prevents them from accepting as a norm any one standard form of family life. In the absence of domestic stability the urban poor are thus deprived of the most valuable resource for moving out of a "culture of poverty" into the mainstream of their societies.

The importance of the family factor cannot be emphasized enough in this connection. Detailed studies on the migratory experience indicate that the family gains new and added significance in the migrants' encounter with a great variety of urban challenges. This was particularly true for those families who tried to secure their livelihood in the informal sector of the urban economy. The necessity to cope with day-to-day problems of urban living, to develop economic skills of entrepreneurship, and to figure out how best to circumvent bureaucratic obstacles erected by governments veering between oppressive merchantilistic policies and the requirements of socialist-type command economies, appears to have fostered new modes of behavior and thought among many. The commercial nature of their work requires forms of self-control, initiative, and interaction alien to traditional rural settings. Reminiscent of Adam Smith's depiction of the civilizing project of commercialism in the England of his time, the new modes of thought and behavior that developed in the crucible of the migrants' struggle for survival in the cities of the developing world today appear to hold considerable promise for the future of their societies.

It is of singular importance to note that both small-scale entrepreneurial activities as well as new forms of interaction occur within the context of the family household. The stability of the family relationships that provides the urban poor with a competitive advantage hence becomes vitally important. Bryan Roberts, for instance, found that among the urban poor in Guatemala City many of the family unions were quite stable despite the fact that a large portion of the couples living together were not married by either church or state.[38] They were found to be particularly stable when a common commercial goal united the couple. Similar findings can be gleaned from studies conducted in Brazil as well as Chile, Peru, and Mexico. The harsh economic and social realities of migrant life in the penny economy require new forms of interaction, of trust, of planning, and of looking toward the future. In acquiring such new forms of thought and action in the context of the household economy, the migrants are able to invent not only new modes of being, they also reinvent the family. A good many studies reveal that a transformation of the traditional family that was part and parcel of "the common human pattern" is currently in process among the urban poor in disconnected parts of the world. Diachronically conducted studies, such as the one by the sociologist Bernard Rosen, indicate that the family type that is in the process of emerging today increasingly resembles that of the conventional family. In his book, *The Industrial Connection*, Rosen presents us with a penetrating description of the stages in which the transformation of behavior and thought occurs in the *favelas* of Rio de Janeiro. After years of research he arrived at the unequivocal conclusion that the family acquired a new significance among the migrant poor.[39] Whereas in the rural setting all aspects of individual and social life were regulated by powerful and often stifling traditions preventing families from transforming themselves from within, in their search for food, work, and shelter in the rough urban environment families were practically forced to abandon practices and attitudes of long standing that had lost their raison d'être. More by necessity than by design, the relationship between husbands and wives, on the one hand, and parents and children, on the other, became more communicative and egalitarian, the importance of individualized socialization and the educational achievement of children gained new importance, and collaborative behavior patterns emerged that made for a strengthening rather than a weakening of family ties. Similar insights can be culled from Peter Lloyd's memorable study of the new towns of Peru.[40] Analogous to the European case, in the squatter settlements of Brazil and Peru a new modern ethos appears to be in the making at the intersection of family and work today and new forms of living together appear to be spreading slowly yet persistently. An analogy to the instrumental role of the proto-industrial family in Western Europe's long road to modernity would perhaps be an act of overreach. Yet case studies like those just cited strongly suggest that the reinvented families of Latin America have the capacity of providing the locale and the instrument for the requisite redefinition of individual and social life. Provided political powers permit (a big "if" in some developing societies, as de Soto forcefully points out), a new and thoroughly modern family, nuclear and conjugal in form, enterprising, commonsensical and forward looking, egalitarian and respectful of the rights of individuals, appears to be in the process of unleashing a new dynamism that augurs well for the futures of their countries.

Reminiscent of the Western case as well, a different set of studies permits us to glean at the singular importance of a religiously-informed ethic in the formation of a distinctly modern manner of life. In his path-breaking book *Tongues of Fire,* the British sociologist David Martin documents the importance of Pentecostal and fundamentalist sects in the cultural transformation process among slum dwellers of Brazil's and Chile's teeming cities.[41] Like similar studies before him, Martin's research strengthens once more the important insight of an earlier generation of scholars that for a society to prosper and modernize it must not only be a moral community—other societies are that too—but a moral community of a particular kind. In cultures ruled by ideals of *machismo* that permit men to relinquish their familial obligations and responsibilities and find refuge from the hardships of poverty in fleeting sexual relationships, the indiscriminate consumption of alcohol, gambling, and idleness, women are typically left alone to fend for themselves and their children. Martin's records indicate that in their quest for deliverance from a seemingly hopeless fate sizable numbers of desperately poor women have turned to the promises of fundamentalist sects in recent decades. The harsh fundamentalist commands of Protestant sectarianism, he points out, requires its disciples not only to work hard, be self-reliant, frugal, sober, and save, they also effect what may be called a "domestication of the senses." That is to say, sexual appetites must be tamed, inclinations toward self-indulgence disciplined, and self-gratification postponed. Though Martin emphasizes the importance of religious yearnings in the Pentecostal phenomenon, there can be little doubt that questions of the family play an exceptionally important role. For basic to all new activities is the unwavering desire of women—and men in due time as well—to create a stable basis for the survival and the advancement of their families. Hence it cannot be accidental that in structure and content the family "of choice" in the developing world begins to look increasingly like the conventional nuclear family we have talked about so much in this book. When in their quest for transcendence marginal men and women are inspired by a religiously-informed ethic that enjoins them to fundamentally change their daily practices and rely upon themselves, they are in the process of developing "a new manner of life." The evidence from a growing number of studies on the Pente-costal phenomenon suggests that among these particular groupings a new kind of familism appears to be in the making that makes for far fewer family breakdowns, less frustration, less apathy, more optimism, and considerably higher aspirations than had been previously assumed. In this, the religious conversion drama unfolding in Brazil, Chile, Guatemala, and other parts of the world today gives hope for whole segments of the population of developing societies economically, politically, and socially.

Conclusions

As we reach the end of this chapter, which sought to provide a brief sketch of the role of the family in the rise of the modern world, we are led to conclude that contrary to the opinions of many the rise of the political and economic institutions conducive to modernization and economic development did not take place in the society as a whole, but through the web of diversified collective social life, in the microcosms of the family and the communities in which families are embedded. It was here, and not at the planning boards of governments and industries, that the syntheses productive of change occurred. At the center of this transformation stood the conjugal, nuclear family that in form and content gave not only rise to a dynamism that made the rise of the industrial democratic world possible, but that also had the capacity to absorb the fallout from the industrial system's various permutations down to our own days. At the same time, a brief excursion into contemporary processes unfolding in certain parts of the developing world today should rid us of the assumption that the Western case is unique and societies bereft of the resources the conventional family has to offer are condemned to lag behind for centuries to come. The family imperative that unites all human beings makes it possible that under circumstances yet to be explored in greater detail, families, wherever they are, have the capacity to engender a dynamism that promises to aid individuals and whole societies alike.

In the course of our pursuit of the unique role of the conventional family in Western history, we also gained a first inkling of the distinctly uncomfortable possibility that the dynamism peculiar to this type of family may be blocked, subverted, or even destroyed. And it is to this topic that we shall turn our attention in the next two chapters.

Notes

1. Peter Laslett, *The World We Have Lost* (Cambridge: Cambridge University Press, 1965); Peter Laslett *Family Life and Illicit Love in Earlier Generations* (Cambridge: Cambridge University Press, 1977); Alan Macfarlane, *The Culture of Capitalism* (Oxford: Basil Blackwell, 1987); Alan Macfarlane, *The Origin of English Individualism* (Oxford: Basil Blackwell, 1977).

2· R. O'Day, *The Family and Family Relationships 1500–1900: England, France and the United States of America* (London: Macmillan, 1994).

3. R. O'Day, op.cit.

4. Rudolf Braun, "The Demographic Transition in the Canton of Zuerich in the 18th and 19th Century," in Charles Tilly (ed.), *Historical Studies of Changing Fertility* (Princeton: Princeton University Press, 1978).

5. Alan Macfarlane, *The Culture of Capitalis*, op.cit. and Alan Macfarlane, *The Origins of English Individualism,* op.cit.

6. Max Weber, *The Protestant Ethic and the Spirit of Capitalism* (New York: Scribner, 1930).

7. See for instance E.L. Jones, *The European Miracle* (New York: Cambridge University Press, 1991).

8. Adam Seligman, *Inner Worldly Individualism* (New Brunswick, N.J.: Transaction, 1995) and Adam Seligman, *The Question of Trust* (Princeton: Princeton University Press, 1999).

9. Colin Campbell, *The Romantic Ethic and the Spirit of Modern Consumerism* (Oxford: Basil Blackwell, 1987).

10. Ann Douglas, *The Feminization of American Culture* (New York: Alfred A. Knopf, 1977).

11. Edward Shorter, *The Making of the Modern Family* (New York: Basic Books, 1975).

12. See Schama, op.cit. Moreover, a good number of the issues of the quarterly *Dutch Journal of Sociology* contain numerous articles on the status of the family in the past and today. None lead us to conclude that the centrality of the family has in any way changed since the historical period Schama wrote about.

13. E. P.Thompson, *The Making of the English Working Class* (London: Penguin edition, 1968).

14. Michael Anderson, *Family Structure in Nineteenth Century Lancashire* (London: Cambridge University Press, 1971).

15. Mount, op.cit., p. 56.

16· See Frank Musgrove, *Youth and the Social Order* (Bloomington, Indiana: Indiana University Press, 1964).

17. Neil McKendrick, "Home Demand and Economic Growth: A New View of the Role of Women and Children in the Industrial Revolution," in Neil MacKendrick (ed.), *Historical Perspectives: Studies in English Thought and Society in Honor of J.H. Plumb* (London: Europa Publications, 1987).

18. McKendrick, Brewer, and Plumb, *The Birth of a Consumer Society: The Commercialization of Eighteenth-Century England* (London: Europa Publication, 1982, p.172).

19. A good American example of this can be found in the person of John D. Rockefeller, as described by Ron Chernow, *Titan: The Life of John D. Rockefeller Sr.* (New York, Random House, 1998).

20. Simon Schama, op.cit., Part Three.

21. Alan Macfarlane, op.cit., and Eileen Power, "The Position of Women," in G.C.

Crump and E.F. Jacobs (eds.), *The Legacy of the Middle Ages* (Oxford: Oxford University Press, 1926).

22. Ferdinand Mount, op.cit., p.241.
23. Schama, op.cit., p.404.
24. Mount, op.cit., p.221.
25. Philippe Ariès, *Centuries of Childhood* (New York: Alfred A. Knopf, 1962).
26. Jacques Donzelot, *The Policing of Families* (New York: Pantheon, 1979).
27. John Locke, *Some Thoughts Concerning Education* (London: Cambridge University Press, 1884 [2nd ed.]).
28. Norbert Elias, *The Civilizing Process* (New York: Urizen Books, 1977—originally published in German in 1936).
29. Brigitte Berger and Peter Berger, *The War Over the Family: Capturing the Middle Ground* (New York: Doubleday, 1983).
30. Thomas Sowell, *Race and Culture: A World View* (New York: Basic Books, 1994).
31. William J. Goode, *World Revolution and Family Patterns* (New York: The Free Press, 1963).
32. Emmanuel Todd, *The Explanation of Ideology: Family Structures and Social Systems* (Oxford: Basil Blackwell, 1985) and Emmanuel Todd, *The Causes of Progress: Culture, Authority and Change* (Oxford: Basil Blackwell, 1987).
33. Janet Perlman, *The Myth of Marginality* (Berkeley: University of California Press, 1976), and Bryan Robert, *Cities of Peasants: The Political Economy of Urbanization in the Third World* (Beverly Hills, California and London: Sage Publications, 1978) offers fine discussions of this claim.
34. Bryan Roberts, op. cit., p. 128.
35. Clifford Geertz, *Peddler and Princes: Social Developments in Two Indonesian Towns* (Chicago: Chicago University Press, 1963, pp. 90–103).
36. Hernando de Soto, *The Other Path: The Invisible Revolution in the Third World* (New York: Harper & Row, 1989).
37. Edwin Eames and Judith Goode, *Urban Poverty in a Cultural Context* (New York: Free Press, 1973). This book presents a useful review of a number of studies on the topic.
38. Bryan Roberts, op. cit., p.142.
39. Bernard Rosen, *The Industrial Connection* (New York: Aldine, 1982).
40. Peter Lloyd, *The New Towns of Peru* (New York: Aldine, 1985).
41. David Martin, *Tongues of Fire* (Oxford: Basil Blackwell, 1990).

Part 3

The Conventional Family Today and Its Future

5

The Modern Family Today

This chapter aims to provide an overview of the current status of the modern family in its conventional middle-class form and ethos. The task will be carried out against the background of the by now familiar question of whether we are to assume with the theorists of postmodernism that recent shifts in individual behavior indicate that this type of family has outlived its usefulness, or whether we are to agree with more conservative observers that the shifts that have occurred are likely to endanger its indispensable role in individual and social life. These drastically opposing views operate on essentially similar premises. Both suggest that we are living at a juncture in history where the institution of the modern family has been hollowed out from within, with the difference that the one would welcome what the other tries to prevent.

This question takes us back to the beginning chapters of this volume, which sought to provide a brief description of how it happened that the conventional family came into disrepute in the course of a few hectic decades. Though it appears at the turn of the century that the counterculture's war against the family is for all practical purposes over and the utility of the family has been rediscovered by many, not all that much has changed. Today, as some thirty years ago, we encounter the same sharp divisions on the role of the modern family. Those informed by classical liberal principles (political centrists, neo-liberals, neo-conservatives, and conservatives) argue for the indispensability of the nuclear family, while those to the Left of center (that motley assemblage of Marxists, neo-Marxists, feminists, and, of late, the theorists of postmodernity in particular) continue to view it in mostly ambivalent, if not negative, terms. The representatives of the communitarian movement, who in recent years have made a fetish out of the community and consider themselves to be neither of the Right nor the Left, on the other hand, decry the selfish individualism this type of family is alleged to have fostered to the same degree that they advocate its revitalization. Though largely in agreement that the conventional family's protective, educational, moral, and social functions have been progressively displaced by the macro-institutions of modern society—the schools, the legal system, the therapeutic empire, the mass media, and so forth—all camps party to the public debate continue to disagree whether this is a good or a bad thing. Those of the philosophical and political Right try with all the legislative and persuasive tools at their disposal to rein in the discretionary power of both the government and its surrogate institutions, while those to the Left claim that the current unsettling degree of fluidity and normative uncertainty makes attempts to restore the conventional family to its once privileged status unworkable. The first refuse to acknowledge the possibility that some of the profound changes that have occurred in the ways we live and interact with one another may not be as pronounced and disastrous as they have been made out to be, and the second persist in seeing the recent public recovery of the conventional family and its equally conventional ethos as either an intellectual annoyance or even as a political disaster.

When one leaves the political arena, however, and inquires how ordinary people have adjusted to the challenges of the past decades, it comes as a surprise to discover that research data after research data show that by far the majority of ordinary men and women—in all walks of life and from the most varied ethnic backgrounds imaginable—have refused to embrace the more extreme positions flaunted by either political camp. Contrary to postmodernist claims, the vast majority have been resistant to abandoning the ideal of a life defined by marriage and a way of living together in which husband and wife, joined by love and mutual commitment, set out to build a private world for themselves and their children.[1] At the same time, when the available research data are controlled for age and social class they appear to indicate that most men and women tend to be considerably less hostile to a good number of the changes that have occurred than conservative thinkers are prone to think. For that vast segment of the population that is neither of the Left nor the Right, the meaningful question today is not so much whether to resurrect or destroy the conventional family, but rather how an ideal of married life can be realized without being compelled to surrender the freedoms that have been gained. As a consequence, ordinary people find themselves frequently at a loss as to what to make of the very different claims advanced on their behalf by either of the sparring parties.

On the Ambiguity of Research Findings

Given the magnitude of the discrepant claims around the conventional family and its future the question arises as to whether and to what degree we are today better equipped to understand contemporary family trends. The answer is mixed. As far as our knowledge of particular aspects of family life is concerned, we know today more than ever before, perhaps even too much. There exists hardly any aspect of family life that has not been researched and re-researched and then ad nauseam. Yet that knowledge is by no means as self-evident as it may seem at first blush, nor are its implications as clear-cut as many analysts would like to make them out to be.

Why is that so? For one, while there always existed a distinction between professional knowledge and policy advocacy, the upheavals of the sixties have fundamentally reshaped the academic study of the family. Ambitious theoretical claims on the grand scale have given way to narrow studies, conducted mostly by special interest groups concerned with statistical groupings held to be oppressed— women, minorities, lesbians, and gays. And with this shift, strategic and ideological considerations have come to dissipate the core fund of knowledge gathered by earlier generations of scholars. Moreover, contemporary researchers who should—and do—know better are loath to publicly acknowledge findings that run against the currently received wisdom culminating in the diagnosis that the conventional family is in a state of acute crisis.

The misuse of research in policy advocacy is not precisely new in the history of the social sciences. In a much-noted essay, "The Continued Utility of Mythical Numbers," Peter Reutter brilliantly documented a few years ago how easy it is to manipulate research findings to suit the argument a particular author wishes to make.[2] One does not have to abide by the frequently-uttered dictum that "there are lies, there are damned lies, and then there are statistics," yet as the argument of the present chapter progresses it will become obvious that even the best of research data lend themselves to widely-divergent interpretations when political passions and interests enter into the equation. When it comes to the affairs of the conventional family, in particular, the most ostentatiously-flaunted data are not necessarily the most reliable!

In view of the mass of contradictory claims and emotions swirling around the status of the family, the question arises how it is possible to obtain a more balanced picture of the current status of the conventional family. In recent years it has become apparent to many that we can neither rely upon the opinions of intellectuals who remain comfortably ensconced in the ruins of a view of the family that is clearly out of touch with reality, nor are we able to trust those who seek to resurrect a family that in its imagined bliss has a decidedly mythological ring. Yet it is also self-evident that the best of the available research data in and of themselves do not tell us much unless they are informed by an ordering principle. The previous chapters on the nature and history of the inner dynamics of the conventional family have made it evident that the customary structural analysis of marriage and the family needs to be supplemented with a perspective that is able to incorporate the role of values and norms in the life of ordinary men and women. This methodological requirement applies not only to the understanding of the family's role in the past, it applies to the life of the contemporary family as well. Hence our inquiry of the status of the family will start with providing a brief demographic overview of the significant structural and normative shifts that have taken place in recent decades. After having wound our way through a minefield of potentially contradictory demographic data and normative shifts, we shall proceed to find an answer to the question of why in an age of great freedom and tolerance the vast majority of men and women continue to hold the ideal of the conventional family in such high esteem that they enter voluntarily, if not even with great eagerness, into a married life that neither promises unrestricted personal freedom nor tolerates much deviation from its core norms.

Through the Looking Glass More Sharply: Twentieth-Century Demographic and Normative Shifts and Their Implications

The twentieth century, as we have learned from the first chapters of this book, has not been kind to the family that stood at the cradle of the modern world. As the century progressed it became increasingly clear that the enormous achievements of industrialization and democratization did not come without cost. Far-reaching demographic and normative shifts of some standing began to manifest themselves ever more sharply in the ways in which individuals tended to organize their private lives.

On the *structural level* we see:

> *A notable decline in mortality*: People live longer and are healthier and more active today. As a consequence there has been an increase in the numbers of the elderly, who either live alone, in institutions or with their children or relatives, just as there has been a progressive fall in the infant mortality rate with the result that virtually all children reach adulthood.

> *Significant shifts in household structure*: Families and households are smaller in size and there has been a concomitant decline in extended and multi-family households to the same degree that there has been a significant growth in the numbers of single-person households.

> *Significant shifts in sexual behavior:* The advent of modern contraception made for an increase in abortions just as a growth in leniency in all sexual matters made for a growth in cohabitation as well as in single motherhood due to divorce and an increase in births outside of marriage.

> *Significant changes in the marriage structure*, with prevalence for later marriages, increase in the divorce rate, as well as in the proportion of remarriages amongst all marriages and the consequent growth in married-couple stepfamilies.

> A *growth in the cohabitation* of single parents with changing partners; the creation of cohabiting-couple stepfamilies.

> *Significant increases in the number of women in the paid labor force*, including the percentage of mothers with young children.

And on *the normative level* the following broad range of shifts in attitudes and values manifest themselves:

> A *greater societal emphasis on the needs and desires of the individual* and an increased desire for personal autonomy and unlimited freedom on the part of the individual and a concomitant resistance to accept obligations prescribed by tradition.

A *greater emphasis on equality, including gender equality, and a loss of deference for age* (a growth of anti-hierarchical sentiments in general).

The *blurring of the boundaries of social roles*, including the weakening of gender-specific roles, including such family roles as the "mother role" and the "father role."

A *greater willingness of both men and women, mothers as well as fathers, to rely on surrogate institutions in the care, socialization, education, and guidance of children*, including a general increase in the reliance upon the state.

A general *decrease in the family's control over its members*, the weakening of traditional norms guiding marriage resulting in the weakening of the marriage bond, and the acceptance of divorce.

The *separation of sexual relations from both the biological function of procreation and the legal institution of marriage*.

An increased tolerance and acceptance of all forms of lifestyles, including a *greater tolerance of all forms of sexual behavior* such as homosexuality and lesbianism.

Looking at these two sets of shifts as a whole, a number of questions arise. First it has to be noted that although many have been long in coming, the most massive changes occurred in the post-World War II period. Having for years focused all their attention on waging a bitter war against Nazi Germany, most Western nations were preoccupied with the reestablishment of political and economic normalcy and little thought was given to the consideration of long-term social trends. To many it seemed that a strong state and a distributive economy were the key to solving the social problems that had begun to surface with increasing frequency. As a consequence, the slow but steady triumph of liberal political theory celebrated the individual and strengthened the state, but had little faith in either the conventional family as an institution or its equally conventional ethos. As time went on, however, it became ever more evident that governmental involvement in the organization of private life did not suffice to stem the tide of problems that began to flood the societies of the West. As is the custom of governments when faced with challenges of undetermined origin, in this instance as well Western governments responded by getting ever more deeply entangled in social and individual problems until the realization finally began to set in that the state is a limited and highly imperfect surrogate for the family.

It is also important to appreciate that regardless of cultural differences, the direction of the trend was similar in every democratic industrialized society of the West. Though it may be argued that governmental policies and the vagaries of policy fashions may have served to magnify some of the consequences of the demographic shifts in particular countries like the United States, it now appears that many of the observed shifts are part and parcel of the modernization process. What remains an open question is to decide whether these shifts—or at least some of them—may have been temporary in nature and to determine which of the observed shifts have been so severe in their consequences that they have the potential to undermine the continuity of those values and freedoms Western societies have come to cherish. Only when this sorting out has been accomplished can one hope to tackle the policy questions foremost in the public mind today.

Hence it is of considerable importance to determine which of the measured changes in the structure of the family and individual behavior are likely to impair the core features of the conventional family and its important functions in the lives of individuals and society alike. There is, of course, some validity to arguments from structure. So, for instance, as recent revisions in laws covering divorce, welfare, and taxation show, changes in the law did have an effect on certain aspects of modern family life. By the same token, it can also not be denied that changes in the economic environment serve to influence the birthrate as well as the employment rate. And, of course, the rise of a new class of professionals competing with the family in the performance of its traditional tasks has not been without consequences either. Yet as the following deliberations will show these shifts have not destroyed the core principles upon which the conventional family rests. As we have already seen, it was the genius of the modern family to hold in *balance* the often-contradictory demands of its core themes revolving around love, liberty, responsibility, individuality and equality. The modern family's remarkable capacity to adapt itself to the ever-changing demands of an exploding industrial system and the fortuitous balance it was able to provide between individualism and social responsibility, between authority and equality, and between limitless "liberation" and a commonsense practicality became the most outstanding features of industrial democracy. Needless to say, such a balance had always been precarious to a certain degree. Each element in the balance could potentially escalate or be radicalized in such a way as to make the balance impossible.

This is precisely what is at issue today. It appears to many that with the measured shifts in behavior and norms the celebrated balance the conventional family used to provide has fallen by the wayside, and perhaps irretrievably so. Modern individuals are held to be irredeemably narcissistic, socially irresponsible, by nature predisposed toward inequality, and unable to make enduring commitments. It goes without saying that if these suspicions should prove to be true, a myriad of problems that already exist on every level of social life should increase and do their destructive work. Yet before one can join in the jeremiads of either political camp, it is useful to establish whether and to what degree the conventional family has indeed lost its capacity to keep the contradictions of modernity at bay.

The Issue of Family Cohesion

The fact that people in the highly-industrialized societies live longer, are considerably healthier, and lead more active lives than ever before has been a source of celebration and joy. On the other hand, the decrease in family and household size, the trend away from multi-generational households, and the considerably higher prevalence of people living alone, are held by analysts across the political divide to be symptoms of the loss of family cohesion. Some, like those located in the conservative camp, are inclined to attribute this loss to government intervention programs (such as the expansion of government-sponsored social security measures and the guaranteed income for single parents),[3] while those in the political center and on the Left argue it to be an inevitable consequence of the modernization process and hence put pressure upon the government to step in where the family has failed. Yet looking at the family from within, a more nuanced interpretation suggests itself.

The fact that significantly more individuals—both in their younger as well as in their older years—live in separate households reflects not only a general growth in affluence in the society at large, but should also be seen as a welcome solution to a variety of issues posed by the extension of the lifespan and the trend to start a family at a later age. From this point-of-view it is hard to imagine how modern men and women could be inclined to quarrel with those gifts of modernity that provide freedom, choice, and a modicum of economic security at one and the same time. Far from feeling shunted to the side, most of the elderly, but most decidedly all of their younger counterparts, prefer to gain, or retain, their personal autonomy. If finances permit, this includes for most the ability to control their living arrangements, even if this choice should imply the loss of some family warmth and fewer intimate contacts with kin. While a family is a wonderful and good thing to have, some distance to the intensity of familial relationships may also come as a welcome respite at times, particularly if this respite neither harms the sense of family nor the relationships it fosters.

To strengthen this argument one only has to look at a good number of micro-studies available today that suggest that the preference of people to live in separate households gives in no way support to the contention that the family is in danger of losing its cohesion. Two famous empirical studies, one conducted in England and the other in America—the first by Michael Young and Peter Willmott exploring post-war domestic changes in the working-class housing estate Bethnal Green, England, and the second by Mary Jo Bane and her associates on the demographic shifts effecting American family life in the second half of the twentieth century—convincingly demonstrate that neither the shrinking of the family nor the trend for older as well as younger people to establish separate households necessarily imply that family ties are on the verge of breaking.[4] Despite significant changes in the way most of us live today, family members tend to communicate and interact with one another often and intensively, perhaps even more so now than ever before in the past. To be sure, such communications tend to occur on the telephone and during frequent family get-togethers rather than around the village well held in high esteem by nostalgic anti-modernists. But they do occur, nonetheless. Readers of nineteenth-century novels by writers such as Honoré de Balzac, Jane Austen, and Nathaniel Hawthorne have been relatively immune to falling prey to the romantization of a past that in many ways was more oppressive than supportive.

By the same token it also has to be observed that the cornucopia of modern technology and "the rising economic tide that lifts all the boats" hardly drove the wedge of alienation into family relationships. To be sure, technological progress removed the place of work out of the household and the wage-earning economy provided individuals with a new independence from the family. Yet it also equipped individuals with more choice and freedom and relieved women and men, and the first in particular, from the drudgery of the household. Technological inventions and their diffusion into all layers of society provided ordinary folks not only with goods and services that in earlier times had been the prerogative of the elite alone, they also strengthened and expanded that sense of equality that had been the hallmark of the conventional nuclear family and, by extension, of Western society at large. Such changes should hardly give cause for lament but to the most ardent utopian dreamer who imagines the world to have been a better and more equitable place when "Adam cleft and Eve span."

Most recently the sociologist Thomas Luckmann was able to document in considerable detail that the Western family has neither lost its function nor its cohesion. On hand of an impressive investigation into the lifeworld of ordinary individuals in the German Federal Republic he and his research associates could document that in the vast network of shared communicative interaction processes of the conventional family modern individuals continue to acquire their personal identities, basic moral matrixes, and their capacity to maneuver through the labyrinth of life in postmodern society. This highly-theoretical and deeply- informed treatise makes it evident that the family has gained a new and vital function in the continuing pluralization of the modern lifeworld. Not only is it able to make sense of the multiplicity of disjointed and often contradictory ideas and images floating about in an information-sated world, but it also has the capacity to integrate a great variety of experiences modern individuals have in disparate spheres of life. Luckmann argues that there simply are no other institutional competitors available that could perform this indispensable integrative function in an ongoing fashion.[5]

At the same time, there exists a clearly identifiable category of people in the United States—variably labeled "the underclass" or "welfare dependency class"—whose existence is marred by bundles of problems difficult to sort out in terms of cause and effect. While liberals hold poverty and racial discrimination to be the root problem of all their woes, conservatives tend to attribute the cause of their troubles to behavioral shortcomings. No matter which side of the debate one is inclined to come out on, here it should be simply noted in purely descriptive terms that the underclasses' most striking feature is the absence of family cohesion and the lack of the interactive and communicative dynamics typical of conventional families. At this point in the present argument it will have to suffice to emphasize that the emergence of a population category called "the underclass" confirms rather than repeals the continued importance of family cohesion and that of the conventional family in general.

The Organization of Intimate Relationships: Sex, Love, and Marriage in the Postmodern Age

Much has been written about the human passions through the ages, how it is necessary to distinguish between expressions of raw sexuality and the various types of love, and how different cultural traditions tend to give shape and meaning to both. In our own time legions of theologians, scientists, anthropologists, psychologists, and poets continue to be busy with their varying attempts to unravel the mysteries of sexuality and love and how they relate to each other. Many wise—and, alas, all too frequently not so wise—things have been said about both. For our present purposes it is important to emphasize the degree to which these three elements are interlinked in Western societies in the past and continue to be so to this day. Though technological inventions undoubtedly make it possible to separate sexual relations from the biological function of procreation today, it is also important to keep in mind that the present-day tolerance of all sorts of sexual practices inside and outside of marriage was greatly influenced by changing notions of human freedom and personal autonomy. While marriage in the Western past also tended to be based on the free decision of individuals, both sexuality and marriage from medieval times onward had come increasingly under the control of church and state. Yet despite stringent attempts to contain sexuality in marriage, it was very often transgressed against, especially by men. The large number of children born outside of marriage frequently spelled disaster for their mothers and the stigma of illegitimacy was real and lasting. Today, in contrast, the free practice of sexuality has become a matter of individual rights and it is up to individuals themselves to decide whether and to what degree they are inclined to follow the injunctions imposed by either state or church. To the same degree that sexuality is no longer restricted to marriage, marriage itself is no longer held to be an absolute prerequisite for having children. In the public view the essence of Western marriage today lies more in the freely undertaken decision of a man and a woman to enter into marriage in some sort of expectation for companionship that will go on more or less indefinitely, and which, with young people, is expected to lead to children if they should decide to do so.

At least since Freud we appear to have accepted the view that sexual appetites can be easily tamed or repressed either by design or by force. While for centuries the churches and the governments of Western bourgeois societies labored long and hard to dampen sexual appetites and relegate matters of sexuality to the confines of marriage—with draconian methods that frequently bordered on physical and mental terror—it was quite impossible to repress the sexual urges of whole generations for any length of time by means of government or ecclesiastic fiat. With the advent of the twentieth century some form of truce had been established in most Western societies whereby "official" society upheld binding sexual standards that grew more lenient as the century progressed. When the 1960s came around it was already possible for those who stood in the vanguard of critical theory to openly declare that the violence modern man does to human sexuality will have dire consequences for the future of Western civilization. In his extravagantly successful *Eros and Civilization*, the German-American philosopher Herbert Marcuse openly proclaimed that a successful culture presupposes the liberation of sexuality from all control,[6] and cultural revolutionaries of the sixties celebrated the unrestrained pursuit of primal passions. Sexual promiscuity was declared to be a liberating, natural, and a good thing and the restrictions of bourgeois society were held to function as the assassins of genuine sexual passion and love.

While most ordinary people hesitated to accept the more extreme countercultural notions, there can be no denying that in virtually every industrialized society of the West something of a sea change occurred vis-à-vis sexual mores in both individual as well as public attitudes. Though recent years have witnessed something of a backlash against the unfettered practice of sexuality, it has become an accepted fact of modern life that sex can be regularly enjoyed without the benefit of clergy or registrar. Many of the more liberal notions that emerged in the crucible of the sixties continue to permeate current understandings. We can observe today a far greater tolerance of the expression of carnal appetites outside of marriage, just as we can find a considerably greater acceptance of sexual practices that had been the subject of legal persecution and public opprobrium in the past. Although the notable relaxation in the public attitude toward all things sexual certainly antedated the 1960s, it frequently appears to many as if a progressive slide of sexual behavior toward a point where boundaries no longer apply has become an established fact in the public mind. While there continues to exist considerable confusion among ordinary people about what to make of such critical issues as "cohabitation," "gay marriage," and abortion, it also has become implausible for many to agitate for the resurrection of those rigid sexual codes the prudish Victorian already felt distinctly uncomfortable about.[7]

To say this in no way implies an endorsement of the type of laxity in sexual matters that has crept into the public discourse since the sixties, nor does it imply an endorsement of the agenda of the conservative movement as it has developed in recent years. To subscribe to the first, one would be obliged to disregard not only the values most people hold but also to overlook the appalling consequences the celebration of unbounded sexuality has brought to individuals, if not entire groups. By the same token, as many have come to realize that there is more to family values than sexual behavior, it seems unlikely that modern men and women will easily return to the kind of Victorian moralism some contemporary advocates so avidly seek to promote. The first would fly against the human being's innate sense of boundaries and decency and the second would amount to a denial of the genuine achievements the relaxation of oppressive sexual codes have brought. Today we can neither go home again to a world in which church and state tried to police intimate relationships, nor can we, or would we wish to, proceed yet further down the path of unrestrained sexuality and excess that more often than not has led to grief and destruction. Regardless whether one bemoans or welcomes the changes that have occurred, it is important to understand the impact of the shifts in sexual mores—both in practice and in public opinion—and ask to what degree these shifts have undermined the viability of the conventional family.

The most important thing to note in this context is the fact that in the celebrated freedom of the postmodern age in which uncensored sexual practices and sexual mores are in flux and unopposed, most contemporary men and women continue to express an unfeigned longing for a life defined by the bounded love between two individuals. By far the majority seek stability and personal meaning in a family life based upon the commitment of two individuals to each other and they are willing to be guided by ideals and restraints which in content and form are strongly reminiscent of those of the conventional family.

The measured reality of personal values shifts the focus of the discussion from that of sexuality to the discussion of important aspects of love. As we have seen in the introductory chapters of this book there exists some sort of consensus across the political divide that a new postmodern self is in the process of being reformed in the chaotic transition of the industrial system to a postmodern one. We hear relatively little about the once widely-endorsed proposition that men marry for romantic reasons and women for security—tendencies once held to provide a fortunate matrix for childrearing in the nuclear family, with the man offering security to the woman who, in turn, appeals to him on an emotional basis. In this day and age it is no longer possible to argue that modern women marry for security—only a brief glance at divorce, labor-market, and earning statistics will dispel this notion—just as it would take some effort to show that men marry for sexual and romantic reasons only. In an age as free and tolerant as ours opportunities for brief and unencumbered romantic encounters abound, especially since no strictures against such fleeting practices exist in the public mind any longer. By the same token, we hear a lot today about the dangers of romantic love, though these dangers are given a decidedly distinctive slant by different writers. On the one hand, Robin Norwood, whose best-selling *Women Who Love Too Much* can be held to be representative for mainstream feminism, diagnoses the "disease of loving too much" to be the modern woman's principal emotional problem as it is held to endanger feminism's very achievement. On the other hand, there are books such as *The Abolition of Marriage: How We Destroy Lasting Love*, in which the more conservative Maggie Gallagher faults

the modern emphasis on romantic love for having replaced old-fashioned marriage with its emphasis on duty and moral obligations.[8] In
a paradoxical way, both in the feminist as well as the conservative
mode, romantic love tends to be viewed as being "dysfunctional"
and a danger to guard against. This somewhat joyless conclusion
receives a particularly sinister twist in the writings of postmodernist
theorists who argue that the increasing fragmentation and disorganization of modern life has led to the rise of a postmodern self characterized by a lack of passion, blankness, pessimism, and cynicism.
Far from loving too much, postmodernists for their part argue that
modern individuals are incapable of forming any lasting deeper relationships. While there may be short-lived physical passion in this
brave new world we are about to enter, love with all its romantic
baggage, they argue, has become a thing of the past. The dwindling
numbers of individuals who still marry for love are held to be guided
by nothing more than fleeting impulses and shifting expectations.
And as we have already had occasion to note, all camps, regardless
of ideological provenance, typically trot out the skyrocketing abortion and divorce rates of the past decades and the increasing frequency of cohabitation as empirical evidence of the changing nature of human relationships.

The voracious media targeting popular consumption—witness the
explosion of Harlequin novels, television soap operas, movies, ad-
vise tracts, and women journals—indicate very contradictory notions about love in one garbled form or another as well. While romantic love may be dysfunctional, indeed, the fact that this luxuriant repository of pulp fiction finds a ready audience suggests that
people can't get enough of it. In an endless stream of songs, novels,
and movies—low brow, high brow, and in between—the same ideas
about love and its woes are repeated over and over again and then
ad nauseam. What is more, by all accounts vast numbers of individuals hunger for reading and hearing not only about love in all its
many guises, but most continue to "fall in love," passionately and
with romantic abandon. In sifting through mountains of literature on
the topic, it appears that the modern individual's capacity for love is
neither diminished nor shallow. Despite the fact that both men and
women may delay in getting married and seem to be more easily
inclined to cohabit and divorce, love continues to blossom in our
midst! All predictions to the contrary, more often than not, romantic

love tends to lead to marriage. And if individuals decide to divorce, most are eager to recommit themselves to another exclusive relationship. Whatever else may be said about modern marriage, one thing is for sure, neither convenience nor interest, but love is its basis.

In an interesting treatise on *Love, Passion, Action: The Meaning of Love and Its Place in Life*, the Australian philosopher Eric Dowling explores why that is so. In an intriguing line of reasoning he tries to show why love, almost by definition, tends to marriage even in a society where "free love" and cohabitation no longer receive the odium they once did.[9] For to love someone truly and deeply, he suggests, calls forth in us the desire for being together with that individual as much and as long as possible. While across cultures and through the ages people have always fallen romantically in love, only in societies where individuals enjoy a modicum of freedom is it possible to move from "falling in love" to taking the vows of marriage freely and, at times, at great resistance.

As will be remembered from the preceding chapter, Peter Laslett and his associates were able to document that the freedom to marry for love has long been one of the distinguishing characteristics of the nuclear conventional family. In Western-style marriage it was love that provided the glue. It not only served to tame insatiable sexual appetites, but it was also love that fused two separate individuals together into a union stronger and more enduring than any other. Already close to four hundred years ago the great English poet John Milton found marriage to be a covenant that can neither be based on economic considerations nor on the performance of duties and obligations alone. It was the freedom to marry the individual one loved and to build a home together that made for the adaptability and strength of the conventional nuclear family through the centuries. To this day, perhaps more than anything else, it is this freedom to marry the one one loves that makes the Western way of life so attractive to individuals whose cultures have traditionally failed to provide them with similar options. It has caught on in societies like contemporary India, China, and Japan. Even in the polygamous societies of Africa, yearnings are reported to spread today that resemble those familiar to Westerners for long. Romantic love and individual choice in marriage is perhaps the single most important export of Western culture!

Yet freedom, ultimately, also implies the recognition of necessity. The innate human need for institutional boundaries makes it inevitable that men and women who freely commit themselves to each other also set limits to their freedom if they desire to preserve their love relationship. Without being aware of it, their sincere desire to make their free, romantic, and, perhaps also passionate love, last, sets men and women off on a course of action in which love becomes habituated, routinized, and, ultimately institutionalized. Institutionalization, almost by definition, superimposes formal as well as informal requirements and it is not accidental that the moral right to liberty was based upon the notion of a person's responsibility for his or her actions. In the Western tradition individuals are thought of as free agents capable of making rational choices because of their awareness of the consequences of their choices. This linkage between choice and responsibility may be harsh and unforgiving, yet it is a linkage that provides the conventional family with the capacity to keep in balance the contradictory impulses flowing from its core principles. As we shall see in the next chapter, the institution of marriage in its Western form is endangered only when individuals are no longer held responsible for their actions.

Marriage in the West then, today as in the past, is based on love, choice, and responsibility. Love is as essential to the modern family as liberty is to Western societies as a whole. As the romantic love that propels individuals to marry matures and changes into a more realistic acceptance of the partners once the honeymoon is over, the solemnity of the marriage vow becomes necessary to admonish individuals to hold fast to their commitment to love and care for each other and their offspring in the long haul of life ahead. The institutionalization of love in marriage engenders a transformation whereby love in its first form is turned into the love of marriage with its strictures, duties and obligations. Even in an age like ours where we have a surfeit of information and instruction on the most minute details of intimate life available, few individuals are aware of the transformations in store for them when they freely chose to set out on the journey of married life. Yet that often-rocky journey will be greatly aided by the love that joined two individuals together to begin with. In the words of Eric Dowling, the philosopher, "The Western family has been described as a haven in a heartless world but it's not the family as such that's the haven but the love that's found in, and only in, the family."[10]

What happens to love in marriage then is an altogether different story. In the humdrum existence of everyday life romantic illusions are bound to fall by the wayside rather sooner than later. Yet if the two individuals who have freely committed themselves to each other are lucky and wise, their love will mature and persist and provide the lasting basis for the life they wish to share. The transformation from romantic love to mature love does not happen by itself nor does it do so in an instant. It is a process that requires work and effort. More often than not it is an incremental process that occurs at levels which may seem meaningless and trivial at times. Though in the postmodern world men and women struggle hard to retain their separate identities within the shared life of marriage and the family, they nonetheless devote a great part of the day to "working" at it. A flourishing marriage counseling industry provides ample documentation for the desire to keep marriages together. According to Barbara Dafoe Whitehead's research, an anti-marriage bias has developed among counseling professionals in recent decades and hence their efforts, she claims in her much discussed *The Divorce Culture*, have been destructive more often than not. [11]

Marriage in the Postmodern Age: Questions of Identity, Freedom, and Equality

When two individuals enter into marriage today they embark on a journey that requires special and, at times, even extraordinary efforts. Whereas in former times the same social life pulsated through the house, the street, and the community and men and women almost automatically knew what married life involved, in our present age things are vastly different. Once firmly embedded in a social world in which there existed little difference between private and public life, today each family constitutes its own segregated subworld that must be constructed, maintained, and, at times, reconstructed on the sole basis of the efforts of the two individuals involved. In an earlier age clear and socially-prescribed roles governing the requirements of marital and familial life made the transition from romantic love to married life relatively easy. In contrast today, individuals are on the one hand continuously compelled to strike a balance between their highly-individualized understandings of what life together involves, and the very different demands posed by their separate lives in the outside world, on the other.

This requisite is greatly complicated by what social scientists call "the pluralization of the worlds of social experience." This term is used to describe the social tendency to divide modern social life into two spheres, the private sphere of the family and the public sphere in which the macro-institutions of work and politics dominate.[12] This division requires modern individuals to perform divergent, and frequently contradictory, social roles in the course of a given day that, depending upon the requirements of the specific social contexts, elicit different skills and forms of attention. While the public sphere demands instrumental, rational, and impersonal forms of conduct, in the private sphere of the family the personal, expressive, and emotional is emphasized. Though these antithetical normative requirements have a way of spilling over from one sphere into the other—that is, sentiments and habits that by rights should be confined to the private make their appearance in the public sphere, and vice versa—there can be little doubt that the pluralization of the lifeworld holds a number of disquieting implications for the conventional family.

For one, there are peculiarly modern problems connected with the effort to make a marriage work in the postmodern age. While the entry into marriage entails practically no legal and few economic problems today, interpersonal and social uncertainties loom large. Each of the spouses arrives at the port of embarkation with their own biographical baggage and expectations and each is required to make adaptations and concessions if the marital enterprise is to come off. Since their personality makeup has already been formed to a large degree during the long years of childhood as well as the history of their separate past experiences, this task is problematized yet further. If the partners backgrounds are fairly similar, and each knows approximately what to expect, the process needs not necessarily be an exacting task. But if husband and wife should come from different social worlds of experience, as is frequently the case in societies as mobile and diverse as ours, then the negotiations between the two can become a long and drawn-out affair and major concessions are in order. The entire venture is further burdened by the absence of clear-cut social understandings of what a family is and what precisely is involved in its construction. Since a good variety of family forms appear to be possible and acceptable today and the boundaries and content of each form are fluid and indeterminate, husbands and wives setting out to weld together the many parts a common life entails are thrown back upon their frequently meager personal resources and knowledge. Despite the wealth of advice literature available, few seem to be able to convey the message that there are not only two individuals involved in this monumental task—the husband and the wife—but that there exists a third, as it were "silent partner" as well in the form of the institution of marriage itself. This institution must be considered as a separate entity that has a life of its own and makes demands in its own rights. To put it more sharply, what becomes essential in making a marriage work today—perhaps even more significantly so than in the past—is the appreciation that the family, ipso facto, is "a thing in itself" (in the Durkheimian sense) that is larger than the individuals involved. It not only requires concessions on the part of all, but must be given attention and care if it is to flourish and become a new and binding reality. To this end, as the British sociologist Bernice Martin has observed, each family must develop its own distinctive rituals ranging from the trivial to the significant. While some, like the adoption of distinctive family signals and the organization of more or less ritualized routines have the potential to turn into family customs ("the Smith's always use a chestnut stuffing in their Thanksgiving turkey," "in times of crisis the Clayton's brew a cup of tea," "Lopes boys never cry," etc.) may be the product of individual idiosyncrasies and accident, others, like the celebration of high holidays and significant family events reflect essential meanings, frequently of religious origin, infuse a higher purpose to the mundane unit of the family. Habits, rituals, customs, and meanings, as they are worked out and given form by the marriage partners, now aid in the creation of the reality of the social world of a particular family.

It is for reasons of this kind that every marriage requires *some form of socialization and resocialization* on the part of those involved regardless of time and place. What is new about marriage in the postmodern age is that individuals have to actively participate in this process rather than accommodate themselves to existing rules of conduct as was the case in earlier times. In other words, the two marriage partners are the architects, the builders, and the owners of their future together. What is more, once this new reality has come into existence, the task is not finished. For the new reality is not posited once and for all, but in order to be maintained, it requires further adaptations to ever-new demands that are brought to it from within and without. In this the family is what sociologists have called "a greedy institution," an institution that requires enormous amounts of energy, devotion, time, and care. The greedy quality of the family expands exponentially when children enter into the picture. For now the needs of children, (grossly underestimated by the unchilded!), test the viability of the unit the husband-wife team has labored to build. The massive presence of children exerts new pressures and demands on parents, and father and mother separately and together have to work out their individual solutions to these new requirements.

For another, there is the distinctly modern problem of how to retain one's personal identity in a marital relationship. It requires not only that each partner accepts and accommodates him or herself to the ways and views of the other, but also makes it necessary that the two will construct a common marital profile. This effort tends to overlay or even block out their previously separate identities. In all mundane matters a particular partner thinks about and acts on in everyday life the thoughts, attitudes, and wishes of the other have to be considered and correlated. In summing up the effect of this process Peter Berger and Hansfried Kellner, two phenomenologically-inclined sociologists, conclude: "In meeting these requirements the identity of each now takes on a new character, having to be constantly matched with that of the other, indeed being typically perceived by people at large as being symbiotically conjoined with the identity of the other."[13] In other words, the very fact of marriage initiates an identity transformation process that few individuals are able to apprehend with any degree of lucidity.

It is this identity-threatening dimension of marriage that has caused so much discomfort and antipathy to modern individuals. While in pre-modern societies a concept of the "self" apart from the roles performed was an alien thing since individual and role were held to be one, the pluralization of the lifeworld in modern times has made it close to impossible for individuals to achieve their identity by means of an unquestioned identification with a particular social role. Not only do modern individuals—men as well as women—perform a great variety of social roles inside and outside of the home in the course of a single day, the marital roles themselves are open to individual interpretation. Inasmuch as individuals are obliged to define and redefine their respective marital roles in an ongoing fashion, marriage has become problematized to a measure unknown to previous generations. The resulting navigations through uncharted waters have turned modern married life into a complicated balancing act which, almost by definition, is bound to proceed in a seesaw fashion.

As if all these new factors were not reason enough to complicate marriage in the modern age, there are yet further challenges to the continued viability of the conventional family. In addition to the broad societal forces that have deprived the conventional family of its traditional functions, the contemporary *Zeitgeist* carried forward by waves of freedom and equality appears to have rendered hopelessly out of step an ethos based on the voluntary curtailment of personal interests and freedom. As noted, it was precisely this limiting function of the conventional family that has evoked much resentment and anger among some highly-educated, middle-class women in the West. Though modern technology and a growing service industry succeeded to increasingly relieve women from many of the demanding chores of the household and provided them with a degree of autonomy and freedom unimagined in an earlier age, intellectuals working in the tradition of Rousseau and Bentham argue to this day that the requirements of the conventional family tend to subvert the principles of freedom and equality upon which life in the postmodern order rests. Not surprisingly the domestic sphere has been turned into the primary arena where the much-flaunted battle for gender equality and liberty is carried out today.

As we shall look at some of the critical issues feeding the culture wars of today in the next chapter, we shall emphasize here merely once more the social fact that the conventional family in no way forces out cherished notions of freedom and equality. As argued earlier, from the vantage point of history there exists not only a fortunate "fit" between the conjugal nuclear family and the structural requirements of the modern industrial system in which a universalistic valuation of skills and individual rights has come to be progressively important.[14] It cannot be repeated often enough that it was this type of family that was the chief carrier of the industrial way of life and its cherished ideals of individual freedom and equality. Norms of fixed hierarchical relationships and the division of labor that serve to guide human behavior in virtually every part of the world to this day were in the Western case weakened over time as a new respect for individual ability and performance gained in importance. Growing demands for skilled and adaptable labor tended to work against traditional barriers of ethnicity, class, and race in the labor market. They made for more egalitarian relations in virtually all spheres of social life in general, but in the microsphere of the household in particular. Here an increase in the equality between husband and wife, on the one hand, and parents and children, on the other, occurred simultaneously to the degree that rigid notions of gender roles appear to have become a thing of the past. In this great transformation process previously available egalitarian tendencies were reinforced and promoted and they continue to be so to this day.

The frequently slow and incremental nature of this process is held to be inadequate by some today. In recent years once diffuse lamentations about gender inequality have given way to a variety of more stringently-defined actions by feminist groups focusing on women's equality in the economy and in politics. In the economic arena their objective has been reduced almost exclusively to maneuvers in favor of income parity (the comparable worth of different job categories to which men and women are typically drawn), to battles against discriminatory hiring practices, and to break through the "glass-ceiling" barrier women encounter in the higher echelons of the corporate world. When it comes to politics, on the other hand, we hear today relatively little about the political discrimination against women but a lot about the need for a more equitable representation of women on the national and local political level. Whenever broader issues of equality are involved, however, the more narrowly-defined special interest groups join rank with a luxuriant variety of feminist groups whose major purpose is to target the gender trap in the household and the culture in general. Concerns vary from doing battle against domestic inequalities flowing from gender specific conceptions of marriage in mainstream feminism that are argued to make for two types of marriages—"his" and "hers"—to the more radical feminism's determined construction of a genderless future. In the first instance, marriage is seen to be in trouble as long as in the prevailing hostile cultural climate men coming from "Mars" do not know how to communicate with women coming from "Venus" and thereby relegate the genders to live in segregated enclaves and universes of discourse.[15] In the second instance, the continuing war against nature expresses itself in ever-new attacks on established gender roles based on notions that female behavior is driven by special propensities for nurture and care. Regardless of these varying nuances, however, all factions continue to be convinced that repressive and unequal family obligations prevent women from achieving their rightful place in a genderless postmodern world.[16] All—including those mainstream feminists who have recently rediscovered the importance of the family in the life of modern women—assume, more or less indiscriminately, that participation in the paid labor force is not only the life-agenda of every woman but that the escape from what Betty Friedan has called the "comfortable concentration camp" into the paid labor force is the only chance for women to achieve autonomy and equality. Inasmuch as this agenda seriously interferes with traditional household and childrearing duties, all factions persistently argue that household and caregiving tasks have to be divided equally between the spouses. Household tasks—mostly prominently those involving the nurture and care of children—that neither spouse is able to attend to due to their respective work obligations, will have to be performed through arrangements with state-subsidized out-of-home providers. It is argued that the hierarchical relationships that inevitably tend to creep up on the domestic level can be prevented by such devices as the establishment of separate discretionary power for men and women (including separate accounts, payment of separate taxes, and the signing of a "marriage contract" that obliges the partners to carry out their predetermined duties).[17]

Facing the alliance of activists for whom the conventional family continues to be a shelter of gross gender equality is today a loose conglomerate of more conservative groupings who defend the traditional family and its lifestyle. They range from a collection of neoconservatives and the centrist Institute for American Values to the ultra-conservative wing represented by the Rockford Institute and the Family Research Council. In recent years these defenders have entered the political arena with a vengeance and the latter group's co-director, Gary Bauer, sought to make the resurrection of traditional family values and the revocation of legal abortion the central issue of his run for presidential election in 2000. Although frequently divided philosophically, all are opposed to their opponents' vision of a genderless future. They are convinced that biology does make for different predispositions in men and women, with women being more inclined to nurture and care and men more pronouncedly oriented toward the external world. Despite these similarities, however, they differ both in emphasis and in their line of argumentation. While the conservative as well as the neoconservative wing of this loose alliance rejects the gender role resocialization program of their political opponents, traditional conservatives rely more exclusively on arguments from biology and bluntly ascribe much of the responsibility for the current crisis in the family to the gender driven agenda of their opponents.[18] The centrist and more moderate neoconservative wing, on the other hand, prefers to stay away from such arguments. In this they reveal something of a libertarian streak as they define marriage as a domestic partnership between economically interdependent men and women which confers certain rights and duties upon each and requires from both parties mutual adjustments to the joint enterprise. Moreover, they prefer that individual couples find marriage arrangements that best suit their inclinations and circumstances.[19] While for hard-line conservatives the term "feminism" is a symbol of everything wrong with contemporary society, neoconservative activists like to see themselves as feminists as well, though they understand their feminism to be in a different key from that of their opponents and think themselves to be more in tune with contemporary realities. Both wings, the neoconservative as well as the paleo-conservative, see little wrong with traditional gender roles and would prefer women to care for their children and home themselves. "True" conservatives tend to see traditional gender roles more in terms of a moral obligation, while neoconservative feminists, for their part, see human beings to greatly differ in what is productive and meaningful and the issue of gender equality, to them, is a matter of individual choice.

The implications of the various political agendas for *social policy* have been expertly analyzed by Neil Gilbert in his *Welfare Justice: Restoring Social Equity.*[20] Though Gilbert is able to show that the support for the traditional hierarchy of male dominance has long fallen by the wayside and, "true" conservatives excepted, equality between the sexes has become a taken-for-granted aspiration in all spheres of social life, he also documents that the Left-liberal policy approach remains firmly wedded to the notion that individual interests must be defined in economic and political terms alone. In their relentless pursuit of a genderless future, he argues, the family re-mains a stumbling block in the realization of a better future. Hence policy experts working in the Left-liberal mode seek to enlist the state and its legal-contractual instruments for bringing about the struc-tural changes they hold to be necessary for this purpose. In the neoconservative understanding, on the other hand, the family is seen to be a covenant based on ties of affection, commitments to share the benefits and burdens of family life, and as a social entity in which the interdependence of male and female relationships figures promi-nently. They hold that the organization of domestic life with regard to work outside of the home is a matter of choice, and issues of basic law aside, individual couples themselves will have to decide how to resolve the tensions arising from the dual commitment to family and work. Though Gilbert's focus is on American domestic politics, it is worth mentioning that the research conducted in a good number of highly-advanced industrial countries other than the United States clearly indicates that the vast majority of Western women would prefer to be given the choice how to handle their family and work problems. From the perspective of an impartial observer who looks at these alternative policy visions in terms of their implications for the stability of family life, it is easy to see why the neoconservative approach is significantly more in harmony with those core principles of the conventional family that have been so instrumental in the life of individuals and society in the past. The sentiments and prefer-ences of the vast majority of contemporary women appear to be in support of such a position to boot.

Has the Modern Family Become a Victim of Destructive Individualism?

The significance of the focus on the inner dynamics of the con-ventional family becomes nowhere more apparent when one exam-ines more closely the currently wildly-fashionable view that the in-dividualism inherent in Western culture has unleashed materialistic tendencies that threaten to devour the institutions upon which it rests. It is further argued that in no other society is this materialistic indi-vidualism more rampant than in the present-day United States. Re-gardless of the political location of the critics and regardless whether their arguments are coached in the language of "social capital," "cul-tural capital," or "moral capital" (i.e., that set of resources inherent in family relations and community organizations that are held to be useful for the cognitive and social development of future citizens), all theorists subscribing to the "revolution in values" school of thought concur that forces external to the family are responsible for the progressive failure of the family as an institution. So, for instance, inspired by the rational actor model of analysis, sociologists like James Coleman have argued that vast transformations in the macrostructure of society have led to the depletion of the social capital upon which the Western industrial order depends.[21] The family's key function to protect its members against the hazards and uncertainties of life, it is argued, were severely fractured, first by the historical shift from household to industrial production and, subsequently by the rise of an individual-based welfare and social security system. Moreover, the recent massive movement of women into the labor market, Coleman in particular argues, has had similarly destructive consequences for the cohesion of the family. Modern men and women are not only claimed to be increasingly unwilling to have children (which would explain the decline of the birthrate), but they are equally argued to be reluctant to invest their resources, time, energy, and emotions in them. Based on the interpretation of large-scale demographic shifts, Coleman and theorists like him arrive at the conclusion that ours is a culture in which a "revolution in values" has sacrificed the needs of children in favor of the celebration of adult needs for liberation, self-fulfillment, and sexual gratification.

Though quite distinct in emphasis and purpose, neoliberal communitarian theorists like Robert Bellah, Amitai Etzioni, and Robert Putnam are equally in agreement that an increasingly untrammeled individualism has spread like wildfire through middle-class America. This new kind of individualism, they submit, must be held responsible for the decline of commitments to those supra-individual moral prerequisites that hold democratic society together.[22] So, for instance, the sociologist Robert Bellah emphasizes that the "cancerous" individualism and greed rampant in the West today must be seen as a consequence of an intolerable disarrangement of "the large structures of the economy and the state," which, by implication, are those of democratic capitalism. Similarly, Amitai Etzioni, another sociologist, exhorts both parents and communities (including the state) to be more mindful of the dimensions of communal life to the same degree that he admonishes communities and the state to promote and undertake public efforts that enable parents to meet their childcare requirements. And Robert Putnam, the Harvard political scientist, argues that the same rampant individualism that is destructive of family and community is likely to have serious consequences for the future of the democratic political order. In more conservative camps one equally encounters numerous expressions of concern with the cultural crisis created by a crass individualism that threatens to suffocate all that is good and noble in American society. The culprit for this turn of events, however, is located in different quarters. For conservatives like William Bennett or Gary Bauer, the genderless ideals of radical feminism and the rapacious embrace of greed and avarice among the career-oriented youth of today are held to have replaced a natural division of labor and gender complementarity. And West European academics, for their part, posit that the culture of modernity itself is the carrier of its own destruction. For the purposes of the present argument it is hardly necessary to elaborate their nuanced arguments yet further. Ultimately, all—Left, center, and Right—arrive at the same conclusion, namely that in the wasteland of suburban middle-class America the grossly self-centered spirit of the marketplace has served to dissipate the social institutions that have made for the country's strength and resolve. All appear to be convinced that contemporary rescue attempts must begin at the top, and all are trying to put pressures on the body politic to do whatever needs to be done, albeit by vastly different methods.

While these varying prognoses of the social and political consequences of the rampant individualism set loose at this point in time may well give pause to many, the question arises of to what degree such views can stand the test of closer scrutiny. As it was the case with other critical issues, when the empirical evidence is examined through the analytical lens of the inner dynamics of the family, it becomes quickly apparent that the core contentions of the various scenarios of doom leave much to be desired. Not only can it be shown that their analytical assumptions rest on shaky ground (they are almost exclusively derived from large-scale survey data), but many of the inferences drawn—over and over again and repeated with blithe certainty—are grossly overstated.

Let us begin with the claim that the self-serving individualism of modern men and women has led to their declining commitment to children. To bolster this argument survey data on the entry of women into the labor market along with data on (1) the decline in the birth-rate, (2) the increasing unwillingness of parents to invest in children, and (3) the neglect of child-raising responsibilities, are typically trotted out and correlated.

As to the first, there is little doubt that the reproduction rate of all industrial societies has sharply declined in the course of the past two hundred years.[23] In the United States, for instance, the number of families with six members and more declined from 49 percent in 1790 to 2.3 percent in 1990.[24] This trend has been a general trend in all highly-industrialized societies, as the cases of Italy, at one end of the globe, and Japan, at the other, clearly show. The "Baby Boom" of the post-World War II period and the mini-baby boom of the 1975 to 1985 period excepted, such fertility reduction rates make eminent sense from a rational actor model perspective. Inasmuch as it can be shown that with increasing prosperity people tend to make a tradeoff between the number of children (quantity) and the time, attention, and investment they allot to them (quality), the "demographic transition" model sketched here in its simplest possible terms appears to hold.[25]

Yet it would be a fatal mistake to assume that the overall decline in the birth rate provides evidence for a retreat from the family. Detailed analyses in countries such as France, Holland, Germany, and the United States make it evident that while people have fewer children, they do have children nonetheless. Instead of having two or more children per family, as it was the norm in the middle part of the twentieth century, by its end, the family with two or less children had become the norm in all industrial societies.[26] This general trend makes exceptions to the rule problematic (such as the increase in single-parent families in the United States where mothers are unmarried, unemployed, and in need of public support), yet it hardly signals a retreat from the family.

It is equally difficult to accept the claim that today's parents tend to invest less in their children in terms of resources, time, and commitment. If the number of years in which parents are involved with the direct care and support of their children can be taken as a measure of their commitment, then the polar opposite is true. While at the turn of the century parents still could expect their children to leave the family household by the time they reached the age of sixteen—in the case of the middle classes at the age of eighteen—this period has been extended to the legally-binding age of eighteen across the class divide. Among the middle classes it is not infrequent to hear the wistful questions today of when the time will mercifully arrive when grown-up children will be on their own, emotionally and financially, and provide exhausted parents with much needed respite from worry and care. By the same token, educational requirements in the postmodern age have dramatically magnified the financial cost of children in all industrial societies,[27] and the fact that middle-class parents have been able to manage financially at all must be attributed to the willingness of wives and mothers to enter and stay in the paid labor force. To be sure, such a course of action takes mothers away from their children, particularly during those early years of childhood when children are most sorely in need of individualized care and stable relationships. The trend opens up a Pandora's box of childcare issues which will be addressed in the next chapter, yet for the moment it is important to appreciate that the mothers' decision to do double duty puts both parents—and not only mothers—under enormous stress that can only be mastered when all the individuals involved are ready and willing to cooperate.

When one turns to the raising of children and their preparation for life in the postindustrial order one cannot but be awed by the degree to which this task exacts an inordinate amount of care, discernment, and time from both parents. It is hard to imagine that anybody else but parents would have the capacity, the persistence, and, above all, the unselfish love to undertake both the chores and the commitment the task requires. The raising of children has developed into something akin to a fine science that propels parents to subject every aspect of the childrearing repertoire to close scrutiny. Questions about what is good for the child—and not the parent—are foremost in the minds of modern fathers and mothers. In an earlier age commentators on childrearing argued that the relationship between parents and children was burdened by a generational conflict that was triggered by the child's quest for greater personal autonomy from their parent's authoritarian tutelage and economic independence. Their contemporary critical counterparts, in contrast, bewail that children have gained too much personal autonomy and discretionary financial powers. Parents are said to have lost control over their children's consumption behavior, including most dramatically, the consumption of television programs and ever-novel varieties of entertainment. There is hardly any middle-class household today where parents and children do not have words over the amount of time allotted to the watching of television, the purchase of records, discs, and all sorts of other paraphernalia that may appear to be vile and dangerous to a generation socialized into different tastes. Yet the conventional fathers and mothers of today are well aware of the potential dangers a loss in parental control entails and they try with all their might to strike a fair balance between the exercise of necessary controls and leaving their children with enough space for personal autonomy. While there can be little doubt that parental control has been considerably weakened when compared to a hundred years ago, the trend in and of itself does not indicate that those parents who take their conventional pedagogical obligations seriously have lost their power to influence and shape their children ethically and morally. Thomas Luckmann's earlier cited pathbreaking study on "Morality in Everyday Life" documents in great detail how the transmission of norms and values continues to occur in the everyday situation of the contemporary conventional household.

By the same token, cross-national studies indicate that despite a considerable increase in geographical and occupational mobility the communication between parents and children tends to be intensive, positive, and, in most cases, lifelong.[28] If we are to trust the studies available, it appears that with the exception of divorced fathers and the stormy teenage years during which children are determined to find their own way, today's parents and children have succeeded in establishing an intimate and lifelong relationship built on reciprocal love and trust. Most children love their parents, like to be with them, and even admire them. Moreover, once children have left the parental household, the communication between parents and children does not come to an end. Though they no longer live together in a common household, the two generations continue to be in close contact with each other, seek advice from each other, and take it for granted that they can rely upon each other whenever the occasion should arise.

When one steps back from the cacophony of laments about the decline of child well-being and family decline and looks at current family trends through more sober eyes, one cannot fail to reach a conclusion that is strikingly at odds with the received wisdom of the day. As long as families adhere to the core requirements of the conventional family, they persevere and even thrive, and that despite the many internal and external challenges posed by our complicated age. That is to say, a family based upon the love of two individuals for each other, who enter into a partnership defined by the mutual obligations of a conventional marriage, with both partners committed to each other and the well-being of their children, is not only the option most ordinary people prefer, but also the best guarantee for individuals to weather the taunting challenges of modern life. When they abandon the lifestyle the conventional family ideal encourages, families tend to have more problems, and for longer periods of time.

To return to the start of the argument: while confirming the claims of the demographic transition model that with increasing prosperity people tend to make a trade-off between the number of children and the time and attention they afford them, these findings hardly provide evidence for the claim that a revolution in values has occurred in the society at large. Modern men and women have neither collectively decided that children are a nuisance, nor does the majority see them as standing in the way of career and pleasure. When one considers the extraordinary cost children entail in terms of emotions, time, energy, and money, one is impressed by the degree of commitment that motivates modern men and women to voluntarily enter into a state of virtual slavery for years, if not decades, to come. Perhaps more than in any other period in history, they are willing to make personal sacrifices in favor of a life that revolves around the family.

In the light of these realities, currently popular attacks on the rise of a rampant individualism, egotism, and "consumerism" have a decidedly hollow ring. One of the chief reasons for this jarring note must be located in the reluctance of cultural observers to acknowledge that despite the many structural and ideational shifts that have occurred in the course of the past one hundred years or so, the conventional family with its middle-class companionate marriage ideal and its child-centered focus is alive and comparatively well today.

New Myths and Old Realities

To sum up the foregoing discussion, a century of change that transformed social life in major ways has also transformed many of the features once held to be typical of the conventional family. As it is the case with other major institutions, the family's structure has become more permeable and the considerable control it once exercised over the life of its individual members was weakened commensurably. As the family weakened, there also occurred significant shifts away from relying upon the family in all aspects of life. In the course of the twentieth century we see a growing reliance upon the state to organize, finance, and deliver efforts for the care and education of children, the protection of the weak, and the promotion of the interests of those who, for whatever reasons, have been discriminated against in the past. Yet this new porousness of the conventional family should not be judged to have been as debilitating as conservatives today are prone to do, nor should it be understood as the harbinger of the coming of a brave new postmodern order that excites the visionary Left. The weakening of the family's control over its members, the blurring of gender roles and hierarchies inside and outside of the family, and the insistence upon the equal treatment of women in politics and the labor market neither implies an end to social cohesion and the imminent loss of social order, nor does it spell the death of the modern family in its conventional form. Despite the shifts in the daily organization of family life, changes such as they have occurred remain—by and large—on the surface and do not violate the core principles of this type of family. The powerful lure of perennial visions of unencumbered individualism, personal freedom, and abstract notions of equality not withstanding, the vast majority of modern men and women continue to be committed to a freedom bounded by love, an individual autonomy tempered by an overarching commitment to the family, and to endeavors to ascertain the equal treatment of all its members in a commonsensical way.

After more than fifty years of viewing the family as standing on its last legs, with individuals reported to defect from it in droves, it has become obvious for anyone who has eyes to see that the family continues to play a paramount role in the lives of most ordinary people. Though modified in form and weakened in its claim to authority, the core principles of the conventional family have remained largely intact. The latest empirical evidence confirms with "hard" statistical data that even in the volatile climate of the present-day United States, educated Americans—middle America, that is—have largely remained immune to the scourge of illegitimacy (only about 2 to 4 percent of the children born to non-Latino white college graduates are born out of wedlock); statistically, divorce, while often a personal tragedy and admittedly high, has never been as severe a social problem in this particular group as among socially more marginal groups, and there exist indirect signs—as, for instance, in the strongly conservative shift in the received wisdom about the effects of divorce on children—that the divorce rate is likely to drop. Moreover, more traditional forms of childrearing among this group seem to have made a strong comeback, even among the countercultural generation of the sixties. And although the evidence is still anecdotal, it suggests that career mothers are beginning to figure out ways to stay home with their young children, even if it means the interruption of their careers for a while.[29] More and more young women appear to be looking for husbands who are willing to share in the tasks of childrearing and housekeeping, just as more and more young husbands have not only accepted that their wives work and have careers of their own, but they also have adjusted their own careers to realize this common goal. While it may not always be easy to maintain a balance between a commitment to both the family and a career, it appears to be within the reach of most.

In other words, neither the pressures emanating from a rapidly-changing economy nor the messages from radical critics advocating the superiority of all sorts of new lifestyles seem to have greatly succeeded in devalidating the ideal of a life which revolves around a family which in structure and style resembles the conventional nuclear family to an amazing degree. The old virtues may be in retreat in some areas of contemporary life, yet they still animate modern minds when it comes to the organization of their personal lives. Though there has been much hand wringing and accusation that today's Westerners are less loving and more egoistic than their predecessors, more hedonistic and narcissistic, the evidence marshaled in support of such positions has always rested on shaky grounds. More remarkably even, in an age where neither tradition nor economic necessity forces people to marry and lead a conventional way of life, most have neither abandoned the modern family nor the conventional lifestyle associated with it. To be sure, some marginal social groups were more affected by the consequences of the prevailing shifts than others and it is true that the family as an institution is faced by a good number of somber challenges. Yet contrary to postmodern and conservative myths, modern individuals have neither lost their capacity for love, trust, and commitment nor have they abandoned the family. Today the lifeplans of a new generation of men and women may well be compared to a model that resembles a team of mountain climbers who must be prepared to have careers that require flexibility, lateral moves, and lengthy rests at base camps if they wish to attain something of a "good life," which, almost by definition, revolves around the family.

To sum up the argument of this chapter one may conclude with the observation that the core features of the conventional family today, as in the past, rest upon ideals of freedom, equality, and love. These three core components blend into each other in a multiplicity of ways. Contrary to the high priest of individualism, John Stuart Mill, for whom "the only freedom which deserves the name, is that of pursuing our own good in our own way," the family perspective central to this book permits us to see how modern individuals as free agents are tempered by the timeless love of two individuals for each other, their children, and the world they together seek to build. People who love, freely put themselves voluntarily into bondage. This bondage cannot be compared with life in a prison or worse, as it has become so fashionable to aver today. In the words of Eric Dowling, the philosopher, whom we had occasion to quote earlier, "Everybody who is freely devoted to the service of someone they love gets pleasure and satisfaction without seeking it as the freely given care and devotion of mother to child shows." And after all has been considered, one can only agree with Dowling's concluding insight that "it is not so much that love flourishes in the nuclear family, it is the nuclear family flourishes where there is love."[30]

Modern men and women have come to realize that the lover who encourages independence in the ones he loves, who helps them do their own things, improves the quality of their love and thereby the quality of their life together. If that love should get lost, the family is in trouble, just as the family will be in trouble when all kinds of extraneous demands and expectations are brought to it from the outside. But more about this in the next chapter.

Notes

1.   In poll after poll, most Americans (more than 90 percent) express their desire to get married, and that percentage has held steady for close to forty years now. What is more, in recent surveys close to three-fourths of Americans expressed their belief that, extreme circumstances excepted, marriage is a lifelong commitment that should not be broken.

2.   Peter Reutter, "The Continued Utility of Mythical Numbers," *The Public Interest,* 74, spring 1984. More recently, in his much acclaimed *Damned Lies and* Statistics (Berkeley: University of California Press, 2001), the sociologist Joel Best wrote a fascinating book about the abuse statistical data lend themselves to.

3.   See the "Social Security and the Family" debate between John Mueller vs. Allan C. Carlson, *Policy Review* 42 (Fall 1987).

4.   Michael Young and Peter Willmott, *Family and Kinship in East London* (London: Pelican, l962); Mary Jo Bane et al., *Here to Stay, The American Family in the Twentieth Century* (New York: Basic Books, 1978).

5.   Thomas Luckmann, *Moral im Alltag* (Gueterslohe, Germany: Verlag Bertelsmann Stiftung, 1998).

6.   Herbert Marcuse, *Eros and Civilization* (Boston: Little Brown, 1966).

7.   In defense of the Victorians, however, it should be noted that their emphasis on "virtues" was largely motivated by their zeal to root out the vestiges of drunkenness, thriftlessness, and shunning of family responsibilities they assumed to be responsible for the "beastly" state of England's poor.

8.   Maggie Gallagher, *The Abolition of Marriage: How We Destroy Lasting Love* (New York: Regnery, 1997).

9.   Edwin Dowling, *Love, Passion, Action: The Meaning of Love and Its Place in Life* (Melbourne, Australia: Australian Scholarly Publishing, 1995).

10.   Ibid., p. 76.

11.   Barbara Dafoe Whitehead, op.cit.

12.   Peter L. Berger, Brigitte Berger, and Hansfried Kellner, *The Homeless Mind: Modernization and Consciousness* (New York: Random House, 1973).

13.   See Peter Berger and Hansfried Kellner, "Marriage and the Construction of Reality," *Diogenes* 46:1-13, 1964.

14.   W. J. Goode, *World Revolution and Family Patterns* (New York: Free Press, l96l); and Bernard Rosen, *The Industrial Connection* (New York: Aldine, 1982).

15.   See, for instance, John Gray, *Men Are from Mars, Women Are from Venus* (New York: Harper Collins, 1992).

16.   Susan Okin, *Justice, Gender, and the Family* (New York: Basic Books, 1992); and Cynthia Fuchs Epstein, "Toward a Family Policy: Changes in Mothers' Lives" in Andrew Cherlin (ed.), *The Changing American Family and Public Policy* (Washington, D.C.: Urban Institute Press, 1988).

17.   A good summary of the divergent view on marriage can be found in Neil Gilbert, *Welfare Justice: Restoring Social Equity* (New Have: Yale University Press, 1995, chapter 1, "Strengthening Family: Social Security and Gender Equality").

18.   See the various publications of Gary Bauer and Lou Dobson in *Focus on the Family,* a publication of the Family Research Council.

19.   Elizabeth Fox-Genovese, "Feminist Rights, Individualist Wrongs" *Tikkun* 7, no. 3 (1992): 29–34.

20.   Neil Gilbert, *Welfare Justice:Restoring Social Equity* (New Haven: Yale University Press, l995).

21.   James Coleman, *Rational Choice Theory: Advocacy and Critique* (Beverly Hills and London: Sage, 1992).

22.   Robert Bellah, et al., *The Habits of the Heart: Individualism and Commitment in American Life* (Berkeley, Ca.: University of California Press, 1985); and Robert Bellah, et al., *The Good Society* (Berkeley, Ca.: University of California Press, 1992); Amitai Etzioni, *Socio-Economics: Towards a New Synthesis* (New York: M.E. Sharpe, 1993); Robert D. Putnam, *Bowling Alone: The Collapse and Revival of American Community* (New York: Simon & Schuster, 2000).

23. Simon Kuznets, "Notes on Demographic Change," in Martin Fedlstein (ed.), *The American Economy in Transition* (Chicago: University of Chicago Press, 1980).

24. U.S. Bureau of the Census, Household and Family, *Current Population Series* no. 447, 6.

25. Gary S. Becker, *A Treatise on the Family* (Cambridge, Mass.: Harvard University Press 1981).

26. Hans Bertram, *Familien Leben* (Guertersloh: Verlag Bertelsmann Stiftung, 1997) and S. Kusnetz, op.cit.

27. For the United States see Victor R. Fuchs and Diane M. Reklis, "America's Children: Economic Perspectives and Policy Options," *Science* 255, 1992; For Germany see Hans Bertram, op.cit, 1997, chapter 4,2 and 4,3.

28. Bertram, op.cit., 1997, Leopold Rosenmayer, op.cit., 1980.

29. See Charles Murray, *Commentary*, November 1995.

30. Eric Dowling, op.cit., p. 98.

6

Critical Contemporary Issues

In recent years more and more people have become convinced that the well-being of the public life lays at the mercy of private life. Many have started to realize that a good number of today's pressing social problems can only be solved by means of a restoration of the conventional nuclear family to its once pivotal role. Yet it remains an open question precisely which of the changes in the organization of contemporary private life must be held responsible for recurring symptoms of social disorganization. All too frequently social problems have been ill defined and poorly measured and recent events have made it painfully evident that a considerable amount of caution is advisable when one makes use of the mass of studies floating about today. Even in those cases where we can pinpoint a clearly identifiable cause, it is hard to decide which of the proposed policy mechanisms have the capacity to do more good than harm. What is more, when one takes stock of current policy thinking one cannot help wonder whether the proposed measures stand in a realistic relationship to the targeted problems. If the recovery of the dynamic role of the family is the ultimate goal, past experiences have taught us that it will neither do to disregard deep-seated human propensities and values, nor will it be useful to pretend that a return to some family practices of the past is all that desirable.

In this policy limbo it would seem that the insights that can be gleaned from the deliberations in the previous chapters have the capacity to provide a guide through the maze of claims and counter-claims swirling around diverse family issues without falling prey to an unqualified partisanship for either of the positions dominating the public discussions today. When one looks at critical family issues through the theoretical lens developed in this book, many of the hotly-debated problems take on a decidedly different hue from those bandied about by either of the camps participating in the current debate. At the risk of violating the political sensibilities of all, in what follows an attempt is made to explore some of the policy issues held to be critical for the future of the family in the same spirit of objectivity that has guided the writing of this book. We shall start with the definition of the contemporary family and explore to what degree a redefinition is in order.

The Definition of the Contemporary Family

As every good policy researcher knows, policy issues—along with the data that can be marshaled in their support—depend largely upon the definitions used. Few instances reveal the accuracy of this basic research postulate more dramatically than the official definition of the contemporary family. Since the 1960s we have heard a lot about how the "traditional" two-parent family is about to disappear, how marriage has just become one lifestyle choice among many possible others, and how modern men and women no longer wish to marry and commit themselves to each other and their children. The claim that children are no longer likely to grow up in a two-parent family, in particular, has caused much hand wringing and confusion and it seems that practically every few months another report sees the light of day that gives proof to the claim that the conventional two-parent family is about to disappear. The major result of all this turmoil around the family has led to a redefinition of the family along the lines of what Daniel Patrick Moynihan has called "defining deviancy down." When applied to contemporary domestic arrangements, Moynihan's revealing term reflects the public capitulation to behaviors that once were regarded as acutely offensive, immoral, or illegal, as acceptable and normal. As we have seen in an earlier chapter, with the redefinition of the family from the two-parent conventional "family" to "families" of the most varied compositions, the family was turned into just another lifestyle choice. With this redefinition, policymakers who sought to bring public policy in line with changing private practices gave the official signal that the family in its conventional form had reached its end.

Yet some twenty years later prophecies of the disappearance of the two-parent family appear to be way off the mark. As the data cited in the previous chapter show, despite a century of far-reaching shifts in the ways we organize our lives, the conventional family in practice and ideal continues to be dominant in broad segments of the population today. And those segments who have deviated from its core behavioral features have done so to their own detriment. Hence it is of some importance to start our review of critical issues with taking a look at the data that have led to this fateful redefinition.

In a remarkable essay, "Myths of Marriage and Family," the Australian family specialist Moira Eastman presents us with an informed analysis of why a myth has come to prevail in her country that only a small portion of children live in an intact household with their biological parents (less than one third, as the myth claims, over against the more than 80 percent of Australian children who actually do). Her account of the spread of this myth is paradigmatic as it reveals that the same tendencies to misinterpret the wealth of available data are at work in other Western societies, including the United States, as well. Some of the misperceptions, Eastman argues, are due to problems in definition. Extremely narrow and confusing definitions of "family," "traditional family," and "two-parent family" tend to slide imperceptibly into each other with the consequence that only a family with a bread-winner husband, homemaker wife, and dependent children living in the home can qualify to fit the "traditional family" definition. This statistically precise definition excludes those families where mothers work in the paid labor force, fathers work part-time, or one of the parents has died but who, by any other definition, would also qualify for that label.

There are yet further factors that add to the confusion. So for instance, the lack to differentiate between "household" and "family" has the consequence that people living alone in a household are counted as constituting a family. And if this were not enough, an even greater confusion is generated by the tendency to totally ignore the fact that all families follow a lifecycle of their own. "What could be more 'traditional' than the life cycle?" Eastman asks and she goes on to argue "The phase of rearing young children is only one part of the life cycle. How then, can passing through the various stages of that life cycle—being single and childless, being a childless couple, being the parents of children over age seventeen who are living at home (parents of nondependent children are routinely used in statistics to bolster the "non-traditional families" sector), being the parents of adult children who have left home, being a widow or widower, being grandparents—be counted as evidence of not being in a 'traditional family'?" And summing up her argument she concludes that "it is ridiculous to define the family only in terms of one phase of that life cycle and conclude, on the basis of the fact that just under half of all households do not include dependent children that the traditional family has almost disappeared."[1]

In the United States we are confronted with a similar confusion. To this very day one set of social scientists contradicts the measurements of the proportion of children growing up in two-parent families used by those of another: some claim that a mere 7 percent of all American families fit the conventional two-parent model, while others point to a national figure of 73 percent—that is the vast majority of American children—live in a home with married parents. In an age that relies for every public measure to be taken almost exclusively on the basis of research data and statistical measurements this discrepancy is vast and truly remarkable. When one tries to find out why this is so, one discovers that analogous to the Australian case described by Moira Eastman the disparity is a consequence of the definition of the conventional family. The 7 percent figure is based upon the narrowest definition of the conventional family imaginable. Only those families qualify to be subsumed under that label that consist *exactly* of a father, a mother, and two (not one or three or four) children and then only if "the mother never works, not even for two weeks during the year helping out with the Christmas rush at the post office."[2] Moreover, such a narrow definition disregards the fact that though it has become common practice for mothers to work outside of the home on a full or part-time basis, by far the majority can still claim to lead a conventional family life in which husband and wife are committed to each other and the welfare of their children.

A further example of the contentious nature of the current family debate can be found in the mixed reception accorded to the most recent U.S. Bureau of the Census report that shows that the trend of the 1990s is in the direction of people settling down into families of married couples with children. So, for instance, it is reported that the rapid growth in the percentage of single-parent families and in family breakdown has halted and the claim is made that there exist clear indications that after two decades of upheaval families in America have become more stable again.[3] While more conservative policymakers hail the Census report as a welcome documentation of the effect of their many efforts on behalf of the traditional family, more liberal scholars claim that "It's really nonsense to say the traditional family is coming back because there is no such thing as a traditional family any more" and they conclude with apocadictic certainty that "We can't pretend that families haven't irreversibly changed, and it does a disservice to everybody . . . to suggest it's otherwise."[4]

In the face of this persisting battle over the definition of the family it will not suffice to simply observe that the use of questionable statistics has provided ideological and material opportunities to a wide spectrum of special interest groups who greatly benefit from defining what could be a problem as essentially normal. Fluctuations in the organization of private lives are not new in history. Provided that a given family system has the capacity to be adaptable to new environmental challenges, readjustments typically occur after periods of dislocation and disorientation. This was historically the case in the aftermath of wars in all societies we know of, just as it was, and continues to be, the case in the migration of large groups of people to new and alien environments. To confuse such normal readjustment processes with genuine and lasting shifts in behavior and values to the degree that an official redefinition of the family becomes necessary is not only premature, but also perilous. Not only does such a redefinition do little to reduce the problems held to have been a consequence of the earlier definition, but all too frequently serves to magnify and distort the same.

When social historians of the future look back at the twentieth century they will no doubt point to the demographic trends and the weakening of social processes that made for the porousness of the institution of the conventional family. And, to some degree, they will be right. As noted in the previous chapter, the conventional family has become smaller in size, significantly less stable, men and women get married and start having children later, gender roles have become considerably more flexible both inside and outside of the home, and, as an institution, the conventional family has received considerable competition from not so conventional arrangements of living together. Yet the real story was and always will be the degree to which the conventional family has managed to withstand the onslaught of these macro pressures. Despite the much heralded sexual revolution, modern men and women continue to fall in love, and this love propels them to choose marriage rather than alternative lifestyles as the ideal way to organize their life; marriage itself is expected to be enduring, to entail economic and emotional reciprocity, and to rest upon the mutual dependence of the spouses upon each other; children and their well-being remain central; and with some modifications, a more or less conventional family life— in which the home and common activities figure prominently— remains the preferred choice for most. As we have gleaned from previous chapters, it was the genius of the modern nuclear family to be able to adapt itself to an ever-changing environment without damage to its constitutive features. While there is simply no possibility to recapture all the many nuanced expressions of the family lifestyle of the past—structure, values, and ideals included—the fact that most moderns continue to order their lives along the lines of its core elements tells us a lot about the symbiotic relationship that exists between modern society and the modern family. In other words, though the details of conventional family life have changed considerably during the past century, in its essentials the institution of the conventional family has weathered the onslaughts against it remarkably well. No matter how many changes have taken place and no matter how momentous the challenges to the family may have been, life in the modern era seems to require the kind of social arrangement the conventional family appears to be able to provide in special measure. More than any other institutional arrangement it seems to be able to correspond to the deeper yearnings of modern men and women for an exclusive, lasting relationship based upon love and mutual commitment while at the same time being able to respond to the values of individuality, equality, and personal freedom they cherish to such a high degree. The modern family continues to revolve around the welfare and progress of children and while it can accommodate voluntary childlessness, it is the combination of the modern family's reproductive function and its unique socializing capacity that endows the institution with its central social mission. This central and foremost role brings to the fore not only the reasons why the institution of the modern family is more than a *modus operandi* for the channeling of the most elemental properties of human nature but also why the family in its conventional form persists to be an institution that deserves to be protected and promoted by the modern state.

Cohabitation: A Danger to the Institution of the Family?

Between 1970 and 1994, according to the U.S. Bureau of the Census, the number of people who live together as unmarried couples has increased from 523,000 to 3.6 million, and among persons under the age of 25, there occurred a fifteenfold increase.[5] In view of these figures the question arises of to what degree they contradict the much more benign vision of contemporary marriage argued in this book.

Aside from the current demographic trend to marry late and to divorce more readily (two factors that tend to skew the numbers of people living alone) it has become commonplace among family specialists and demographers to argue that marriage may be going out of fashion. Recent research data collected in selected European countries and the United States appear to support the argument that it has become attractive to a growing number of men and women to enter into some informal arrangement to live together without state-registered ceremonies marking the beginning and the end of marriage. Cohabitation, the specialists' term for this arrangement, is argued to be the outgrowth of a trend in which two consenting adults either do not wish to make the commitment marriage requires, or who, for whatever reason, may not be in a position to do so. That observation is correct to a point. Yet it is important to keep in mind that while cohabitation appears to be a growing phenomenon, indeed, the percentage of couples living together is relatively small if compared to the number of people who actually take the leap into marriage.

Moreover, if one takes a closer look at records of interviews with men and women who actually practice cohabitation, one finds that even in an age alleged to be adverse to making long-lasting commitments the most ardently expressed wish of most is the wish to marry eventually. Consequently, professional sociologists talk frequently about cohabitation as an informal arrangement in a sex tolerant age where two people want to find out how they get on when living together. In most instances individuals enter into cohabitation with a view to marriage if they prove themselves loving and compatible. It is for that reason that it may be argued that cohabitation should be viewed as "trial marriages" (in contradistinction to casual mating) which more often than not leads to marriage. All the data available give evidence that the wish for having a family still ranks highest among all possible lifestyle choices available. The vast majority of

Americans, more than 90 percent, continue to fall in love, get married, and have children. Hence, this writer, like other sociologists, is inclined to suggest that rather than viewing the growth in the proportion of a man and a woman living together informally as signaling an end of marriage, the practice of cohabitation should be viewed as a new part of the courtship pattern or as a prelude to marriage. To be sure, the institution of marriage as such has become less rigid and prescriptive in specific aspects, yet it most certainly has not lost its attraction and power, and, in all likelihood, never will.

Two highly-respected researchers, Barbara Dafoe Whitehead and David Popenoe, reported recently that there is reason to believe that cohabitation tends to lead to a significantly higher rate of marriage breakup. They speculate that cohabitation slowly erodes both the people's ability to make firm commitments as well as their faith in the institution of marriage itself.[6] Their report adds credence to a 1997 study released by the National Center for Health Statistics that found that among couples whose marriages dissolved within five years, 22 percent had lived together before marriage, while 10 percent had not. If future research should confirm this correlation, the rather optimistic view of cohabitation argued here would be seriously put into question. At this point in time, however, this writer is inclined to doubt that the correlation will hold up for the simple reason that the divorce rate has stabilized since 1980 while the rate of cohabitation has gone up. If such a direct correlation would exist, one could plausibly expect that with increasing cohabitation the divorce rate would accelerate. And this has not happened. While one may have many reservations about the institutionalization of cohabitation, as I for one have, there simply does not exist conclusive evidence as of yet that cohabitation itself tends to lead to divorce.

This position should not be taken as a blanket endorsement of cohabitation. Particularly for the young, cohabitation poses unexpected problems and uncertainties. Appearances to the contrary, today's young neither dispose over the necessary emotional maturity nor do they have the practical wisdom to handle fluid relationships and situations for which codes of behavior have not yet been established. An almost pathetic insecurity and vulnerability is hidden under the hard veneer of modern savoir-faire. This fragility does not inspire confidence that the sexual passions of starry-eyed youngsters can withstand the challenges of the unscripted social relationship called cohabitation. When mature and responsible adults opt for this alternative form of living together, one would assume that they know what they are doing. The young, in contrast, most certainly do not. Yet regardless of whatever preference one may have in the matter of cohabitation, at this point in time there exists little evidence that cohabitation as such is harmful to the continuity of the institution of the conventional family.

Gay Marriage

Some homosexual men and women, who hope that their loving attachments will be recognized as genuine marriages in law and public opinion, have with increasing urgency argued that if they live together like conventionally-married couples then they are entitled to the same positive recognition of their relationships. To withhold such recognition, they claim, would amount to blatant discrimination. Making use of all the legislative tools available in a liberal democratic society, representatives of gay organizations are currently trying to base their case on the argument that the acceptance of gay marriage amounts to little more than a long-overdue legal recognition that homosexual men and women are living in domestic arrangements akin to the family.

This argument, however logical it may seem, overlooks the fact that just as it is impossible to discuss the family without reference to marriage, it is also impossible to discuss the family as if it were nothing more than marriage. As we have seen, the family, almost by definition and regardless of history, location, and form, revolves around the procreation and upbringing of children. Any other definition, I would insist, is just a play with words. It is this central mission that fuses private behavior with public needs and makes the institution of the family a matter of public concern. To hold to this definition does not suggest that homosexual love is less deep or valid than love between heterosexual men and women. Yet their living together does not start a train of events that should be of general public interest. Theirs is an essentially private relationship if contrasted with heterosexual marriage and the latter's fusion of the private with the public and the personal with the social. While this line of reasoning does not equip us to judge the merits of such public practices that enable homosexual couples to register as "domestic partners"—as it is for instance done in San Francisco, Boston,

and Cambridge, Massachusetts and the state of New Hampshire today—it allows us to state unequivocally that homosexual domestic
arrangements have little to do with the procreation and care of children and hence they cannot be subsumed under the definition of the
family offered here. To be sure, marriage is a creature of the law
wherever we go. In modern Western societies, however, marriage
laws deal less with marriage itself than with the disposition of children and property in case of separation or divorce. There is no earthly
reason why in the absence of children the state should get involved
in the entirely private arrangements between two adults, be they now
hetero- or homosexual.

There are a number of arguments that are frequently advanced by
gay activists today that beg an answer. So, for instance, they ask, if
children are so central, why do heterosexual couples who are either
too old or do not intend to have children still receive the state's im-
primatur of marriage, whereas homosexual couples do not, or why
homosexual couples who are willing to adopt children and commit
themselves to their well-being are not worthy of being called a family. These are admittedly difficult questions that defy an easy solution. Yet in view of everything else we know, they do not devalidate
the argument that the state should without embarrassment provide a
privileged status to the conventional family consisting of a man and
a woman. Both law and public policy should accommodate people
who deviate from this norm and appropriate measures should be put
into place to safeguard the rights of people who prefer to live an
unconventional life. But none of these lifestyle choices deserves the
same status as the conventional family does.

Abortion

Abortion, the measure to terminate pregnancy, has been practiced
legally and illegally as long as we can remember. In a 1998 report
the Alan Guttmacher Institute, America's principal research organization in the fight for a woman's legal right to birth control, including abortion, estimated that of the estimated 210 million pregnancies occurring each year globally, 38 percent are unintentional and
22 percent end in abortion. While abortion laws differ from country
to country, the rate of abortions is fairly similar in comparable countries. Developing countries are typically more restrictive than developed countries, though the highest abortion rates are reported to

occur today in the countries of Eastern Europe (90 abortions per 1,000 women of childbearing age over against 11 per 1,000 women in Western Europe, and that despite similar abortion laws).[7]

While an argument can be made that the abortion issue transcends the family in many ways, in current American debates on the family, abortion has become a central, if not the central family issue. Though having been a contentious issue through the ages, fraught with grave moral and legal complexities, nowhere has it become more divisive than in the present-day United States where the 1973 Supreme Court's ruling in *Roe v. Wade* granted women the constitutional right to end pregnancies at will. This decision engendered not only a fiercely-waged battle over the sanctity of human life, but is said to have altered the American moral landscape as well.

The way the 1973 abortion law was legally framed unwittingly served to tear apart the uneasy moral consensus that had existed prior to that date for some time. In subsequent years the hardened political oratory of organized "pro-life" and "pro-choice" action groups succeeded to create a cultural climate in which "pro-life" activists compare the defenders of abortion rights to the butchers of the Holocaust and "pro-choice" advocates, in turn, accuse their opponents of violating the fundamental human rights of women and of incitement to murder. To this day their diametrically opposed positions are based on theoretically contradictory doctrines. Each of the warring factions is determined to use the coercive powers of the state to have their respective understanding of the issue encoded in the law, with pro-choice groups working hard to uphold existing abortion rights and pro-life activists passionately toiling for their reversal to the *status quo ante*.

In an earlier book co-authored with Peter Berger more than fifteen years ago I made the attempt to work out a moral position on abortion that made common cause neither with the pro-life nor the pro-abortion side in the abortion debate. The Supreme Court ruling, it was argued at the time, had turned the mystery of human life into a simplistic issue of individual rights. It opened the doors to contentious and essentially unsolvable arguments about "whose" life we are talking about, that of the mother or that of the child, with the pro-life side arguing on behalf of the rights of the fetus and their opponents defending a woman's right to decide whether to abort or not. As the subsequent years have shown, this is precisely where the debate has been stuck to this day. Our very different position then—as today—was based on what we called "the postulate of ignorance," that is to say, an ignorance about the very foundations of human existence. We argued, since we do not know what human nature is, we cannot know when a human being begins (and by the same token, when a human being ceases to be). Hence modern men and women find themselves in the unenviable position that they do not know with any measure of certainty at what point in the nine-month cycle the human fetus should be regarded as a *person*. We concluded our argument that whether we like it or not, making moral judgments about abortion today presupposes, by necessity, a postulate of ignorance.

Yet while the postulate of ignorance implies a rejection of both the flat and amoral utilitarian calculations of the pro-abortion advocates *as well* as the divinely revealed claims of the pro-life camp, it does not imply that we are unable to make any judgments at all. With the exception of those who base their moral judgments on allegedly inspired certitude, very few people find it believable to say that a fertilized ovum fifteen minutes after conception constitutes a human person entitled to all the protections of the law. Curiously, even those who would say this and who regard the abortion of this fertilized ovum as an act of murder are unlikely to want the act punished as if it were murder in the ordinary sense. It would seem that even they would look upon such an abortion as murder of a special sort. On the other hand, very few people who are not complete fanatics on the pro-abortion side would maintain that a fetus carried for nine months is a human person fifteen minutes after delivery but *not* fifteen minutes before. This side of doctrinaire certitude, then, it would seem that our ignorance diminishes as we approach the beginning and the end of the normal period of pregnancy; our ignorance is greatest when a reasonable dividing line is to be drawn through this period.

At the time we wrote that book, we strongly felt that both a moral and a practical lesson could be drawn from our considerations based on the postulate of ignorance. Not much has changed since then. Close to three decades after the enactment of the controversial Supreme Court ruling, the issue of abortion continues to defy the possibility that a moral consensus can be reached by law. Much to the chagrin of feminists and liberals it has become only all too evident that the law can express and codify morality, but it cannot create morality. Many people continue to be rigorously opposed to the abortion laws as currently framed.

By the same token, it has also become evident that the abortion issue cannot be resolved by science, as pro-life activists had hoped. Recent evidence—such as DNA code, brainwaves, and other biological properties of the fetus—strongly suggests that human life begins much earlier than it was thought in the past, and the advances of medical technology have made it possible to sustain human life from early in the gestation period. Yet despite all of this, we do not see any indications to date that public opinion is about to move into a complete pro-life direction. All we can see is a society in danger of being torn apart over this most central issue of human life. This need not be so. Obviously, the fetus is human life and has the potential for personhood. Yet the issue is not life, but personhood. The law protects human persons, but not human life. The "postulate of ignorance" pertains precisely to the question of at what point does human life become a person. The new evidence does not and cannot settle this question.

Already the terminology used in the current debate reflects the depth of the confusion on abortion. The term "pro-choice" is confusing for it begs the question at what point we are dealing with a person. Obviously a woman does not have the right to strangle her week-old baby, yet the question remains up to what point does she have the right to choose to abort the fetus? Equally confusing is the widely-accepted norm of a woman's right to her own body. No one disputes that. The issue is whether the fetus is part of her body or someone else's body. The same confusion reigns in the "pro-life" camp. As indicated earlier, it confuses life with the notion of personhood. An appendix is also human life, yet it does not follow that one should not have an appendectomy.

The virulent and lasting clash over abortion has made it clear that this issue is more than a question of abstract morality and law. As Emile Durkheim has taught us, all human communities are moral communities that are created and maintained by an ongoing consensus about central issues of social life. Wherever that consensus breaks down, coercion must take its place. If the breakdown is at the margin, the moral community at the center is preserved by coercing the offender responsible for the breakdown by the various means at its disposal. But when the breakdown threatens the center itself, as the abortion issue does, the ordinary instruments of "marginal" coercion fail to solve the problem and more massive coercion becomes necessary. This is always a difficult matter, but it is doubly difficult in a democracy whose very political legitimacy depends upon consensus. In order to preserve what Arthur Schlesinger has called "the vital center," it becomes necessary that some kind of compromise on abortion be reached.

If one take's the postulate of ignorance to heart, it should not be as impossible to achieve such a consensus as the warring factions tend to assume. In fact, a good argument can be made that a broad moral consensus on abortion has already been reached at this point in time. So, for instance, polls consistently show that while the vast majority of Americans think abortion to be morally wrong, especially when it is used as a form of birth control, most continue to be firmly in favor of the legal right to abortion. Despite the evidence on the beginning of sustainable human life, only a small percentage is willing to return it to its earlier outlaw status. Even though the catapulting rates of teenage pregnancy and abortion of the past two decades have greatly dismayed many Americans, relatively few feel this worrisome trend to be sufficient cause for the repeal of *Roe v. Wade*. At the same time, however, most people feel deeply conflicted over a woman's unfettered right to abort. So, for instance, the debate over late second trimester or "partial-birth" abortion indicates that by far the majority of men and women are loath to endorse such radical last-ditch efforts at terminating unwanted pregnancies.

Beyond these key points, there exist a number of issues, where it is not quite clear yet how a moral consensus will emerge as reliable data are notoriously hard to come by. Among these two issues, parental notification in cases of teenage pregnancies and the morality of the legalization of RU 486, the so-called day-after drug a woman can apply herself, figure most prominently.

Mindful of the postulate of ignorance the moral and practical lessons that may be drawn from all that has been said here suggest that public policy on issues of abortion should move in directions as follows:

- *Abortion should remain a legal, though limited device to terminate pregnancy*. A fairly narrow time frame (certainly not beyond the first trimester and probably below it) needs to be set that most certainly excludes the controversial procedure of partial abortion. In other words, the law should, as far as possible within the bounds of concern for the mother and other family members, lean to the side of conservatism in presuming at what point the fetus is to be regarded as a person. But within the time frame set, the decision on whether to abort or not must be left to the pregnant woman who proceeds in consultation with whomever *she* chooses. The reasons for this should be clear enough. If the fetus is presumed to be a person, neither the mother nor any other individual has the right to kill that person. But if the fetus is presumed not to be a person, it must be presumed to be part of the pregnant woman's body, in which case no one else has the right to make decisions regarding it.

- *Abortion should be discouraged whenever possible and alternatives to abortion be encouraged.* While the already existing network of homes for unwed mothers and adoption services are a good beginning, more and better thought-through services are needed: in the case of unwed mothers marriage should be encouraged whenever possible and be economically rewarded by means of a revision of the tax code that favors marriage.

- *In the vast majority of cases parental notification should be a legal requirement.* The parental notification laws passed by twenty-four states (as of June 1999) give evidence of the return of a modicum of commonsense on this matter that is less tricky than is commonly argued. Though parental notification considerably reinforces parental rights, it also opens up new channels of communication between parents and their children and reinforces the sense of mutual obligation and love between them. It is quite absurd to consider that for liability purposes parental permission is required in virtually every run-of-the mill activity a teenager is engaged in outside of the home (such as permission to participate in school outings, non-academic programs, and extracurricular activities) but is held to be inoperative in such a crucial matter that deals with the consequences of an unwanted pregnancy, which, incidentally, involves far more than the medical intervention itself. The fact that according to a California study two-thirds of pregnant teenage girls were impregnated by adult men not only opens up questions of statutory rape and who is to press charges, but drives home the need for parental protection with great poignancy.

The ruling reached by the Supreme Court in a series of decisions that bars states from giving parents of unwed minors an absolute veto over abortions and further ruling that parental consent cannot be required without providing some alternative (such as letting the

minor seek a judge's approval instead) makes good sense and should
not be changed

- *The use of tax dollars for the financing of abortions here and
  abroad should be guided by the same commonsense rules on abortion spelled out above.*

- *RU 486, the much-debated "day-after" pill, should be made available as soon as possible.* While there may be some as yet unforeseen side effects, its availability promises to make the depersonal-
  ized act of abortion less gruesome. How the responsible supervision of RU 486 will be administered and handled is still an open
  question that needs to be handled with exceeding care.

A final point on this haunting and tragic topic is in order: the
postulate of ignorance suggests that it is time to abandon the stance
of dogmatic arrogance, the shrill tone, the habit of threatening mutual excommunication from the ranks of the truly humane, that has
accompanied the abortion debate for years. It is as irresponsible to
talk of a "culture of death" as it is irresponsible to talk about a
woman's constitutionally guaranteed unfettered right to abortion (a
right which according to the Center for Reproductive Law and Policy,
the major national pro-abortion litigating organization, should extend to include even minor children). The evidence available suggests that the great majority of people have already been able to
arrive at an ethically-defensible position despite the absence of any
responsible public guidance. Their refusal to see the abortion issue
in Manichaen terms of good and evil appears to be based on convic-
tions that come close to the postulate of ignorance advocated here.
In practical terms this means that while *Roe v. Wade* may be defended in some aspects, it certainly cannot be defended in others
and some revision of this fateful legislation is clearly indicated.

Family and Work

With the movement of ever-larger numbers of mothers into the
world of work and the decision of many to stay in the labor force
during the demanding early childhood years, three sets of questions
have come to the fore: first, there is the basic issue of gender equality
in labor force earning, which is a basic human rights issue; next, there
is the issue of "what women want," which, by and large, is an issue
that pits family values against women's interests; and finally, there is

the child-development issue that poses the question of to what degree a mother's decision to stay in the labor force while her children are young has negative implications for the normal development of her children. Since close to three-quarters of American mothers are currently employed (and 64.8 percent of mothers with children six years old or younger worked outside the home according to a 1997 Bureau of Labor Statistics survey), these three sets of questions have come to intersect with one another in a particularly sharp manner. They also have become a perennial topic of public controversy and debate. For economists like Gary Becker, who claim that the economic dictum that divided labor is efficient labor applies also to marriage and family organization.[8] Yet from the perspective of this book the issue of motherhood and work, while interconnected, is neither an economic nor a labor issue but one of personal values and judgment. Hence each of the themes connected to family and work must be reviewed separately.

The issue *of gender equality in labor force earnings* has incited much dispute in recent years and not among feminists alone. As already pointed out, it is an issue of basic human rights and deserves to be treated as such. From the outset any discussion about equal payment for equal work has to acknowledge the fact that no matter in which way economic analysts cut their data, the evidence shows that in all advanced industrial societies there continue to exist clear gender differences in economic earnings despite the fact that women have come a very long way economically, indeed. At the same time, the data also show unequivocally that much of the gender differences in earnings in nearly all occupational categories is linked to factors of marital status, lifecycle, and family characteristics. Hence these two sets of data indicate that what at first blush appears to be a human-rights issue, becomes a family issue at closer scrutiny. To put it differently, while at the turn of the twentieth century the women of advanced industrial societies have an abundance of work and career opportunities before them—indeed, never-married women appear to have achieved wage parity with never-married men in virtually every job category examined (single never-married women even seem to have a wage advantage over men)—the fact remains that the gender income ratio varies widely by marital status. So, for instance, the wage gap for married, separated, divorced, and widowed men and women remains quite large. On the average, working, married-spouse-present women earn considerably less than men and the number and spacing of children tend to affect the gender wage differential even further. Moreover, factors of the lifecycle kick in as well. While only a small wage differential occurs in early work phases, it expands over the working life until about age forty, at which point wage differentials begin to decline.[9]

In sum, while there can be no doubt that regardless of the gender economic inequality that existed in the past, women have made enormous strides toward closing the gender earning gap. Whatever differences persist in advanced industrial societies today must largely be explained in terms of family-related factors. Present-day young women are investing in human capital skills at unprecedented proportions (the most recent data show that women are about to outdistance men in schooling and the acquisition of professional credentials) and most enter the labor market with expectations of staying in it even after they marry and have children. Yet the decision to have a family puts them at a slight, though noticeable, economic disadvantage. Hence, political liberals and feminists try with considerable ingenuity to put political measures in place that they hope will counterbalance all earnings inequities caused by family commitments. Their proposals range from the reassessment of the comparable worth of jobs to family leave, the establishment and support of public childcare, and the enactment of child subsidies. As to be expected, all have been perennial issues of public debate and continue to be so to this day. The fundamental question of at what point private choices become public obligations, however, remains an open issue.

The empirically indisputable fact that present-day wage disparities are caused by family commitments obliges us to take a closer look at the question of what women value more: a career or having a family. And here the data appear to be quite clear. After one has sifted through the mountains of data and published treatese about what women want, and tries to control for all sorts of tangible and intangible variables, one is left with the rock bottom insight that while the talents and interests of women are roughly comparable to those of men and that women value their independence and their earning capacities in equal measure, they tend to value a life that includes a husband, children, and a home even more. This insight needs some explaining.

The reasons why women enter the paid labor force are many. They range from the wish to make money to a quest for autonomy and self-fulfillment, from escape from boredom to genuine career interests, from desires for individual achievement to those for making a contribution to knowledge and society at large. Some, though surprisingly few, opt for having only a career or only staying home. The majority hopes that they can "have it all": a family as well as a career.

The contradictory nature of their values places women into a peculiar quandary: since they are committed to participate and stay in the labor force—and there is little indication that this will change significantly anytime soon—few are ready to quit the workplace on a permanent basis when family needs arise. Most oscillate between periods in which desires for personal autonomy and having a career are replaced by even more powerful desires for having a family and a home. What is more, this observed shift in priorities might be repeated more than once during the lifetime of a given individual. Indeed, women go to enormous lengths to prepare themselves for a career only to discover that in most cases love for children and for family comes to take precedence. Yet once they think they have the most pressing needs of their children under control, the lure of the workplace gains in strength once more. Juggling between two worlds, that of the family and that of work, they frequently make heroic efforts to do justice to both. While desperately clinging to their autonomy, they also try to contribute to the emotional and economic well-being of their families. Some take up jobs that permit easy exit from and reentry into the labor market or that offer opportunities for part-time and flexible work schedules, and that, in sum, can be reconciled to a lifeplan in which the family plays a central role. Others embark on a life of doing double-shift duty. In some rough-botched union between work and family most women, in their own ways, seek to make the best of a very difficult situation. They love their husbands, children, and their larger family by extension, but will sometimes sacrifice them all a bit (along with themselves) for the sake of work and vice versa. The new lifestyle of turn-of-the-twentieth-century mothers involves more often than not the necessity to secure some forms of paid childcare, though they worry a great deal whether they are doing right by their children.

The fact that women of all social classes are today much less likely to slow down for their pregnancies and much more likely to continue to stay in the paid labor force has provided cultural pundits of all stripes with yet further evidence of an uncaring individualism on the rise. This is an accusation that reveals a good deal of historical ignorance. Today's widespread tendency to assume that the needs of small children can only be taken care of by their biological mothers is of fairly recent origin. To be sure, households in the past were larger than today, with all sorts of people milling about who could be expected to keep an eye on children and for the more well-to-do the help of servants was always available. Yet as the French social historian Jacques Donzelot has been able to document, two major considerations—the one relating to the mind and the other to the body—encouraged the rising middle classes of the nineteenth century to become directly involved in the rearing and socialization of their offspring. Leaving the care of children to servants and other hired help, as it had been the custom of the well-to-do for long, was increasingly rejected as it was held to have a deleterious influence on a child's acquisition of desirable character traits. At the same time, an emerging core of medical professionals spread the message that the hygienic and nutritional requirements of children could best be met within a parentally-controlled environment. This growing conviction about what it takes to prepare children to acquire the habits and the knowledge to compete in an increasingly achievement-oriented social order turned childrearing into the rising bourgeoisie's primary task and mission.[10] It was precisely this preoccupation with the child's well-being and development that set the socialization patterns of the growing middle classes apart from those of the aristocracy as well as the lower social ranks. With their reliance upon servants, wet nurses, tutors, and the like, the first continued the soon-to-be discredited routines of the past, while the latter neither had the leisure nor the knowledge to reflect upon the inadequacies of the childrearing practices of a rapidly disappearing rural world. And for those who had migrated to the cities in search of work and opportunities, it would take some time to adapt themselves fully to the new patterns of modern social life.

At the same time, it is of some importance to keep in mind that although a child's well-being and progress was central in the life of the middle-class family, at no time did the nurture and socialization of children exclusively depend upon the biological mother. Those who could afford it made use of the services of hired help in easing the pressures created by the routine tasks of middle-class house-keeping and when it came to their children's schooling, it was taken for granted that only the most competent and inspired teachers would do. The all-encompassing mission of childrearing and housekeeping, incidentally, provided middle-class women with new forms of power and status. In the vast literature on the evolving childrearing practices in the modern order, Frank Musgrove's *Youth and the Social Order*, stands out for the clarity of the description of the social class dimensions in this area of social life.[11]

Though it has become fashionable of late to pronounce that it "takes a village" to raise a child, the combined insights of two hundred years show that it takes a great deal more to bring up a child in the contemporary industrial world than a reliance on the simple networks of an imagined rural past. Modern childrearing is an exceedingly strenuous, time-consuming, and intellectually-demanding task. It demands the establishment of a congenial yet organized family environment in which children are allowed to develop their very individual talents and competencies and to acquire those virtues that make for decency and responsibility. By definition almost, it must be very individualistically oriented and it requires the love and devotion only a father and a mother are able to provide.

That said, it is also of great importance to recognize that the shift in contemporary work patterns that takes both fathers and mothers out of the home does not imply that today's parents do not meet their parental duties. Though it was admittedly easier in the past to provide for a stable home and close supervision when mothers stayed at home, the new practices do not invariably spell doom for the future of their children. Perhaps even more than their predecessors, present-day mothers and fathers are striving with all the strength and means at their disposal to ensure their children's well-being, happiness, and progress. So, for instance, the amount of time mothers report spending with their children in 1998 has not changed over the past forty years despite the fact that three-fourths of the women with children younger than eighteen are in the workforce today.[12] In reply to the question of how working mothers find the time, the author of the study, the sociologist Suzanne Bianchi, reports that today's working mothers sleep five or six hours less each week than mothers who are not employed and they have up to twelve fewer hours of free time at their personal disposal. They also vacuum less. In other words, today's conventional parents are in no way different from their predecessors, if anything, they work harder and worry more. To be sure, to provide for their children's physical and supervisory needs, many may have to rely to a greater degree upon out-of-the home care by strangers over whom they may have little control. Yet to a far greater degree than in the past, today's parents are fully cognizant of the importance of providing children with sound fundamentals, the capacity for individual judgment, and with skills and values that prepare them for an unknown future. Some current parental practices and arrangements may appear to be misguided to some present-day observers. Yet as long as they meet basic requirements for safety and individualized care and an abundance of love, the current problematization of every childrearing issue flowing from a mother's decision to stay in the labor force and have a career appears to be superfluous.

While the question of motherhood and work is thus a non-issue from the point-of view of this book, the third issue in the motherhood and work debate, the effect of out-of-home care upon young children, is a much more difficult question to tackle. To be sure, mothers have always worked. Yet work in highly-advanced industrial societies takes women—like men—out of the house, and whether they like it or not today's mothers and fathers must rely on the help of others in the care of their preschool-aged children during the long stretches of the day when both are at work. The search for responsible and loving childcare remains a major headache for most working parents. And therein, of course, lies the rub.

Childcare

During the past two decades all sorts of family support mechanisms have been put into place and a growing number of businesses and organizations have made daycare facilities and flexible work-time schedules available to parents in their employ. Moreover, projections about the changing nature of work in the postindustrial world suggest that in the not too distant future growing numbers of fathers and mothers will have the option to work out of their own homes. While such predicted changes would undoubtedly provide parents with some welcome respite from present-day childcare dilemmas, they are not available to most as of yet. As the percentage of married mothers in the workforce has nearly doubled over the last thirty years (from 38 percent in 1969 to 68 percent in 1996 according to a 1999 White House Economic Advisers study), the question of how to secure safe and affordable childcare remains a major problem for most parents.

As the record shows, different social groups have found different solutions for their childcare dilemmas. Some, like the ethnic poor, prefer to rely upon the help of relatives, neighbors, and friends, while more affluent career-oriented upper-middle-class couples try to secure affordable and competent in-home care in the form of retaining the services of nannies, housekeepers, au-pairs, and the like. A sizable number of middle-class mothers seem to have been motivated to temporarily interrupt their careers, work part-time, make use of flextime schedules, form neighborhood childcare collectives, and a good number of couples are reported to have been able to arrange for work schedules that make it possible that either one of them can take charge in successive turns. Yet the reported more than four million preschool children who were enrolled in an assortment of public and private daycare and nursery school arrangements in 1996 (over against a mere 500,000 in 1964) make it abundantly evident that a rapidly-increasing number of parents feel compelled to make use of the services of the expanding out-of-home childcare industry.[13] For most fathers or mothers the option to stay at home to care for their preschool children appears to be increasingly less realistic. Such a decision would imply a drastic reduction in the family's living standards that only a few feel to be able to afford.

No matter how today's parents manage to solve their childcare dilemma, virtually all learn fairly quickly that the substitute arrangements they are able to put together are less than ideal. Questions on how best to solve this predicament remain a major source of dispute between the spouses. Though all take considerable pains to find suitable arrangements, most feel caught between a rock and a hard place. Even books deliberately designed to put a stop to endless debates about a mother's "proper" place, have not done much to lessen the ambivalent feelings harassed and guilt-ridden mothers hold.[14] Concerns for the well-being of their children are simply too deeply rooted and the messages floating about are too mixed and frequently ominous to allow for peace of mind. It does not come as a surprise then that a small, though significant, number of the more affluent young

mothers have been recently reported to have decided to either interrupt their careers or to reduce their working hours during the devel-
opmentally-critical years of childhood. In the vanguard of this most
recent trend appear to be mostly professional women who prefer to
abide by the parental equivalent of the Hippocratic oath that fore-
sight is better than hindsight.

Yet this latest trend, however laudable it may be, does not necessarily imply that those mothers who continue to work during their
children's infancy are likely to inflict lasting damage on their children. When one scans the available evidence on the effect of
nonparental care on small children, one is led to conclude that the
avalanche of research has failed to date to document that the children of working mothers do less well than those of mothers who
stay at home. After decades of sifting and weighing the available
data, Frank F. Furstenberg, one of the leading "hard-nosed" American family researchers, arrives at the conclusion that it is not at all
clear that parents are paying less attention to their children today
than in the past: "True, parents are less likely to be in the home than
they were a generation or two ago. It is easy to forget, however, that
earlier in this century death, demanding work conditions, illness,
and most of all large families meant that children were frequently
put in the care of relatives, neighbors, strangers, or left on their own.
Smaller family size, more flexible work schedules, and greater commitment to child care responsibilities, lower requirements and standards for domestic duties, and greater opportunities to subcontract
household responsibilities could be offsetting some of the deficit in
the time available to children created by women's work outside the
home."[15] All things considered then, the problematization of
childcare arrangements contemporary parents are able to put into
place appears to be unnecessary if not misplaced.

As every parent knows, there is no one right way to bring up a
child. Aside from innate propensities that differ from child to child,
much depends upon a complex bundle of factors that shape a particular child's disposition. The constellation of conditions influenc-
ing the circumstances under which a child is reared, the degree and
type of parental commitment, as well as the parent's capacity to ad-
just their parenting skills to the ever-changing needs of the growing
child, just to mention the most obvious, have an effect on the development of a particular child. As pointed out in an earlier chapter,

once the minimal imperatives of childrearing have been met (as, for instance, the imperatives of physical protection, stability of structure, interaction, love, and a modicum of consistency in the ways in which these basic requirements are carried out), one may squabble about the significance of one factor over and against that of another. It may very well be, as John Bowlby and other psychologists insist, that in the earliest phases of a child's life the biological mother is the "natural" agent for the "bonding" a small child needs for his or her emotional growth. It may also be that the emotionally-stunting "separation" effects Bowlby so hauntingly describes are severe and lasting. By the same token, the findings that small children in out-of-home daycare perform a higher degree of aggressive acts than those that spent the first three years in the home sound intuitively plausible as well.[16] Yet different sets of researchers have also been able to trace the negative effects mothers have on their child's development, when they overly identified with their children, when they mollycoddle and dote on them, or try to control every aspect of their lives. Although researchers are in fundamental agreement that a one-on-one relationship in a stable, structured, and nurturing environment is best suited to meeting the basic needs of the early stages of individual development, it is impossible to determine the degree to which a particular child is dependent upon the exclusive care of his or her biological mother. Little is also known whether a father, or any other committed adult for that matter, can serve as a long-term substitute "mother figure" for creditably meeting the unrelenting and seemingly insatiable needs of the infant with the kind of love, patience, and consistency that seems to come so natural to most mothers. While experience has taught us that the love and care parents are able to give willingly and joyously—and free of charge to boot—are hard to replace and even the most virulent defender of out-of-home care must admit (reluctantly perhaps) that a child's biological parents are the obvious candidates for this job, it is hard to determine the degree to which surrogate maternal care may disadvantage a child permanently. It is no longer uncommon that one reads that today's young fathers have risen to the challenges of infant care. Fathers of all social classes have been reported to be increasingly willing to take equal share in the rearing of their children and though the evidence is largely anecdotal still, they appear to get considerable satisfaction and joy from these no longer novel male tasks.

Though the popular media continues to spread confusing messages, earlier controversies over the wisdom to send children to preschool programs have all but disappeared in the professional literature. Commonsense tells us that even within the same family children are likely to respond differently to the same childcare arrangements. While it may be possible in individual cases to determine the degree to which out-of-home childcare may be good for both mother and child, or may be good for the mother and not so good for the child, or may be good for neither, it is next to impossible to arrive at a generally-binding formula for childrearing. At the end of the day, most parents know only too well that it is impossible to guard against all imaginable dangers. By the same token, every responsible childcare analyst knows that the inner dynamics of a particular family make it impossible for outsiders to decide which type of childcare arrangement will work for one family over that of another. To be a parent implies that one has to take risks. Though it may be a hard fact for modern men and women to accept, children present them with the most formidable reality principle they are ever likely to encounter.

What are the *policy implications* of this brief summary review of the modern-day childcare dilemma? I think they are rather simple and straightforward.

- First, *childcare today is no longer a liberal or conservative issue.* In contrast to close to three decades of fierce political battles between feminists and their allies on the liberal left and traditionalists on the political right, with the first calling for greater governmental involvement in the affairs of the family and the second resisting many, if not most, of such policy initiatives many, though not all, of the once hotly debated childcare issues have been superseded by newly-created realities. In retrospect one often wonders what all the fuss was about. In the aftermath of the turbulence of the 1979 Carter White House Conference on the Family all sorts of family support mechanisms were either revised or new ones, like the Family and Medical Leave Act of 1993, put into place with far less fanfare and discord. With the government already involved in a great number of childcare issues—issues of nutrition, health and safety regulations, provisions of child support for the poor, and so forth—the issue today is no longer the question of the government's involvement in the affairs of the family but rather what form this involvement should take.

- Second, and perhaps most importantly, it has to be reconfirmed that guarding *the welfare of their children is the parents' moral and legal obligation and right*. The vast majority of today's parents take it for granted that they, and they alone, are morally and legally responsible for their own children. As the record shows, most will fight with all the power at their disposal to defend the parental rights they justifiably hold to be natural.

Like generations of parents before them, the present generation of parents is likely to discover that there are no shortcuts in the business of raising children just as they are likely to discover that there exist no clear-cut formulas for successful childrearing. Only a very small number of fathers and mothers are willing to abdicate their parental responsibilities. If, however, it can be conclusively demonstrated that fathers or mothers do not or cannot meet their parental obligations, it falls upon the agencies of the state to assume parental responsibilities on "the best interest of the child" principle.

- Third, caring parents of all social classes need all the information on childcare that is available. Some sort of public referral system should be made available that allows parents to consult with experts about which type of care may be best suited for a particular child. *In collecting the necessary information on childcare resources and making it available to the largest number of people, free of charge, governmental agencies could be of considerable help to families.*

- Fourth, *as childcare becomes de-politicized, mechanisms should be made available that allow the greatest amount of choice to parents*. As in all other issues of public policy, the same political-philosophical divide typical of American political life resurfaces in the public debate over the future of childcare as well. Those Left of center continue to turn to the authority of the state—on all levels of politics, the federal, the state, as well as the local—to provide for a wide spectrum of child support and care services, to finance and supervise them, while those of the political Right prefer the use of tax mechanisms and advocate the subcontraction of childcare services through the marketplace. To put it differently, one set of participants in the policy debate find their ideal policy model represented in North European countries such as Sweden, where childcare is considered to be a major responsibility of the state, whereas the other set voices considerable opposition to most public solutions.

In the United States, where more mothers work than in other comparably-advanced industrial societies, the combination of pressures flowing from career requirements, the difficulty of finding competent and affordable childcare, and the uncertainty of research findings on the effects of out-of-the-home care, the present-day childcare dilemma defies an easy solution. Add to these already formidable factors the pluralistic nature of American society as well as the country's own brand of democratic politics, and one is led to conclude that there simply are no uniformly binding formulas available. Given these facts and weigh them against the real needs of ever larger numbers of American families, it seems indicated that some mechanism be established by and through the state that allows for the widest choice possible. Those families where either husband or wife wish to dedicate themselves to the care of their small children should have the option to do so; those who wish to make use of relatives, neighbors, or a patchwork of arrangements in which husband and wife take turns, or where sets of young couples organize childcare collaborative, or where parents turn to out-of-home care either in the workplace or in the many privately and publicly organized childcare centers, should have the option to do so as well. In a pluralistic society like the United States, where individual initiative and responsibility are woven into the cultural fabric, where concerned parents in all walks of life seek to do the best for their children in the different ways and understandings at their disposal, *it would seem that mechanisms of tax credits (rather than a childcare voucher system) are the preferred option.*[17]

Marriage and Divorce

A marriage based upon a fusion between romantic love, personal freedom, and the egalitarian partnership of spouses is by definition more vulnerable to pressures and tensions than a marriage understood to be either an insoluble sacrament or a marriage held together by the forces of convention and community. Already, close to four hundred years ago, John Milton in *The Doctrine and Discipline of Divorce,* argued forcefully: "Where love cannot be, there can be left of wedlock nothing but the empty husk of an outside matrimony, as undelightful and unpleasing to God as any other kind of hypocrisy."[18] Yet even after divorce became legally available in the Protestant countries of Europe in the early modern period, few men and women sought it for some time to come. And the Roman Church with its doctrine of the sanctity of the marriage vow continues to passionately oppose divorce down to our own days, even though it too recognizes through the concept of annulment that some marriages cannot be saved. For a long time public sentiments and social mores simply were too firmly entrenched to make divorce an easy way out of a relationship that either partner—or both—held to have "irretrievably broken down."[19]

In the course of the twentieth century, however, one can observe a steady increase in the number of men and women turning to divorce to end that special relationship they had entered into with high hopes and expectations. Regardless whether that increase was the result of our changing visions about marriage or whether it was a consequence of burgeoning notions of individual autonomy, once visions of a life unencumbered by obligations and restraints became increasingly attractive, dissatisfaction with the married state also became ever more pronounced and divorce started to run rampant. A mass of statistics reflects the sorry evolution of cultural propensities in which an act once held to be a last desperate measure became for many the solution of choice for putting an end to a situation held to be unpalatable.

Whatever the pathways of cause and effect may have been, there is little doubt that the very same features that made Western conventional marriage so unique, also made for its fragility. With the arrival of the sixties cultural revolution, this fragility became ever more accentuated. When one adds to this the effect of the waning power of parents to control their maturing children and the fact that entry into and exit from marriage is no longer subject to economic considerations, then we arrive at a juncture in history where Western-type marriage has become unhooked from its once powerful social moorings. When one further adds to the cauldron of culturally destabilizing forces the fact that all Western legal systems since the 1960s saw fit to permit nonpunitive exit from marriage regardless of the consideration of the welfare of third parties—that is, children—it does not come as a surprise that the gates were opened to the "divorce revolution" we hear so much about today.

According to Barbara Dafoe Whitehead, whose book *The Divorce Culture* has garnered much attention recently, the explosion in the divorce rate in the seventies was mainly the product of the confluence of two forces: the relentless promotion of values of personal liberation and self-realization and the triumph of the therapeutic vision of life we had occasion to talk about already in an earlier chapter.[20]

Though Barbara Whitehead's tendency to attribute the catapulting divorce rates of the seventies and eighties to the eruption of countercultural notions of self-actualization and personal happiness may be overstated, it is hard to dispute her argument that these notions served to undermine yet further whatever sanctions on marital breakup had remained in place until then. Under the influence of a surfeit of publications and advice from advocates of ideas of dubious psychological origin, many started to abandon an ethic of obligation to others in favor of an obligation to the self. In certain quarters, she argues, a tendency ensconced itself to judge family bonds in terms of "their capacity to promote individual fulfillment and personal growth." It is one of Whitehead's notable achievements that she was not only able to bring the middle-class provenance of the seventies divorce revolution to the fore but that she also was able to draw our attention to the devastating consequences divorce had on children.

Other observers in England, Australia, and the United States, like Norman Barry, Bryce J. Christensen, and Mary Ann Glendon, are more inclined to attribute the divorce revolution to changes in the law, and here most prominently to the enactment of "no-fault" divorce in the early 1970s. Changes in the rules for ending marriage affect the rules for marriage, these scholars argue, and with such changes the intentions and expectations of those who enter it are inevitably changed as well. As a consequence, no-fault divorce changed marriage as a union of a man and a woman held to be qualitatively different from any other private or public arrangement or contract into something that is not much more than "just as piece of paper." They somberly conclude that in absolving individuals from the moral and actual consequences of their actions, no-fault divorce laws, enacted with the intent to "reduce the acrimony, hostility, and bitterness in the divorce process," brought about, unintentionally perhaps, a perversion of the moral ideals of liberty. They deplore that in taking such a course, the supposedly value-neutral state indirectly encourages individuals to follow their impulses and desires, while absorbing the costs that accrue from their broken marital promises.[21] And yet others, mostly those with postmodernist inclinations, aver that high divorce rates coupled with measured increases in cohabitation, late marriages, and the rate of the never-married are the inevitable consequence of shifting realities that signal the end of marriage as we know it. As discussed in an earlier chapter, in embracing this shift the last set of advocates are predisposed to promote the "normalization" of divorce as an inevitable feature of modern life.

No matter what side one comes down on, it is safe to say that recent history has demonstrated that divorce is much more than just a matter between a man and a woman who no longer can abide the idea of being be married to each other. While divorce may be the right and necessary remedy for fundamentally-flawed marriages and, at times, even be a good thing for individual divorcing partners—a proposition seriously questioned by Whitehead, for instance—there can be little doubt that divorce takes a heavy toll on children. After two decades of disputes and data collection, the evidence from a slew of studies undeniably confirms that the fallout from divorce has had an indisputable devastating and long-lasting effect upon the children of divorce. [22] Similar to children growing up in other single-parent households, their standard of living typically plunged, their parental relationships unraveled, their loyalties were severely tested, and many were emotionally traumatized. Equally important, the data also show that divorce in most cases deprived children of the environmental stability they sorely need for the development of stable selves and their progress in school and life beyond. Many children appeared to have greater difficulties in achieving educational and occupational goals and they were more insecure and plagued by more severe emotional and behavioral problems than their counterparts growing up in intact families. While it is of some importance to note that not all divorced mothers and their children suffer equally from the trauma of divorce—highly-educated and psychologically-strong and resilient mothers seem to have been more or less successful in minimizing some of the effects of divorce on their children—divorce remains an emotional and economic burden for most nonetheless. Although a sizable number of divorced women with children remarry, the available scant evidence on the development of children in "reconstituted" families is not precisely encouraging to date.

To make a long and rather depressing story short, the recently secured evidence confirms what ordinary people have known for long: all children, and small children in particular, are in need of a stable family in which mothers and fathers take on the many and ever-changing tasks of childrearing actively, lovingly, and persistently. In other words, children need the kind of care that the much maligned conventional nuclear family appears to be so uniquely equipped to provide. Legislators and politicians, who by virtue of their responsibilities are forced to deal with the fallout from divorce in the explosion of welfare dependency, have in recent years redis-covered the value of a conventional family lifestyle as well. Although the divorce rates themselves have somewhat stabilized since the 1980s, in the words of the British economist Patricia Morgan, di-vorce remains in the minds of many "a great destroyer that is eating the heart out of society as well as savaging children's lives."[23] Like others before her, she urges that marriage in England be restored to its privileged and respected legal status and that legally-binding rules be created that protect the interests of wives and children in cases where marital termination seems to be inevitable. The United States as well has witnessed the rise of a "defense of marriage" movement in recent years whose proud achievement was the 1996 "Defense of Marriage" Congressional Act. In recent years there has been much talk about the introduction of two types of marriages: one that offers easy entrance and exit, and the other, the more serious "covenant marriage," that permits divorce only for very serious reasons and then after extensive counseling and a long waiting period.

The growing calls to restore marriage to its past unchallenged status raise a throng of questions that have no easy answer. Aside from approbations to reclaim the cultural ideal of marital perma-nence, the burgeoning movement for the restoration of marriage has to face up to two competing concepts of marriage: marriage as a contract or marriage as a vow. That is to say, the movement is con-fronted with the question of to what degree marriage is a private or a public matter. While marriage can be seen as a binding commitment under either canon or traditional civil law, with the enactment of no-fault divorce, the courts officially declared the marriage vow as non-binding and hence divorce was turned into a private matter that could be obtained at will. Regardless of the specific mechanisms entailed in the various restoration proposals, all imply that a basic reconfiguration of the meaning of marriage is in order. All agree that there has to be a move away from a mere contractual understanding of marriage that can be repudiated at will and without penalty and back to the traditional meaning of marriage as a solemn vow that cannot easily be broken.

At the same time, it is of some importance to note that a great many people are loath to abandon the no-fault divorce laws that many fought hard to get enacted. They strongly advocate that marriage and divorce remain legally private matters. Modern marriage, they claim, will remain inherently unstable regardless of the anti-divorce measures introduced. In this they are right for a variety of reasons. For one, there is little doubt that marriage in the future will remain to be based upon love and choice and hence is likely to come into conflict with the modern individual's continuing pursuit of freedom and personal happiness. For another, frequently immature and unprepared people, who should not get married, at least not to each other, will persist in getting married. In other words, though enduringly popular, because of the mercurial and contradictory nature of modern marriage, its constitutive features, its lack of a clear definition, and the heightened yearnings for personal freedom, marriage will continue to be a risky venture for many. Moreover, without serious economic, legal, cultural, and moral obstacles to deter them, it is more than likely that modern men and women will continue to find it easy to give up when the sailing gets rough.

The contradictory understandings of the meaning of contemporary marriage contribute in no small measure to the culture wars of our time. Yet this need not be so as the following elaboration will show.

The most obvious feature of modern Western marriage is that it is *not only* a vow nor is it only a contract: It is a curious mixture of both. While people may wish to reinforce their marriage with a solemn vow, marriage in the West will remain a legal contract and hence divorce is a matter for civil courts, rather than an ecclesiastical issue, as Roman Catholics would prefer. History and experience tells us that couples determined to no longer live with each other have always found a way to get divorced, regardless whether it had to be obtained through civil courts or through appeals to ecclesiastical authorities such as the annulment procedures of the Roman Church, or whether it involved a simple desertion of the common home. At the same time, it is important to recognize that the marriage contract is essentially different from a commercial contract. The analogy between the two, as Norman Barry argues from a classical liberal point-of-view, is a perversion of the moral ideal of liberty: "Originally, the moral right to liberty was based upon the notion of personal responsibility for action. Individuals are treated as free agents capable of making rational choices because of their awareness of, and responsibility for, the consequences of their choices. Yet with the introduction of no-fault divorce the state officially absolved individuals from taking moral responsibility for their actions and what is more, it also absorbed the economic costs that accrued from divorce to a large degree."[24]

Accepting this persuasive line of reasoning it follows that marriage is both a private as well as a social institution that involves the moral dimensions of a vow as well as the legal obligations of a contract. Because of its dual nature attempts to privatize marriage along radical libertarian lines by means of removing the state from the way in which individuals care to organize their private lives are just as doomed as those attempts by ultra-conservatives who seek to use the power of the state to restore the concept of marriage as a vow. In either case, the balance between moral obligations and personal freedom characteristic of the Western ideal would be lost, and perhaps irretrievably so. If the aim is to reduce the currently high divorce rates by means of strengthening marriage without becoming ensnared ideologically, it follows that both entry into marriage as well as exit from it requires a restitution of both the moral and the legal dimensions of the conventional family.

It is for reasons like this that such remedies as early marriage and having children while young, as Danielle Crittenden spiritedly suggested in her recent *What Our Mothers Didn't Tell Us: Why Happiness Eludes the Modern Woman,*[25] are largely beside the point. A person's moral development is largely a function of a lifelong learning process and is in need of constant vigil and reinforcement. It is more than doubtful that modern youngsters who are loath to accept parental guidance in matters of the heart have the moral maturity to understand the weight of their decision to marry. To the contrary, it would appear advisable to impress upon young men and women the importance of delaying marriage—and most certainly not to have children—until a point in time when they are better prepared to differentiate between sexual needs and passions and the very mundane requirements of family life.

By the same token, it would also appear that the contemporary movement to make the acquisition of relationship and marriage skills into a required course in American high schools is a nonstarter from the beginning. Whatever else such a curriculum might do, it certainly does not have the capacity to turn today's divorce culture around. The textbooks currently used in so-called marriage, family, and couples education courses are largely inadequate, if not downright pathetic. For one, the politically correct labels of such courses reveal that aims other than the restoration of marriage are involved.[26] For another, it makes one wonder how schools that have demonstrably failed to teach today's teenagers the rudimentary knowledge of most everything, can be expected to tackle complex issues of love, commitment, responsibility, and perseverance.

To be skeptical about the effectiveness of such proposals does not imply that nothing can be done, particularly when the welfare of minor children is involved. If the restoration of marriage is the issue, as many claim it is, a strengthening of the meaning of the marriage vow would seem to be indicated. Whether this could be achieved by legal means—as, for instance, the requirement of a waiting period, the introduction of more stringent and binding prenuptial contracts, or reform of tax laws to discourage divorce—or by offering couples the choice between two types of marriage regimes ("standard" marriage with virtually unrestricted access to no-fault divorce or "covenant" marriage understood to be a lifelong commitment and designed to be more difficult to enter and to exit) remains an open question. At this point in time the covenant marriage movement is gaining momentum and in 1997 and 1998 respectively, the states of Louisiana and Arizona have made historic changes in their domestic relations laws by enacting America's first "covenant marriage" bill that requires couples to choose between the two. Those opting for the covenant type declare publicly and legally a lifelong commitment to each other. Though still allowing for divorce when necessary, covenant marriage cannot easily or hastily be broken. Stipulating that marriage is more than a simple agreement between one man and one woman it acknowledges the fact that individuals need help to be moral. This covenant marriage contains the dimensions of a vow and implies the willingness of couples to be guided by religious doctrine.

Yet covenant marriage has been publicly opposed by progressives, traditionalists and religious leaders alike, although for very different reasons. Some fear, not without justification, that covenant marriage takes a treacherous first step toward a plurality of marital regimes that could lead us down the slippery road of legally recognizing all types of arrangements, trial marriages, marriages of convenience, or even polygamy to ultimately arrive at the privatization of marriage. That is to say, the end effect of the covenant movement could easily lead to polar opposite results than its advocates intended. Others, in turn, argue that covenant marriage constitutes a form of emotional blackmail in which a reluctant man or woman is pressured into the contract and later regrets it. [27]

While one may argue about individual aspects of the proposals to restore marriage and their long-range potential, only the future will tell which of the measures open to us are best suited to put a stop to the casual attitudes toward marriage and divorce that have captured certain segments of society. What cannot be argued about, however, is that the legislative procedures for divorces involving minor children need to be revised and tightened. Divorces involving children are qualitatively different from divorces that do not. When the interests of children need to be protected, the state has not only legitimate reasons to intervene, but is indeed obliged to do so. This charge could be achieved minimally through the adoption of a meaningful waiting period for entering into and exiting from marriage, tax reform in favor of two-parent families, and perhaps mandatory marital counseling.[28]

A little more has to be said about the utility of no-fault divorce laws. While the repeal of no-fault divorce might protect the welfare of children to a greater degree, as some argue, it is doubtful that such a measure in and of itself would do much to bring the divorce rate down from its currently still high level. No-fault divorce laws neither created the divorce revolution of the 1970s and early-1980s— the divorce rate went up close to a decade before their enactment— nor are there good reasons to assume that their repeal alone would do much to bring the current rates down still further. It is true that the divorce rates went up after the laws were enacted, yet they went down again in the mid-1980s while no-fault divorce laws remained in place. No-fault divorce, as Lenore Weitzman correctly observed some years ago, made it easier for battered and frequently poor women to escape an untenable situation.[29] To revert to the *status quo ante* would in all likelihood make their already precarious situation still worse. It would also bring the heavy hand of the state back into marital affairs. Experience has shown that courts are singularly ill-equipped to serve as arbiters in deciding who is more at fault in a particular case of marital breakdown. Aside from making divorce a messy and costly affair, such a repeal would in all likelihood reward the party with the better lawyer rather than penalize the guilty party. In any case, the problem is not so much no-fault divorce as such but the fact that the measure was perverted into "divorce at will" by well-educated, middle-class women who by virtue of their class location and education could have been reasonably expected to be aware of the moral dimensions of the marriage vow and the restraints the institution of marriage places upon individuals. (To this day close to two-thirds of all divorce petitions are filed by women.) It is doubtful that a repeal of no-fault divorce laws would suffice to strengthen the meaning of marriage.

Clear-eyed observers of shifts in social values know that Western societies are unlikely to return to the low divorce rates of fifty years ago just as they know that it will not be politically easy to effect those legal changes necessary to make "divorce at will" more difficult to obtain, even when the welfare of innocent children are at stake. Nonetheless, efforts to make marriages more stable and divorce rarer have to be looked at with an open mind and deserve to be encouraged. In view of everything we know today it is hard to imagine that the citizens of democratic societies would be willing to forego the chance to strengthen marriage and prevent unnecessary divorce. With the rediscovery of the conventional family in the court of public opinion there is reason to expect that the divorce rate may decline yet further. If there ever was a divorce culture, as Barbara Dafoe Whitehead insists, then we can hope that it was of brief duration only. Signs are favorable, though mostly anecdotal still, that ordinary men and women have come to realize that with all its tensions and demands, marriage is still the best thing we have got.

In view of the foregoing considerations, the brief policy recommendations that may be formulated here are guided by the search for finding a satisfactory balance between two of the conventional family's outstanding features—its capacity to provide for stability and its driving spirit for individual freedom—without endangering its unique social mission.

- First: *divorce is here to stay*. It has to be accepted as an inherent feature of Western-type marriage not only legally but it should also not be condemned morally. It is not the business of the state to enforce religiously based vows, though it welcomes the wish of couples to be guided by religiously inspired principles.

- Second: *no-fault divorce laws should be retained*. There is no evidence to date that would let us assume that the repeal of no-fault divorce would lead to a significant reduction in the divorce rate.

- Third: *both law and public policy should make a fundamental distinction between divorcing couples with children and without children*. Though the covenant marriage option could become relevant here, a two-step marriage regime proposed as far back as the early 1970s by Margaret Mead could meet the need to provide special protection for children.[30]

- Fourth: *Divorce should be made more difficult to obtain when children are involved*. The issue is what are the effects of divorce on children.

Contemporary Issues of Poverty and Their Putative Social Consequences

In recent decades there has been much talk about the rising rates of poverty, of crime, delinquency, drug addiction, and educational failure in the highly-industrialized societies of the West. The rates themselves have been fairly consistent in all, with the United States and the countries of Northern Europe outdistancing, by a wide margin, countries such as France, Italy, Germany, and the Czech Republic. [31] In response to this trend a tendency has come in vogue in academic circles to link such increases in problematic behavior to the progressive disintegration of the family and quite a few felt impelled to call for a major revision in the ways we think about the institution of the family itself.[32] Yet when one looks at the evidence more closely, it is distinctly odd to note that on all sides of the political divide many fail to acknowledge that the "crisis of the family" is actually the crisis of dysfunctional families. There exists today a persistent refusal among the most outspoken social critics to accept that the vigorous virtues of the conventional family continue to be the strongest bulwark against this trend. An only cursory look at this poignantly cautionary tale of social amnesia reveals what can happen when political elite, skeptical of the benefits of the conventional family lifestyle, set out to elevate the role of the state. Ardently inspired by desires to save those living at the bottom of society, mostly urban and ethnic poor, many were determined to disregard the importance of the inner dynamics of conventional family life for fear of being accused of bias and Western ethnocentrism. Few had the wisdom or the courage to hold on to the insights of generations that the values and behaviors of the conventional nuclear family, regardless of ethnic origin, religion, and social class, are the values and behavioral requirements of modernity par excellence. It did not help much that the Western elite themselves were susceptible to the siren songs of alternative lifestyles! It was this accidental confluence of trends and factors that got the United States into what has come to be known as "the welfare mess," which the country still labors hard to get out of today.

Welfare in America was first organized during Colonial times along the lines of the English poor laws of 1601. Enriched by an uniquely American spirit of voluntarism, and given distinctive shape by the history of diverse immigrant groups arriving at its shores in subsequent centuries, it remained for long the concern of local communities and religious and ethnic organizations. With the enactment of the Social Security Act of 1935 the U.S. government entered the welfare arena for the first time in a systematic way. The act itself was designed as a straightforward national insurance plan to provide all workers with income in their old age and to take care of widows and their dependent children if the breadwinners should die. Although a number of interim programs—such as Aid to Dependent Children, Aid to the Blind, and Aid to the Permanent and Totally Disabled—were added in later years, it was expected that these programs would disappear as soon as all American workers and their dependents were covered by Social Security.

It is important to keep in mind that well into the 1960s welfare agencies and the general public alike were not only convinced that poverty was linked to shortcomings in the behavior of individuals, but that the best chance to get the poor off welfare was to regulate their conduct. The two-parent family figured prominently in this strategy. Although the generally unforgiving attitude of welfare agencies toward non-middle-class behavior evoked the criticism of the more liberally inclined, the more traditionally informed were able to point to the successes this approach had achieved in the past.

By the early 1960s, however, when it became increasingly evident that the number of people on welfare continued to grow rather than decline a conviction began to solidify among a new breed of social policymakers that the persistence of poverty in the midst of general affluence was to be blamed on governmental neglect. Many found the old approach to be outmoded and to violate the "dignity" of the poor and their chosen lifestyles. Rather than "blaming the victim" as the earlier approach was alleged to have done, the welfare system itself now came under attack. Many at the time were persuaded that what was needed to make poverty a thing of the past was a combination of money, good old American know-how, and, above all, a more active and less punitive involvement on the part of the federal government that would accept the legitimacy of non-middle-class lifestyles. Above all, it was found expedient to uncouple welfare from individual behavior. The new governmental crusade was ill-timed in many ways for it set out to realize its high-minded mission at the very moment when the antifamily visions of the counterculture came to find a receptive hearing in policy and media circles. Bourgeois family ideals revolving around the rearing and education of children as a vital instrument for the prevention of poverty came increasingly into disrepute and it did not take long for many federal welfare programs to abandon their reliance upon the nuclear family model that had served the country so well in the past. In this sense the "war on poverty" declared by the Johnson administration in 1964 reflected not only a new confidence in the government's wisdom and abilities, but also the seductive power of countercultural visions of alternative lifestyles.

Despite the undeniable success of some of the newly targeted programs—such as those designed to reduce poverty among the rural poor and the aged poor—it did not take long for it to become evident that the new approach to welfare was anything but beneficial for the poor, particularly for those located in America's central cities. Although there continues to this day a fierce dispute between those for whom poverty is a function of economic want and those for whom it is a function of behavioral shortcomings, there can be little doubt that at the bottom of American society a new class— variously labeled "the underclass" or "welfare dependency class"— had come into existence in the course of a few decades for whom welfare had become a new way of life. Unlike the poor of the 1930s or the 1950s, this underclass was neither deprived of job opportunities nor could its rise be explained primarily in terms of racial discrimination. The civil rights acts of the 1960s went a long way to outlaw racial discrimination, yet the presence of African Americans in the underclass was not only disproportionally high, it seemed to grow steadily with every year that went by. As a slew of studies available today indicates, in contrast to newly-arriving immigrants to America (Cubans, Cambodians, and Vietnamese, for instance), for whom family cooperation remained of unquestioned importance, the newly-emerging dependency class had turned its back on the traditional path toward self-sufficiency and upward mobility. The once vital reliance upon conventional family dynamics and the support of moral communities in which this type of family is traditionally embedded—the churches, the ethnic, neighborhood and self-help groups for which this country has become justifiably famous—was replaced by a new reliance upon the state.

The debate over the causes of poverty continues to this day. Explanations from demography and structure compete with those based on racism and moral isolation. Yet regardless which side one prefers to come down on, a huge set of data collected over the past decades demonstrates with a considerable degree of certainty that it would be a fatal error to cast the issue of poverty in economic and political terms alone. Though it would be difficult to document that ill-informed welfare policies must be held responsible for the rising rates of welfare dependency, as some have claimed, a good argument can be made that the delegitimization of the conventional two-parent family and its moral code had a lot to do with it. In bypassing the historic imperative of the two-parent family, the substantial expansion of governmental programs encouraged men and women to optimize the monetary advantages these new policies offered to individuals. When it became obvious that the new directions of the welfare system made it unnecessary, if not downright undesirable, for the poor to pool their family resources, some were tempted to follow the rational actor principle. In deciding to "go it alone," they milked governmental coffers for all they had to offer. In this, programs like AFDC created strong disincentives for work and marriage. In the words of one observer, AFDC "converted the low-income working husband from a necessary breadwinner into a financial handicap and has made marriage an economic debit for low-income couples."[33]

The new trend had a particularly destructive effect upon African Americans. In his provocative book, *The Promised Land: The Great Black Migration and How it Changed America,* a study of the post-World War II migration of Southern sharecroppers into the cities of the North, Nicholas Lemann argues that the welfare programs of the 1960s fostered behavior patterns in culturally vulnerable migrants that served to lock them ever more deeply into the mire of welfare dependency.[34] Since behavior leading to dependency was actually rewarded, and public opprobrium against such behaviors had practically disappeared in the larger culture, growing numbers of the "working poor" found it increasingly futile to struggle against poverty on their own. They too found it now more advantageous to obtain available public funding rather than to rely upon the pooling of family collaboration and resources as it was the custom in the past. Slowly and incrementally the availability of government handouts helped in this manner to undermine the social fabric of groups in which cultural taboos and the existence of a strong normative order had traditionally discouraged dependency-related practices and attitudes.

It is hard to overlook the collapse of the two-parent family among the welfare dependent. According to the U.S. Bureau of the Census, the vast majority (90 percent) of "persistently poor" households are composed of women and their children. Since 1960 their numbers have tripled. Two major factors have led to the phenomenal rise in female-headed households: The disastrous increase in the divorce rate and the equally calamitous increase in the illegitimate birth rate, particularly among teenagers.[35] A few statistics may serve to illustrate the relevant dimensions of structural shifts: While the illegitimate birth rate was 5 percent in 1960, it had risen to just under 30 percent nationwide in 1990. If the factor of race is put into the equation, among the white population we find that illegitimate births increased from 2 percent of births in 1960 to 22 percent in 1991; among African Americans the numbers increased from 23 percent in 1960 to 67.9 percent in 1991.[36]

As pointed out repeatedly in this book, a huge set of data on welfare dependency indicates beyond the shadow of a doubt that a host of pressing domestic problems is rooted in profound shifts in the structure as well as the moral code of the American family. So, for instance, two-parent families rarely stay in poverty for extended periods, nor do they show up among the homeless for any length of time[37] and their children have a better start in life than children from single-parent households where fathers are totally absent or play only a marginal role. In contrast, children from single-parent households are two to three times as likely as children in two-parent families to have emotional and behavioral problems. They are more likely to drop out of high school, become pregnant as teenagers, abuse drugs, and become entangled with the law.[38] More qualitative research points to far-reaching changes in their commitment to the family as an institution, attitudes toward work and authority, and the ability to defer gratification. Together these shifts have fused into a devastating amalgam of influences that exerts enormous pressures upon those who struggle to improve their situation.

It is of some importance to note that not all single mothers became clients of the state. A sizable number of divorced mothers remarried or were otherwise able to make arrangements that allowed them to "go it alone" with a modicum of success. Highly educated and employable middle-class divorced women with children, in particular, were able to combine their own incomes with adequate child support payments from their children's fathers, and those who were psychologically strong and resilient seemed to have been able to escape the most debilitating consequences of divorce (though the emotional and economic burdens of divorce, according to Barbara Dafoe Whitehead, remain daunting for them as well). Though shifts in the normative order of society have transformed *all* segments of twentieth-century America regardless of their location in the social hierarchy, the fact remains that large portions of the American middle classes have been able to withstand the most harmful effects of the turbulent decades of the 1960s and 1970s. Those living at the bottom of society have not. While massive government-supported interventionist programs may not have been directly responsible for the creation and diffusion of a new type of permanent poverty, they surely were instrumental in giving expression and shape to its formation. Contrary to everyone's intentions, the American welfare system in its 1960s mode cut all too many individuals loose from their familial moorings, isolated them from communal ties, and drove them into an existential and psychological dependency on the state.

As pointed out earlier, these developments, and the statistics to prove them, greatly served to fuel spreading fears among liberals and conservatives alike that something had gone deeply wrong with the way welfare had come to be organized in the United States. By the mid-1990s the country was ready once more for a fundamental overhaul of its welfare policy, one in which the lessons from the rediscovery of the beneficial effects of family cohesion was heeded. Though we are still a long way away from an adequate appreciation of the role of the conventional family and its equally conventional ethos, commonsense has come to prevail once more. Judging by the evidence available today, the tough welfare policies enacted since the mid-1990s have assisted many of those entrapped in the poverty-dependency cycle in their desire to move into the mainstream of American society. Some have been unable to do so. While it would be foolish to claim that the conventional family alone is able to solve all our domestic problems, a conventional lifestyle most assuredly goes a long way to prevent the worst from happening.

Inasmuch as a subject matter as vast and complex as welfare makes it quite impossible to provide detailed policy recommendations in this context, a few *general policy guide lines* will have to suffice:

- Regardless of the details involved, future welfare policies should *in every way possible encourage the promotion of the two-parent conventional family.*

- In this, whenever possible, public welfare policy should *work through the institutions of civil society, particularly religious and other self-help institutions* that have a proven track record to be able to incorporate needy and marginal people into a vibrant communal order.

This recommendation meets with a dual difficulty: On the one hand, experience has shown that programs and services for the purpose of promoting family cohesion among the poor fare best when they are anchored in the microstructures of communal life. The diverse ethnic and religious nature of American society makes it impossible for the government to establish and deliver the very different types of programs needed for this purpose. On the other hand, the traditional American separation between church and state prevents the consideration of faith-based communities for such purposes. *Hence the welfare of the poor demands the reconsideration of the overly rigid interpretation of this doctrine currently in use.*

Notes

1.   Moira Eastman, "Myths of Marriage and Family," in David Popenoe, Jean Bethke Elshtain, and David Blankenhorn (eds.), *Promises to Keep* (Lanham, Maryland: Rowman & Littlefield, 1996).
2.   See James Q. Wilson's excellent "The Family Values Debate," in *Just a Piece of Paper?*, a publication of the Institute for Economic Affairs, Health and Welfare Unit, London, 1995.

3.   Lynne Casper, "Household and Family Characteristics," U.S. Bureau of the Census, 1998.

4.   Quoted in *The Boston Globe*, Thursday, May 28, 1998, Stephanie Coontz, author of *The Way We Really Are: Coming to Terms with America's Changing Families* (New York, Basic Books, 1997) is a professor of family studies at Evergreen State College in Olympia, Wash.

5.   U.S.Bureau of the Census, *American Almanac*, Table No.143, p.102.

6.   See Spring 1999 Report from the National Marriage Project at Rutgers University as reported by Associate Press.

7.   Associate Press Report, *The Boston Globe*, January 22, 1999.
      For an excellent overview of the abortion issue worldwide see Rita James Simon, *Abortions, Statutes, Policies and Public Attitudes the World Over* (Greenwood, Praeger, 1998).

8.   Gary Becker, *A Treatise on the Family* (Cambridge, Ma.: Harvard University Press, 1981).

9.   One of the best overviews of this much-debated issue can be found in S.W. Polachek and W. S. Siebert, *The Economics of Earnings* (Cambridge and New York: Cambridge University Press, 1993).

10.   Jacques Donzelot, *Policing Families* (New York: Pantheon Books, 1979).

11.   Frank Musgrove, *Youth and the Social Order* (Bloomington: Indiana University Press, 1964).

12.   See the sociological study conducted by Suzanne Bianchi of the University of Maryland, reported in *The Boston Globe*, March 28,2000

13.   See Lynne Casper, "Who's Minding our Preschoolers?" U.S. Bureau of the Census, *Current Population Reports*, pp.70-53, April 1996.

14.   Susan Chira's, *A Mother's Place: Taking the Debate about Working Mothers Beyond Guilt and Blame* (New York: Harper Collins, 1998) is representative of this genre of books. Other writers, such as Carin Rubenstein (*The Sacrificial Mother),* and Joan K. Peters, (*When Mothers Work)* have made similar arguments.

15.   See Frank F. Furstenberg, Jr., "Is the Modern Family a Threat to Children's Health?," *Society* 36 (July/August 1999).

16.   John Bowlby, *Attachment and Loss* (New York: Basic Books, 1969); Jay Belsky and D. Eggebeen, "Early and Extensive Maternal Employment and Young Children's Socioemotional Development: Children of the National Longitudinal Survey of Youth," *Journal of Marriage and the Family* 53, no. 4 (November 1991): 1083–1098.

17.   In an earlier book, *The War over the Family* (op.cit.), I advocated the mechanism of a voucher system. The writings of family advocates like Allan Carlson and Brice Christiansen have convinced me of the inadvisability of this option as it would reward only those who work and penalize others who find a stay-at-home policy to be in the best interest of their children. See Allan C. Carlson, *Family Questions: Reflections on the American Social Crisis* (New Brunswick, N.J.: Transaction Publishers, 1988).

18.   John Milton, "The Doctrine and Discipline of Divorce," in *Prose Writings* (London: Everyman, 1927, p.268).

19.   Lawrence Stone, *The Family, Sex and Marriage in England 1500-1800* (London: Pelican, 1979).

20.   Barbara Defoe Whitehead, *The Divorce Culture* (New York: Alfred A. Knopf, 1997).

21.   Norman Barry, "Justice and Liberty in Marriage and Divorce" in *Just a Piece of Paper: Divorce Reform and the Undermining of Marriage* (London: Institute of Economic Affairs, a Choice in Welfare publication, 1995).

22.   The longitudinal research of Diana Baumrind and her associates deserves to be mentioned in this context. Much of the research findings have been summarized in the works of Barbara Whitehead, David Popenoe, and Patricia Morgan, whose writings are frequently referred to in this chapter.

23.   Patricia Morgan, "An Endangered Species?," in *The Fragmenting Family: Does it Matter?* (London: Institute of Economic Affairs, Health and Welfare Unit, 1998).

24.   Norman Barry, op.cit.

25.   Danielle Crittenden, *What Our Mothers Didn't Tell Us* (New York: Simon and Schuster, 1990).

26.   See the special report on the six most commonly used textbooks in such courses authored by Paul Vitz for the New York-based Institute for American Values in September of 1998.

27.   See Steven L. Nocky, James D. Wright, and Laura Sanchez "America's Divorce Problem," *Society* 36, no. 4 (May/June 1999).

28.   For thoughtful proposals see Richard T. Gill, *Posterity Lost: Progress, Ideology, and the Decline of the American Family* (Lanham, Maryland:Rowan & Littlefield, 1997, chapter 14, "Reclaiming the Family: Principles and Programs).

29.   Lenore J. Weitzman, *The Marriage Contract: Spouses, Lovers and the Law* (New York: Free Press, 1981).

30.   Margaret M. Mead, "Marriage in Two Stages," *Redbook Magazine*, July, 1966.

31.   Population Council, New York 1995.

32.   See David Cheal, "Unity and Difference in Contemporary Families," in *Journal of Family Issues* 13, no. 2, (1992), Special Issue "Rethinking Family as a Social Form"; Judith Stacey, *Brave New Families* (New York: Basic Books, 1990).

33.   Charles Murray, *Losing Ground: American Social Policy, 1950-1980* (New York: Basic Books, 1984).

34.   Nicholas Lemann, *The Promised Land: The Great Black Migration and How It Changed America* (New York: Alfred A. Knopf, 1991).

35.   U.S. Bureau of the Census, Current Population Reports #450, "Marital Status and Living Arrangements," 1991, p. 20.

36.   U.S. Department of Health and Human Services, *Vital Statistics of the United States*, 1991, Vol. 1, *Natality*, 1993.

37.   Christopher Jencks, *Homelessness* (New York: Basic Books, 1994).

38.   For details see Barbara Dafoe Whitehead, op.cit.

7

The Family in the Postmodern Age

We sometimes find the truth concerning problems of considerable importance.
But the problem is that we never know we have found it.
—Fontenelle

We have traveled a long way in this book on the career and fate of the family in the modern age. We started our journey with a brief exposition of the social and intellectual trends that helped to turn the once taken-for-granted conventional family into just another lifestyle choice and we ended with the recent rediscovery of its importance for individual and social life. Setting out to explore the reasons for its extraordinary strength, we felt compelled to look for a lens that allows us to account for the modern family's distinctive dimensions and dynamics. Making use of an analytical frame-of-reference broad enough to include the role of values and behavior patterns engendered by the constitutive features of the modern family it was possible to uncover the existence of a close cognitive and structural fit between the nuclear family and the modern social order. This interpretational device also allowed us to argue that despite the far-reaching transformations exacted by the industrial system's numerous permutations in virtually every area of social life, the core features of the modern family remained relatively intact and the changes that did occur failed to undermine its enduring appeal to modern men and women. Based on the consideration of a great variety of factors we felt justified to reason that the values of this type of family and its corresponding lifestyle will continue to be important in an age of transition from the modern to the postmodern.

In the course of these explorations we were again and again struck by the modern family's extraordinary capacity for self-renewal as well as by its extraordinary culture-creating dynamics. Not only were the values and behavior patterns of the nuclear family instrumental in the shaping of the modern social order they also were able to adapt themselves to the changing needs of every phase of the modernization process. Among the great variety of family types recorded in history, this type of family alone has shown the capacity to provide for individual liberty while restraining the excesses of liberty, the genius to encourage individuals to strive for new horizons while keeping them grounded in reality, and the strength to inspire the modicum of trust and social responsibility necessary to meet the challenges of an unknown future. If nothing else, this journey reminds us how easily social critics can confuse passing cultural moments with lasting transformations. It alerts us to the fact that in ideal and practice the conventional modern family consisting of father, mother, and their children, bound to each other by mutual ties of love and obligations must be seen as being part and parcel of the modern way of life rather than being destined for the dust heap of history.

Turning to thorny contemporary questions of equality and freedom in marriage, this volume sought to argue that while it may be deplorable that true equality between men and women was long in coming, the seeds for equality were planted in the conventional family from the outset. The realization of the ideal became more tangible with every shift in economic and political modernization, and its universal validity is accepted with few reservations today. In reflecting upon the structural and cognitive fit between equality and personal liberty in the conventional family we came to realize that both are based upon the recognition of the complimentarity of familial roles and the need for striking the proper balance between the two. In an age where issues of equality, freedom, individuality, and choice dominate wherever one turns, these reflections suggest that individuals have to sort out their family relationships for themselves and in every particular case anew.

The explorations of this book also provided a necessary antidote to nostalgic longings for a return to the good old family of yore. Some aspects of the world we have lost weren't all that great to begin with and quite a few are no longer viable today. Though traditional "family values" sound good and appealing in the abstract, some exact great costs in personal repression and sacrifice that modern men and women are no longer willing to accept. Attitudes and norms vis-à-vis specific aspects of conventional family life in the past have changed, indeed, and it has become fairly clear that no amount of control by either church or state is likely to motivate modern men and women to return to the *status quo ante* where there existed sexual double standards and hierarchically-ordered relationships between the genders, with men being the sole breadwinners and women applying themselves exclusively to the care of children and home, while children, for their part, were expected to accept the tutelage of their parents in all matters of life. It is neither likely that modern men and women will abandon the freedoms that have been achieved in the domestic as well as in the public sphere in the course of the past centuries nor is it necessary that they do so to safekeep the modern family's enduring civilatory mission. At the same time, there can also be no doubt that in their search for sustenance and meaning the vast majority of modern individuals, today as in the past, will turn to the family in its conventional form for this purpose. Few today would be inclined to contest the diagnosis of Robert Wuthnow, the Princeton sociologist, that the institution of the family has become "porous," that is to say, more permeable and with thinner boundaries, yet most are determined to stay loyal to an ideal that does not substantially deviate from the one that stood at the cradle of modernity.[1]

In the course of our examinations it became time and again apparent that there exists a considerable degree of theoretical blindness among analysts of the modern family, past and present. Because of theoretical shortcomings many modern theorists have accepted without much hesitation Juergen Habermas's much admired dictum that the lifeworld is increasingly colonized by forces of the type of rationality peculiar to the public realm of politics and the economy. Their disinclination to entertain the possibility that the solid world of lived familial experiences that repeat themselves in every generation anew has led to postmodernist speculations of doom and gloom. Those proceeding on the assumption that families are ultimately passive conduits of larger political and economic realities treat the family as if it were simply an unwitting creation of political and economic arrangements and ideological constructions, while those who see the family as an omnipotent force, see in it the source for the destruction of individual potentials and as a hotbed of neurosis. In the complicated linguistic and psychological acrobatics typical of theorists on the road to postmodernism, the two views are all too often united in a self-contradictory vision that sees the conventional family to be all-powerful and helpless at one and the same time—a powerful source of alienation as well as a dismantled fortress of invulnerability. On the one hand, the yoke of its patriarchal past is held to be oppressive of women and children, yet on the other hand, when this yoke is removed, both women and children are argued to be unfairly exposed to the harshness of the world of consumption and production outside the household. Some even go so far as to fault modern capitalism for having made women into victims and oppressors at one and the same time. Lacking in political and economic power and forced to enter into an overly intensive relationship with their children, the argument goes, modern women have now become the molders of narcissistic sensibilities in their children and the creators of a generation of hedonistic pleasure seekers.[2] In the minds of such critics, the conventional family is understood to be both the victim *and* the cause of modern alienation, both a symptom and a disease.[3] On the other hand, when one sifts through the mountains of similar theoretical pronouncements it becomes abundantly evident that there exists a widespread tendency to reduce the wealth of familial sentiments, relationships, processes, and activities to mere functions of power—economic, political, and personal. This pervasive trend has greatly added to lopsided contemporary theoretical views of the modern family. And it is this tendency, as this book shows, that will no longer do.

Hence an effort was made in chapter after chapter to show how such theoretical proclivities have lured academics into an intellectual posture that at one and the same time grossly overestimates the power of the rationality of the public domain and sorely miscasts the family dynamics and relationships set into motion by the modern family. If and when it is recognized that individuals are influenced by yearnings and factors of a very different kind, such expressions are typically held to be indications of human frailty and irrationality. Few analysts today know what to make of a love that is more than a simple explosion of passion or infatuation, of human desires for stable relationships, and of human needs for structure and permanency in an inconstant environment. It may well be that a new global culture is in the process of evolving, yet the needs and yearnings deeply ingrained in human nature have remained remarkably constant through the ages. Baring genetic engineering on a grand scale, there exist no significant reasons to expect that this is likely to change. The disappointing results of individual experimentations in the organization of the private domain and the growing public realization that there are limits to what governments can do, remind us of the statement by William Graham Sumner, whose magnificent statue graces Harvard Yard, that "stateways do not change folkways." This observation holds especially true for the modern family which in form and content appears to respond to a remarkable degree to enduring dimensions in human nature. In several chapters of this book the argument was made that one of the distinguishing characteristics of the modern family in its conventional form is its capacity to respond to the many dimensions of human nature while at the same time being able to reconcile external challenges with its core features in salutary ways. This capacity suggests that there exists a near-symbiotic relationship between the inner dynamics of this type of family and the world it helped to create and maintain. Considering its instrumental role in the rise of the modern world, this should not come as a surprise. At the same time, we also saw that this extraordinary adaptive capacity of the modern family makes for its precarious quality. In periods of turmoil and transition, distinguishing features such as its rationality, individuality, and an incipient egalitarianism are in danger of escalating and becoming radicalized in either political direction. With this radicalization the modern family's unique ability to strike a balance between individualism and social responsibility, between "liberation" and strong communal ties, and between acquisitiveness and altruism, may be challenged if not threatened. What previously was held in balance can thus appear as sets of irreconcilable alternatives: rigid stability against mindless innovation, crass egotism against self-abandonment to a community, adventurism without moral restraints (taking *all* risks) against fearful passivity legitimated by an absolutist morality (willing to take *no* risks at all), and so on. Such seemingly irreconcilable alternatives manifest themselves in different ways at different points in time. A century ago there existed the danger that the conventional family with its emphasis upon propriety, authority, and aversion to exuberant daring could render to become *too* conventional. In our own time there exists a tendency that the same components may become radicalized in the opposite direction to the degree that it frequently appears that balanced rationality is in danger of turning into hyperrationality, individualism into hyperindividualism, and egalitarianism into a merely formalistic concept open to legal manipulation. For a while it may even appear as if the balance the conventional family was traditionally able to provide could be irretrievably lost. Yet experience has shown that bar massive governmental attempts, these disturbances have a way of working themselves out for the simple reason that no other form of living together appears to be able to replace the conventional family functions and appeal.

Because of the modern family's extraordinary capacity to adapt itself to new challenges without abandoning it core features, we came to the conclusion that the modern family is governed by a rationality that differs sharply from the rationality at work in the public sphere or other disparate realms of culture. The failure to recognize this difference has led to either frenzied public measures to stem rising tidal flows of behavioral shifts judged to be untenable or to wild postmodernist speculations about the advent of an era in which morality adapts itself to whatever requirements the public sphere seems to pose. In his recent book, *The Great Disruption,* Francis Fukuyama has argued that excessive radicalizations tend to be "bound back" to the reality of individual human life after periods of disruption and upheaval rather than following the progressively linear developmental path of the political and economic realm.[4] So, for instance, he suggests that the moral behavior of societies seems to be cyclical, with peaks—like the Victorian era—and troughs—like the 1970s. However intriguing and to the point this line of reasoning may be, for those who have followed the argumentation developed in the book before us Fukuyama's conclusions may appear to be somewhat schematic. To be sure, all processes of change occur in a quasi-dialectical manner, with spurts and backlash and reconfiguration following one another ad infinitum. Yet shifts in ideas do not occur in a vacuum, they occur in the context of the lived experiences of everyday life. And as we have come to recognize in the course of this book that this paramount reality is to a large degree determined by mundane factors of family life, we also have come to appreciate the close cognitive and functional fit between the institutions of the modern social order—pre-industrial, industrial, postindustrial, or otherwise—and its human carriers. Hence the basic behavioral and moral principles of the modern social order are not only anchored in the values, customs, and beliefs of the modern family of a bygone era, but the future ahead continues to be dependent upon the circle of shared commitments of institutional arrangements that resemble those of the modern family in its conventional form to an uncanny degree. In a permanently unsettled world like ours, no other form of living together can replace the emotional and practical resources this type of family has to offer to modern individuals. Though more porous and robed in new garb, its structure and dynamics remain essentially the same. While specific aspects of conventional family life may appear to be problematic to some moderns, the fact remains that its core elements continue to respond to the deepest ideals and needs of modern men and women wherever they may be. They may be tempted, at least for a while, to entertain thoughts of an alternative lifestyle. Yet when it becomes obvious that these experiments are unable to replace the combination of seemingly contradictory alternatives held in balance by the conventional family, the vast majority of ordinary people stay loyal—or return—to a vision of private life that entails a marriage that specifies that both partners join and leave it of their own free will, to a life that holds the promise of an enduring relationship that accepts the value of individual freedom, and to a structured environment that provides stability, security, and respect for all of its members. After much talk to the contrary, it also has become evident to all but the most recalcitrant utopian that there simply are no other institutional arrangements available that can better safeguard the well-being and progress of children who have been at the center of the modern family's attention from the beginning.

Ignored as well in recent debates is the fact that the private sphere of the family is not only defined by tendencies and impulses deeply ingrained in human nature but also by religious principles that have served to provide the underpinnings for distinct family cultures in the past. In the Western past, as we have seen, religiously-informed principles that stood in close "elective-affinity" to the principles underlying the conventional family provided the rock-bottom cultural basis for the emergence of a civil society upon which the modern order depends to an exceptional degree. This dependence between public and private remains unchanged today. The danger today is that academic observers tend to view oscillations occurring in times of confusion and transition as real and lasting rather than as manifestations of the struggle of individuals and their families to bring changing circumstances in line with their values and proclivities. Being inclined to attribute primacy to developments in the public sphere, they tend to bypass the proposition that novel and challenging technological and economic shifts must inevitably be bound back to the lived reality of human life for it is the human being who is the producer, the carrier, and the user of the new. It goes without saying that that lived reality continues to revolve around family and the communities in which the family is embedded.

The case for the enduring importance of the modern family in its conventional form then rests on the presupposition that _not all institutionalized forms of living together are equally well equipped to supply individuals with the strength and flexibility to meet the challenges of the modern world._ Neither are all able to provide a happy balance between individual freedom and the necessary modicum of constraint the modern social order depends upon. The mass migration of often desperately poor people to the teeming metropolitan centers of Latin America, Asia, and Africa provided us with a rich source for making this argument. A wide range of studies were cited that reveal that traditional behavior patterns, however admirable and useful they may have been in rural and communal settings in the past, can no longer serve to help migrants to prevail and prosper in their new environments. Unless these newcomers to the modern way of life are able to acquire and nurture behavior patterns and norms that resemble those of the often-maligned conventional family, many are likely to be condemned to live a life in considerable poverty at the margin.

As in the European past, the religious dimension plays an important role in the lifestyle transformation of the urban poor in both the developing as well as the developed world. A growing body of research data give reason to argue that a religiously-inspired ethos resembling the Protestant ethic of Max Weber's fame appears to motivate hapless migrants to take up a new manner of life in which the practices and ideals of the conventional family figure prominently. If this connection, dubbed "the industrial connection" by the sociologist Bernard Rosen, can be substantiated beyond a doubt, it may be argued that the conventional family provides a bridge for a modern order of life to emerge. This trend in the making augurs well for the not yet developed countries in which the broad mass of the population has not yet benefited from the promises of modernity.

The ethnographic research conducted in societies as far apart as Brazil, Korea, and Romania gives evidence of the degree to which the private and the public are inextricably intertwined. It also shows that when governments and the elite ignore this connection and assume the private to be at the mercy of the public, the dynamic forces of the conventional family are consigned to the underground, they become, in Ferdinand Mount's earlier referred to term "subversive." By the same token, studies on the persistence of pockets of poverty in the highly-industrial world of Europe and America indicate as well that the comparative cultural advantage the conventional family provided to the societies of the West in the past can easily be jeopardized if the linkage between the private and the public is forgotten. It does not take much for a depletion of the social capital to occur. No matter how strenuous the efforts of national governments may be, if it is not recognized what the social capital consists of, they are bound to fail. One of the unfortunate consequences of the currently prevailing theoretical amnesia is the tendency of almost every government on the planet to try to substitute itself for parents in some ways. As the record shows, this tendency frequently resulted in baleful consequences for many. It took quite some time until the wrong-headedness of this policy was recognized, however dimly and inadequately. Some still refuse to do so to this day!

It was also argued in this book that one of the major reasons for the denial of the importance of the modern family must be sought in the facile rejection of its bourgeois or middle-class way of life. Hatred of the bourgeoisie—the middle class that is neither upper nor lower, neither so aristocratic that it ignores all conventions nor so poor that it is unaware of their existence—has been a defining theme of modern Western culture since the early nineteenth century. Since then it has been the convention among English, German, and French writers and avant-garde artists to express a pronounced distaste with the humdrum aspects of bourgeois life and their know-nothing middle-class philistinism. Their snobbery along with Marx and Engels' savage political indictment of the bourgeoisie has fed the contempt for the middle-class way of life among the Western cultural elite in general. Yet the times, they are changing: whereas in the past the middle classes were attacked for their vulgar artistic taste, their preoccupation with narrowly defined proprieties, and the crude expression of their material self-interests, today they are attacked for their cultural elitism and their defining role of mainstream culture that seeks to control alternative lifestyles and inclinations. Though the attacks are no longer waged in the amplified screeches of the sixties, their echoes continue to linger on. Though eager to enjoy the material comforts and benefits the revolution of the middle classes has made possible, today's cultural elite are loath to accept its value system. David Brooks, who coined the term "Bobos" (Bohemian bourgeois) to describe this paradoxical mix of sentiments, has caught the manifestations of the current mood well.[5] This contradictory cultural mood has spread beyond the confines of the elite in recent decades and threatens to pull individuals into conflicting directions. The trend has served to render the structurally-weakened family even more porous than it already is. This, I think, need not be so.

To be sure, there can be little doubt that with the rise of the middle classes to influence and status, a family-centered way of life became ensconced in which a considerable degree of stifling prudishness and hypocrisy was hidden behind a public air of respectability and quiet dignity. The new morality made the family into the highest achievement of middle-class life and required modes of conduct that allowed for little deviation from the earlier celebrated virtues of self-control, discipline, and prudence. Marriage based on love and fidelity became the requisite standard and concerns for the welfare and advancement of children took on quasi-religious dimensions. The influence of the new morality was most strongly felt in the mores governing sexual conduct. While the eighteenth century still distinguished between love and sexuality and the open practice of libertinism and erotic adventures had been a source of amusement, especially for the aristocracy, the straight-laced mores of the middle classes would have none of that. Men, who like Rousseau or Kotzebue in the eighteenth century, thought little about fathering children and abandoning them at whim, were castigated as lascivious and immoral as the nineteenth century progressed. Young women who gave birth to children outside of wedlock, which compelled many to abandon their children, were equally chastised for their non-middle-class sexual behavior. Yet when it came to sexual mores, the practice of "double standards" continued way into the twentieth century: men still frequented brothels and engaged in sexual adventures on the side, while women were judged much more severely. In this matter as in any other, reality frequently fell short of the ideal and hypocrisy served to conceal that unpleasant truth. The boundaries set by middle-class mores could be cruel, arbitrary, and unjust indeed.

At the same time, it is hard to imagine in our own times of virtually limitless sexual permissiveness that any sensible person would be willing to advocate a return to sexual mores that ignore the devastating effects of unbridled sexual freedom upon the life of children and women. While the desire to flee the orderly world of conventions and predictability by discovering a sexier, more provocative one, may be understandable, the experiences of the past decades have shown that paradise does not result from life without boundaries and obligations. The excitements and challenges such a lifestyle has to offer all too frequently turned out to be not much more than a mirage. Rather than escaping from the stifling crush of conventions, individuals often found themselves ensnared in a morass of contradictions and ambiguities. This hard-won realization has brought a good number of the 1960s cultural revolutionaries back from the wilder shores of madness. Pursuing surprisingly conventional middle-class careers today, they nostalgically contemplate their youthful ways in the lap of material comfort and affluence. More often than not it was the concern for the well-being and future of their children that motivated them to change their lifestyle and conform to long-established ways of caring and rearing. In this sense it may well be observed that children present the highest reality test governing the modern way of life.

The possibility that the celebration of domesticity occurs at the expense of political engagement and civic concerns has been yet one more issue trotted out time and again by the critics of the conventional family. A life spent underneath the placid surface of domesticity is argued to disconnect men and women from the pursuit of loftier ideals and purposes such as politics, the arts, and the principles of religion and philosophy that guide and enrich life in a civilized world. The new domesticity, such critics hold, turned the attention of individuals inward to the trivial things in life and tended to make them complacent, uncritical, and resistant to change. A cultural family-centered conservatism not only prevented individuals from developing their full human potentials, such critics argue, it also served as the unwitting helpmate in the rise of non-democratic authoritarian political regimes. What these critics neglect to appreciate, however, is that their own critical minds and moral outrage are the products of the very socialization processes typical of the conventional family. From Karl Marx and Friedrich Engels to the student revolutionaries of the 1960s, radical critics themselves were invariably of middle-class origin and the majority had enjoyed the benefits of a conventional middle-class upbringing. Where else could they have acquired an individualism willing to go against the establishment and do battle for what they held to be a principled interpretation of equality and justice? It is precisely the balanced independence of thought—minus the recklessness and unbounded utopianism characteristic of radical extremism—that has been the strength of the modern mode of life. A rapidly changing world needs individuals who are able to combine a questing cognitive style with moral fortitude and social responsibility. All these attributes have distinguished the childrearing practices of the conventional family in the past and there are no reasons to think that this is likely to change in the future.

In recent years the highly-industrialized countries of the West have become magnets for diverse groups of people who arrive in skyrocketing numbers at their borders. This mass migration will undoubtedly reshape the ethnic composition of the receiver countries and hence it has become customary to argue that ethnic changes are likely to produce corresponding changes in the existing host culture. Competition for economic opportunities, political power, and cultural supremacy between dominant and minority cultures are predicted with a considerable sense of urgency and it has become fashionable to advocate for the establishment of a politically correct multiculturalism. While such arguments are not entirely unreasonable, they are only partly to the point. Undoubtedly the societies of the future will differ considerably in their cultural composition from the societies of the past and it is difficult to forecast how individual societies will deal with the formidable challenges posed by this mass movement of people. Yet one thing may already be predicted with a fair degree of certainty today. Despite their different origins and sundry cultural understandings, all migrant groups are united by their determination to create a better future for themselves and their children. As past experience has shown, this determination calls forth the best personal resources in all individuals, regardless of their social origin, ethnicity, or creed. Like other migrants before them, they will unfailingly marshal the resources of the family, will go through phases of accommodation, adaptation, and, finally, integration into the modern way of life. More likely than not, they will achieve their goal by making use of the virtues, habits, and ideals that have distinguished the conventional modern family for long. If they persevere, play their cards right, and are lucky, they will succeed. There exist no earthly reasons why this should change in the future. All the talk and bickering about the dangers or merits of multiculturalism the contemporary media are fond of dwelling on is way off the mark. Far from trying to compel their host society to take on the cultural peculiarities of the society they left behind, the newcomers are sure to embrace those core features of modern society that are likely to provide them and their children with new opportunities. While the going may be hard, very hard for some at times, this one thing is for certain: immigrants' efforts and the family-fueled dynamism that has been the hallmark of modern history will in turn enrich the culture of the country of their choice.

In taking the long view of the history of the modern family and its future we may conclude that the family is more than the sum total of its constitutive parts: it is here where all dimensions of human existence intersect and where the drama of individual life is played out. In addition to factors of procreation and production, the meaning-giving function of the family is of equal significance. In the past families sought legitimation for their worldly practices in religious sanctions, prescriptive as well as proscriptive. In modern times, however, a consensus was forged among scholars of religion and the family alike that as the modernization process progressed the importance of both institutions—that of religion and that of the family—has diminished both in the consciousness of individuals and in their relevance for social life. In the case of religion these views were typically expressed in theories of secularization ascribing the decline of religiosity to the ascendancy of modern scientific thinking that is alleged to have made the world more rationally comprehensible and manageable. In the case of the family, as we have seen, the decline of the importance of the family was either attributed to the progressive displacement of the central functions of the family by the rise of competing new institutions, such as education and welfare, or to the attractions of alternative lifestyles that promise to liberate modern individuals from the tutelage of the family. Even the most thoughtful scholars were convinced that the waning influence of both institutions was real and lasting.

Of late it has become decidedly more difficult to equate modernity with the decline of religion. In the case of religion recent empirical evidence forced social scientists to question the validity of the secularization theory. The upsurge of extremely powerful religious movements in many parts of the world today has become an incontestable fact. With some notable exceptions, the world appears to be as religious as ever, and in some places the waves of religious fervor splash higher today than ever before. This kind of revision has not yet occurred among those who study the contemporary family. To be sure, under the pressure of massive empirical evidence the staying power of the family has been recognized in more or less general terms. Yet the resistance to accepting the singular importance of the modern family in its conventional form as a meaning-giving institution continues to be as widespread today as in the 1960s and 1970s. The various explorations in this book should have made it abundantly clear that the time has come to look at the family in more than functional terms only. While the utilitarian value of the family is undoubtedly unique—both in the life of children as well as of adults—it is exceedingly important to recognize that yearnings for perpetuity and meaning—perhaps the most distinguishing properties of what it means to be human—are anchored in this institution. They link every generation anew to the past as well as to the future and provide the modern family with its overarching mission.[6] In a complex and ever-changing world like ours individuals are in the danger of being consigned to a perpetual state of limbo without an anchorage in the reality of ordinary, structured family life. In our encounters with ever-larger numbers of people in the public sphere of work and bureaucracy, few of the relationships we forge are sufficiently stable and lasting to provide the emotional density and steady backdrop individuals need to acquire their essential identity. Only in the constancy and freedom a conventional family life offers can they hope to find the source for personal meaning as well as the individuality necessary for persevering and moving ahead. It is for this reason that marriage and the family gain a significance which may be even more profound today than in times past. As Charles Horton Cooley observed many years ago, it is in the eyes and attitudes of the "other" that I can discover who I am, it is the "you" who defines the "me." It is in the stabilized and institutionalized loving relationship between two individuals that men and women can hope to firm up and maintain their essential identities.

On the social level as well one only has to consider the fact that the modern world with its sophisticated organizational structures and awesome technological capacities depends upon a large reservoir of people who are psychologically well-adjusted, educationally prepared, and socially competent to execute the kind of performances necessary to acquire and operate the instruments of the postindustrial system. During the past century the industrial system has undergone numerous permutations that exacted social adjustments in the ways we work, where we live, how we live, what and how we consume, and so forth. Regardless of such permutations, however, the social habits, the norms, and the cognitive style peculiar to the conventional family have remained the core features of any social order based on the principles of democracy and the modern market economy. To put it differently, our type of civilization—and by extension any democratic and economically productive society regardless of its provenance, level of development, or geographical location—is dependent upon the behavior patterns and ethos that defines the conventional family. Regardless of origin and history, any family system—be it now Chinese, Japanese, German, Islamic, African, and so forth—can meet the challenges of the future, as long as it contains the core features of the family system that was instrumental in the creation of the modern world. There are no reasons to expect that this will change in the years ahead. Whatever the future will bring, one thing seems to be sure, it will be a system of life in which the principal unit of action is based on individual performance and motivation. Despite the perennial search for community and alternative lifestyles, the mechanism of individualism remains the mechanism of the questing individual seeking more and better frontiers. And again, no other family system appears to be better suited to meeting the need for self-reliant, motivated, yet ethically responsible individuals than that of the ever-adaptable conventional family.

As long as history remembers, scholars have debated the hypothesis that every human society contains within itself the kernel of its disintegration. When applied to the changes that have left their mark on the structure and ethos of the family that stood at the cradle of the modern world the question poses itself of to what degree these changes are likely to affect the future of modernity. Some have argued that these changes have exhausted the conventional family's extraordinary culture-building role and with this exhaustion a depletion of the dynamism of modern civilization with all its achievements and triumphs has run its course. Those who have followed the arguments of this book should be comforted by its conclusion that there are no convincing reasons to assume that modern men and women, regardless of ethnic and national origin and across the social classes, are about to abandon their belief in the lifestyle of the conventional family and the salutary effect of its equally conventional ethos. Their actions and their ideals defy the possibility that this particular prophecy of doom is likely to become reality.

A few years ago the Harvard political scientist Samuel Huntington caused a considerable stir with his proposition that world politics is moving into a period of "civilizational clash" in which the primary identification of people around the world will not be ideological, as during the Cold War, but rather cultural. Now that Western-style democracy and economies have remained triumphant, Huntington argued that conflict will arise not between fascism, socialism, and democracy, but between the world's major cultural groups, Western, Islamic, Confucian, Hindu, and so on. Judging by the attention it caused, Huntington's provocative essay (and later book) "The Clash of Civilizations?" clearly hit a central nerve in the minds of academics and politicians alike. While only time will tell whether and to what degree Huntington's predictions are accurate, his essay performs the crucial service of bringing into focus the role factors of culture play in the affairs of nations. In contrast to Huntington, however, it is important to keep in mind the singular importance of the family in the formation of cultures and civilizations. And this observation takes us back to the major theme of this book. If such a "clash of civilizations" should occur some time in the future, then this clash, at its roots, will be one between different family systems and the ways in which they are able to integrate the properties of human nature and human existence with the requirements of the postmodern world rushing toward us today. In other words, the family is more than just a lifestyle choice. Public life and the fate of nations lie at the mercy of private life.

Notes

1.   Robert Wuthnow, *Loose Connections: Civic Involvement in America's Fragmented Communities* (Cambridge, Mass.: Harvard University Press, 1998).

2.   Christopher Lasch in both of his earlier-cited books presents a typical example of this contradictory view.

3.   Barbara Finkelstein and Remi Clignet, "The Family as Inferno: The Dour Visions of Four Family Historians," a review essay published in *The Journal of Psychohistory* 9, no.1 (summer 1981).

4.   Francis Fukuyama, *The Great Disruption: Human Nature and the Reconstitution of Social Order* (New York: Free Press, 1999).

5.   David Brooks, *Bobos in Paradise, the New Upper Class and How They Got There* (New York: Simon & Schuster, 2000).

6.   See Peter Berger, *The Sacred Canopy* (New York: Doubleday, 1967 p. 6 ff.), see also Brigitte Berger's conceptualization of culture being "twin-born," in Brigitte Berger (ed.), *The Culture of Entrepreneurship* (Institute for Contemporary Studies Press, 1991, p. 15 f.).

Subject Index

abortion, 25, 186ff.,190
alternative lifefstyles, XI, 23, 24, 53, 215, 216, 229, 235, 237
"amoral familism," 106

birthrate, 143, 167

capitalism, 100, 105, 109, 110, 115, 123, 124
    "democratic capitalism," 125
childcare (see also socialization), 88ff, 198ff
childcare policy, 202ff
child protection, 111
civil society, 61, 105,117,229
"cognitive fit" of modern family, 126, 160, 181, 223f, 224, 228
cohabitation, 143, 151, 154, 183ff
"comparable worth," 194
comparative family systems, 71
    African family, 71
    Chinese family, 71, 79, 87
    Indian family, 71, 81
    Latin America, 128ff, 133ff
    Muslim family, 71, 87
counterculture, 10, 11ff, 19ff, 23, 25, 29, 35, 40, 43, 91, 121, 139, 150, 206, 216, 232
cultural revolution, 205ff
"culture of modernity" and modern family, 105f, 126ff
"culture of domesticity", 109, 202f, 223
"culture wars," 58, 160, 186f, 209

democracy and family, 100, 134, 161
demographic transition model, 167, 170
domestication of the senses, 133
domestic partnership, 163
divorce, 153, 154, 172, 184, 204ff, 218
    and children, 207f
    "no fault" divorce, 206, 209

economy and family, 113, 131, 132
equality and family (see also gender inequality), 117, 160ff, 224ff

family, general, 3ff, 235
    bourgeois family, X, 12, 20, 38f, 43, 58, 108, 117ff, 150, 196, 231
    cohesion, 40ff, 109, 110, 146ff
    conventional nuclear family, (see also modern family) XI, 5ff, 10, 12, 15ff, 40ff, 45, 51, 56, 64, 104, 109, 111, 112 ff, 117ff, 133, 134, 139ff, 152f, 155, 160, 169ff, 179ff, 208f, 213, 214ff, 223ff, 235f
    conventional family and identity, 14f, 86, 148, 156, 159
    conventional family and its inner dynamics, 101ff, 104ff, 117, 134, 142, 146, 214
    conventional family and contemporary shifts, 109ff,
        structural shifts, 143ff, 146, 152ff, 167, 181f, 218ff
        normative shifts, 143ff, 145, 165, 218ff
female nature, 20
feminism, general, 12, 14ff, 22
    mainstream feminism, 26ff
    moderate feminism, 28f, 168
    radical feminism, 13f, 19ff, 22, 26f, 28, 51, 54
    and women's liberation. 14ff, 17ff
"feminization of culture," 107f

gender inequality
    in income, 161, 193ff
    in marriage,115, 160, 161, 171
gender politics, 22
global culture, 226f

human nature, 71ff

female nature 20ff
  and instincts, 72ff, 162
  and institutionalization of instincts,
    74ff, 162
  and "instinctual deprivation"
  maternal instinct, 16, 93
  politics of human nature, 15ff, 19ff
human sexuality, XI, 48, 75

individualism, 105, 106, 164ff, 169,
  196, 224ff, 234, 237
individual autonomy, 205ff
industrial revolution and family, 5ff,
  49ff, 109ff, 113

liberty and family, 16, 84ff, 96, 100, 117,
  152, 155, 161, 224ff
lifeworld and its dynamics, XI
  colonization of the lifeworld, XI, 225
  pluralization of the lifeworld, 148,
    157, 159
  rationality of the lifeworld, XI
lifestyle of conventional family, 13, 23,
  24, 30
    and choice (see also alternative
      lifestyles), 20, 24, 29ff, 63, 178

marriage in the modern age, 149ff, 152,
  154ff, 162, 204ff, 208
  and cohabitation, 183
  "covenant marriage," 208
  defense of marriage movement, 208
  gay marriage, 185f
  and identity, 14f, 156ff, 159f, 236
  politics of marriage, 160f, 163, 164,
    208ff
  trial marriage, 183, 212
maternal instinct, 16, 93
migration, 234
modern family (see also conventional
  nuclear)
  core elements, 101ff, 120, 117ff
  defintion, IXf, 9ff, 178ff
  redefinition, 19, 24
  theoretical perspectives on the mod-
    ern family:
    communitarian, 139f, 165f
    conservative, 35f, 40ff, 49ff, 139,
      149, 152, 160f
    liberal-mainstream, 35f, 44ff,
      66ff, 139f, 149, 152, 161f

postmodern, X, 36, 52, 54ff, 139f
  radical (Marxist), 35, 37, 49ff,
    139f, 153
modernity, 35
modernization, definition, XIV, 34, 63,
  125
modernization and family, 6, 33ff, 36ff,
  101
multiculturalism, 54, 60ff, 234

normative shifts, 47ff, 54, 152

"pathogenic family," 15
politics of family, XII, 9, 24, 25, 28
politics of identity, 14
postmodern self, 58ff, 152ff, 206
postulate of ignorance, 188, 190, 192
postmodernism and family, 54, 56, 139,
  140, 152, 160f, 171, 206f, 225f, 228
poverty and family, 24
proto-industrial, X, 100ff, 117, 123, 132
"Protestant Ethic," 104ff, 196, 107, 133,
  230

rational cognitive style, 105, 123
rationality of the private sphere, XI, 228
rationality of the public sphere, XI, 228
religion and family, 229ff, 235f
"Romantic Ethic," 106ff
romantic love, 152, 153, 155f

single-parent household, 143,167
social capital, 164f, 231
social class and family, 105f, 114f,
  118ff, 148f, 168, 196ff, 214ff, 232
social norms, 76ff, 182
social policy and family, 7ff, 19, 25ff,
  28, 49, 144, 146, 216
social rituals, 81f
social roles, 75f, 82ff
socialization and childcare in the conventional family, 75, 85f, 88ff, 113,
  114, 118ff, 167, 169ff, 196ff,
  234
"professionalization of childcare," 91f
state and family, 7ff, 52, 171

teenage pregnancy, 190
traditional family, 179ff

women and work, 14f, 17, 107,110,
  192ff, 199

Author Index

Aries, Philippe, 118

Badinter, Elizabeth, 16
Bane, Mary Jo, 26,147
Bennet, William, 166
Berger, Brigitte, 26,159
Berger, Peter, 26,77, 159
Barry, Norman, 206, 210
Bauer, Gary, 162, 166
Baudrillard, Jean, 57
Bianchi, Suzanne, 198
Bowlby, John 201
Braun, Rudolf, 103
Bronfenbrenner, Uri, 90
Brooks, David, 232
Buytendijk, F.J.J., 72

Campbell, Colin, 107,113
Carlsen, Allan C., XV, 221
Christensen, Bryce J. 206
Coleman, James, 165
Conze, Helmut, 100
Cooley, Charles Horton, 78, 236
Cooper, David, 17
Crittenden, Danielle, 210

Deutsch, Helene, 17
Donzelot, Jacques, 196
Douglas, Anne, 107
Douglas, Mary, 81
Dowling, Eric, 154, 155, 173
Durkheim, Emile, 75, 121, 158, 189
Dylan, Bob, 13

Eastman, Moira, 179
Elias, Norbert, 120
Engels, Friedrich, 37ff., 42, 112, 234
Etzioni, Amitai, 165

Firestone, Shulamite, 18, 23
Flandrin, Jean, 100

Foucault, Michel, 65, 85, 86
Fraiberg, Selma, 26
Friedan, Betty, 14, 26f, 28, 162
Freud, Sigmund, 43ff, 150
Fukuyama, Francis, 228
Furstenberg, Frank F., 200

Gallagher, Maggie, 152
Geertz, Clifford, 129
Gehlen, Arnold, 72, 76
Gilberet, Neil, 163
Glendon, Mary Ann, 206
Goode, W.J., 45, 63, 122

Habermas, Juergen, 50, 225
Hegel, Georg Friedrich, 99, 123
Hewlett, Sylvia Ann, 27
Hobbes, Thomas, 73, 74
Huntington, Samuel, 238

Kavalis, Vyantas, 58
Kellner, Hansfried, 159

Ladurie, Emmanuel Le Roy, 20
Laing, R.D., 17, 43
Lasch, Christopher, 26, 44, 58. 226
Laslett, Peter, 100, 101, 112, 154
Lemann, Nicholas, 218
Le Play, Fredric, 40ff.
Lloyd, Peter, 132
Locke, John, 74, 118
Luckmann, Thomas, 77,148,169

Macfarlane, Alan, 100, 104, 115
MacKendrick, Neil, 113
Maine, Henry Sumner, 41f, 87
Marcuse, Herbert, 150
Martin, Bernice, 156
Martin, David, 133
Marx, Karl, X, 37ff, 87, 112, 123, 234
Mead, George Herbert, 78, 83

Mead, Margaret, 214
Mill, John Stuart, 173
Millet, Kate, 18
Milton, John, 204
Mitchel, Juliet, 18
Moore, Barrington, 51
Morgan, Lewis, Henry, 39, 42
Morgan, Patricia, 208
Mount, Ferdinand, 111f, 115, 116, 231
Moynihan, Daniel Patrick, 178
Musgrove, Frank, 197

Norwood, Robin, 152

Ono, Yoko, 18
Ozment, Steven, 20

Parsons, Talcott, 45, 46, 63
Polanyi, Karl, 34
Popenoe, David, 184
Portmann, Adolf, 72
Power, Eileen, 115
Putnam, Robert, 165f
.
Ravitch, Diane, 61
Reutter, Peter, 1413
Rieff, Philip, 9
Riesman, David, 47
Roberts, Bryan, 126, 131

Rosen, Bernard, 132, 230

Schama, Simon, X, 110, 195, 116
Schlesinger, Arthur, 190
Sennet, Richard, 44
Sherfey, Mary Jane, 16
Shorter, Edward, 109
Smith, Adam, 99, 123, 124, 131
Soto, Hernando de, 128, 132
Sowell, Thomas, 122
Sumner, William Graham, 227

Thompson, E. P., 111
Tocqueville, Alexis de, 100
Todd, Emmanuel, 126
Toennies, Ferdinand, 87

Weber, Max, 70, 100, 104, 105, 123, 230
Weitzman, Lenore, 212
Whitehead, Barbara Dafoe, 156, 184,
    205, 206, 213, 219
Willmott, Peter, 147
Wilson, James Q., 180, 220
Wrigley, Anthony, 100
Wuthnow, Robert, 225

Young, Michael, 147

Zimmerman, Carl Z., 41